L.A. Noir

To the memory of Raymond Chandler,
for supplying much inspiration

L.A. Noir

*Nine Dark Visions
of the City of Angels*

WILLIAM HARE

McFarland & Company, Inc., Publishers
Jefferson, North Carolina, and London

ALSO BY WILLIAM HARE

Early Film Noir: Greed, Lust and Murder Hollywood Style
(McFarland, 2003)

LIBRARY OF CONGRESS CATALOGUING-IN-PUBLICATION DATA

Hare, William.
L.A. noir : nine dark visions of the City of Angels /
William Hare.
p.   cm.
Includes bibliographical references and index.

ISBN 0-7864-1801-X (illustrated case binding : 50# alkaline paper) ∞

1. Film noir—United States—History and criticism.   2. Los Angeles (Calif.)
—In motion pictures.   I. Title: LA noir.   II. Title.
PN1995.9.F54H39   2004   791.43'6556—dc22   2004002806
British Library cataloguing data are available

Cover photograph: Yvonne De Carlo and Burt Lancaster in the 1948 film *Criss Cross*

Manufactured in the United States of America

*McFarland & Company, Inc., Publishers
Box 611, Jefferson, North Carolina 28640
www.mcfarlandpub.com*

Table of Contents

Introduction

While cities like New York and San Francisco are known for their cosmopolitan elements, Los Angeles falls into a different category. The city extends in many directions to various suburbs, making it difficult to tell just which town one is in at a given moment. Los Angeles is a city created by a never-ending migration, which continues to the present; the latest statistics reveal that it has the largest growth figure of any city in the nation and has recently surpassed New York as the largest major metropolitan area in the country.

Film noir came into being at the end of World War II, when Paris intellectuals recognized the unique quality of the world of darkness and the fascinating stories to be uncovered in a nocturnal world of adventure, where seemingly typical people resort to atypical responses, spurred on by greedy self-interest. The tug of war between the forces of greed and those seeking to stop them was memorably etched in stories in a pulp detective magazine from the thirties, *Black Mask*, featuring two authors who became legendary. The first author, San Franciscan Dashiell Hammett, had the advantage of career experience behind his work, having been a Pinkerton detective in the city by the bay, which he called home. The second sprang from a completely different background, but, along with Hammett, he helped spawn the major movement of film noir and became a literary immortal.

Raymond Chandler was born in Chicago and taken by his mother to England, where he was provided with a proper British prep school education at Dulwich College in South London. As a young man, he moved to bustling Los Angeles, which was deeply immersed in spirited growth. Chandler's first home in L.A. was in an apartment hotel on Bunker Hill, overlooking downtown, to which one was transported by the world's shortest railway, Angels Flight. The overtly proper Chandler, who spoke with an upper-class British accent and wore tweed suits, appeared to be thoroughly out of place in the milieu about which he wrote with such commanding diligence; however, a superficial analysis of his appearance would prove misleading. The hard-drinking Chandler was an irreverent and inveterate cynic. When

1

he turned his hand to detective stories, sparks almost flew from his Underwood typewriter to the page.

Dashiell Hammett's stories featured two detectives as lead characters: the Continental Op and Sam Spade, the figure who gained immortality through Humphrey Bogart's enduring portrayal in the 1941 Warner Bros. classic *The Maltese Falcon*, which marked John Huston's directorial debut and which historians call the first noir film. Chandler's alter ego was a granite-jawed, broad-shouldered detective with an inner decency and a cynical outlook enhanced by frequent bouts with the bottle, a condition the author knew about firsthand.

Chandler's Philip Marlowe became the classic example of the hard-boiled detective, frequently emulated but never matched, much less surpassed. The words Pygmalion Chandler put into the mouth of his detective matched his cynical outlook as well as his always-prevailing love-hate relationship with Los Angeles. While he lampooned the area for being unsophisticated and lacking the type of cultural refinement he appreciated, Chandler loved the spirited anarchy of the city, reminiscent of the dusty Old West American territory of Wyatt Earp and Bat Masterson.

As a poet laureate of darkness, Chandler became a perfect candidate for film noir adaptation. Not only were his novels selected for filming; he was put to work as a screenwriter, collaborating with director Billy Wilder on the 1944 smash hit *Double Indemnity*, which revolutionized Hollywood with its hard-hitting noir realism, then resurfacing two years later working under fellow British prep school grad producer John Houseman in *The Blue Dahlia*, both for Paramount.

The first chapter of this noir retrospective featuring Los Angeles covers the Warners adaptation of Chandler's first novel, *The Big Sleep*, which was published in 1939. Director Howard Hawks cared little about plot details and concentrated instead on the fascinating constellation of characters interacting in the fast-moving story. He shrewdly signed up the devastating couple whose charisma lit up the screen earlier in Hawks's 1941 hit, *To Have and Have Not*, Humphrey Bogart and Lauren Bacall. Tough guy Bogart proved a perfect match for film noir, as he had earlier demonstrated in *The Maltese Falcon*, tough and brooding, resourceful and sympathetic, though he sought to hide the last named quality for fear it would make him appear soft. From the film's release in 1946 to the present, *The Big Sleep* has been one of the memorable screen hits in the genre.

The second film covered, *Criss Cross*, helped Burt Lancaster move into the formidable ranks of leading men, a position he continued to hold during an impressive career. The 1948 release, directed with convincing authority by German émigré Robert Siodmak, pitted Lancaster opposite exotic beauty Yvonne De Carlo as a decent man who took a wrong turn, being manipulated by the woman he loved above all else and the rival for his affections, mob boss Dan Duryea. *Criss Cross* takes advantage of the worn, fascinating character of the Bunker Hill area where Chandler first resided after arriving in Los Angeles.

D.O.A., the subject of Chapter Three, involves the unique premise of solving one's own murder. Edmond O'Brien, cast as accountant Frank Bigelow, has been victimized by a lethal dose of luminous toxic poison. As the clock ticks off the precious minutes, he has less than a day to solve his murder before his own demise. This 1950 low budget sleeper directed by Rudolph Maté has become a favorite at film festivals and effectively utilizes some of the most interesting scenery in Los Angeles. New York stage great Luther Adler makes one of his rare screen appearances as the remorseless mob boss fearful of the results of O'Brien's efforts.

Noir natural Bogart returns in Chapter Four in an analysis of the film many close to him said resembled the real man more than any other of his fertile career: *In a Lonely Place*, a 1950 release directed by Nicholas Ray. The film was produced by Bogart's own company, Santana Productions, the original plan was for Bogart, who plays a brilliant screenwriter with a mercurial temper which causes him perpetual trouble, to star opposite wife Lauren Bacall. When studio head Jack Warner refused to provide approval for his leading lady to appear, Ray tapped then-wife Gloria Grahame to portray the actress living across the courtyard from Bogart who falls in love with him and has a complicated affair with the temperamental scenarist.

Chapter Five's *The Blue Gardenia*, a 1953 release, finds brilliant German émigré director Fritz Lang on his familiar noir turf exploring his favorite theme of moral ambiguity. Anne Baxter plays a tormented young woman who, after moving from her hometown of Bakersfield to L.A. and becoming a telephone operator, is wanted in a citywide police hunt as the suspected killer of playboy artist Raymond Burr. Baxter remembers fending off Burr's advances in his apartment before passing out; however, when she regains consciousness, she is unaware of whether she killed Burr. Richard Conte plays a popular columnist for a leading Los Angeles newspaper who implores the woman he has labeled "The Blue Gardenia" to turn herself in.

The Chapter Six selection has been called by many the greatest low budget noir film ever made: the 1955 release *Kiss Me Deadly*, with Ralph Meeker starring in the adaptation of the Mickey Spillane novel as Detective Mike Hammer. Hard-hitting director Robert Aldrich, who the same year saw his bitingly realistic study of Hollywood, *The Big Knife*, emerge in the theaters, demonstrates a deft touch for film noir by featuring the seedy hotel rooms of Bunker Hill, with the superb photography of Ernest Laszlo capturing the darkness of corridors and rooms from an innovative down-sweep perspective.

Stanley Kubrick, an ambitious director in his late twenties, broke into the cinematic big time with his innovative work, Chapter Seven's *The Killing*, a 1956 release starring Sterling Hayden as boss of a highly unconventional gang intent on staging a daring racetrack holdup on the day of the season's biggest race. A major feature of the film, much of which was shot in a seedy section of downtown Los Angeles, is the ingenious by-play between statuesque *femme fatale* Marie Windsor and her sadistically henpecked husband, played by one of film noir's character immortals, Elisha Cook Jr.

As discussed in Chapter Eight, Jack Nicholson delivers one of the definitive performances of his career as Detective Jake Gittes in a 1937 Los Angeles setting in *Chinatown*, with Roman Polanski directing and Robert Towne receiving a Best Original Screenplay Oscar. The 1974 release represented a noir transition into color from the old black and white formula which previously held sway. Cinematographer John A. Alonzo muted his colors to give the feel of old noir black and white in a reformulated setting.

Chapter Nine features the screen adaptation of James Ellroy's potent best-selling crime novel, *L.A. Confidential.* The 1997 film, directed by Curtis Hanson from a script which he co-wrote with Brian Helgeland, provides a vividly realistic look at 1950 L.A., when, in the midst of a wave of police corruption, determined officers Russell Crowe and Guy Pearce attempt to solve the Nite Owl Cafe killings, which reveal inter-department corruption led by would-be city syndicate boss police captain James Cromwell. To join forces, bitter enemies Crowe and Pearce must patch up their differences resulting from their love affairs with the same woman, beautiful blonde prostitute Kim Basinger.

The aforementioned noir classics, along with those also covered in the nine chapters, reveal Los Angeles as a forbidding, brooding city, which looms all the more dangerous when the bright sun has descended and the prospects of temptation, corruption, and death loom large in the land of the palm trees.

ONE

Hawks, Bogart and Bacall

Such a lot of guns around town and so few brains!
The Big Sleep (1946)

The forties were not only the most productive era in Hollywood cinema history but the peak period for Raymond Chandler, the hard-drinking, cynical former oil executive. After being fired for booze and womanizing, he turned to detective fiction to make a living.

Chandler and his legion of admirers discovered that he had a superb knack for tales of darkness. With Hollywood interested in enhancing productivity during its boom period, when the knock came on Chandler's door, he responded to the challenge and received a Best Screenplay Oscar nomination with his adversarial writing partner Billy Wilder for *Double Indemnity*. In 1946, working with fellow British prep school alum producer John Houseman, with whom he formed a comradeship totally unlike his *Double Indemnity* experience with director/co-writer Wilder, Chandler wrote the screenplay for an Alan Ladd and Veronica Lake gangster thriller, *The Blue Dahlia*, for which he received another Oscar nomination.

Raymond Chandler was a man of protean gifts whose propensity for dissipation resulted in him becoming washed up as an oil company executive by the time he was 44 and being fired for chronic alcoholism and extracurricular activities with secretaries. Meanwhile, his one and only wife, Cissy, 18 years his senior, remained his faithful companion until her death in December 1954, predeceasing his demise on March 23, 1959, by some four years.

A proud graduate of Dulwich College, a prep school in South London, and a man familiar with the classics, Chandler turned to writing in the then-popular pulp detective field as a means of making a living following the abrupt termination of his oil executive's career. As a classicist, he was embarrassed by writing for *Black Mask*, the popular pulp detective magazine of the thirties, but his survival instincts took over and he studied carefully the work of its most famous author, Dashiell Hammett, the former San Francisco detective who featured the exploits of Detective

Sam Spade, an alter ego representation of himself during his days in the field. Chandler established a detective of his own based on personal experience, but of a different nature. At Dulwich College, he stayed at Marlowe House, named for the great sixteenth-century English playwright-poet and contemporary of William Shakespeare, Christopher Marlowe. Chandler, who lacked Hammett's authentic detective's background, called his detective Philip Marlowe.

Hammett might have had the practical experience as a detective, but Chandler wove more imagination and rich characterization into his work. As a result, his writing was elevated to the level of literature and ultimately read in college classrooms, a previously unheard-of phenomenon as scholars had formerly restricted detective writing to what they deemed a lowly genre category. While the exploits of Hammett's Sam Spade were set in San Francisco, a cosmopolitan city of greater order said to be representative of New York City or Boston, Chandler's settings for his stories featuring Philip Marlowe were located in the sprawling and unruly Los Angeles and its environs some 400 miles to the south. Unlike more-structured San Francisco, Los Angeles, at the time Chandler settled there as a young man, was a rapidly growing melting pot, attracting a large number of new residents from the Midwest and South.

Not long before his death, film noir tough guy Robert Mitchum, who played Marlowe in *Farewell, My Lovely* (1975) and in a less-successful later version of *The Big Sleep* (1978) set in London, appeared on the Arts and Entertainment Network's popular *Biography* series in a segment devoted to Chandler entitled "Murder, He Wrote." Mitchum, who was born and raised in Bridgeport, Connecticut, and lived as a Depression-age roustabout, traveling to many places and holding many jobs before ending up in Los Angeles and gaining ultimate immortality as a prominent cinema leading man, exclaimed, "My first home was the Midnight Mission downtown. L.A. was a loser's town…. If you couldn't make it somewhere else, you could make it in L.A."

At another point in the same docu-biography, Mitchum recalled a visit Chandler made to a Hollywood drinking spot where he was bartending. Noting Chandler's tweed suit and cultured British accent, twin trademarks, Mitchum understood that Chandler did not fit in. Rootlessness and an inability to fit in, disadvantages in most settings, can be successful allies to a creative writer, someone who skillfully reports on the inside from things he or she observes from the outside. Chandler's Marlowe emerges as a laureate of alienation, with sprawling, rootless Los Angeles the perfect venue for his detective activities.

While Mitchum noted his first Los Angeles home at his arrival at age 17 was the Midnight Mission, a young, struggling Chandler arrived there in 1912 at 24. His first residence was an apartment hotel on Bunker Hill, overlooking downtown L.A. below, reachable by the famous funicular railway, the shortest in the world, Angels Flight. In the words of Los Angeles historian Lawrence Clark Powell, "By the time Chandler came to write about it (Bunker Hill), decay had set in; the old dwellings and hotels had become cheap boardinghouses, the seamy setting of many incidents in his novels."

With Bunker Hill becoming a home for small-time criminal elements and life's losers who frequently interacted with them, Chandler found one of many symbols for his corrosive narrative. Imaginative filmmakers would capture the gnarled poetry of Bunker Hill and the Angels Flight railway. As will be later observed, director Robert Siodmak used the setting to advantage in the 1948 noir classic, *Criss Cross*, while seven years later, the area would be featured in Robert Aldrich's probing tale of darkness, *Kiss Me Deadly*.

The Big Sleep marked Chandler's debut as a novelist, coming when he was 51 in 1939. He endeavored to keep his age secret in a trade he considered to be the province of younger men. His bitingly nihilistic prose reaches its zenith at the book's end, with Chandler striking in full force, succinct and with a formidable wallop:

"What did it matter where you lay once you were dead? In a dirty sump or in a marble tower on top of a high hill? You were dead, you were sleeping the big sleep, you were not bothered by things like that. Oil and water were the same as wind and air to you. You just slept the big sleep, not caring about the nastiness of how you died or where you fell.... On the way downtown I stopped at a bar and had a couple of double Scotches. They didn't do me any good."

HAWKS, BOGART AND BACALL

While Chandler would never receive the opportunity to adapt his first novel to the big screen, the creative process by which *The Big Sleep* would assume a life of its own and ultimately become a cinema classic fell into excellent hands. Young veteran Howard Hawks, who had spent his entire working life in the film industry, not only tapped a future Nobel Prize novelist to help write the screenplay, he played an effective winning hand in the equally important casting area. Great directors exercise brilliant creative instincts that their less-imaginative professional colleagues do not possess, and the astute Hawks was able to continue an effective game plan he developed one film earlier.

Jack Warner and the studio hierarchy were tickled by Hawks's decision to team an experienced screen tough guy with a tall, sensuous newcomer whom the director had chosen from the modeling ranks. The slender lady of 19 met the experienced man in his forties and two kinds of magic were instantly generated: the romantic variety, with the two ultimately marrying, and the screen magic displayed when the two appeared together. The team of long-limbed former model Lauren Bacall and cinema's no-nonsense tough guy, Humphrey Bogart, exploded on screen in Hawks's *To Have and Have Not*. No sooner was the first film completed than Warners, playing its hot hand with its dynamic duo, had Hawks put them in action again, the second film being *The Big Sleep*.

Anecdotal legends abound concerning Howard Hawks and his creative activities during the periods of involvement in both *To Have and Have Not* and *The Big Sleep*. In relation to *To Have and Have Not*, a story has been told and retold con-

Director Howard Hawks shrewdly returned to his dynamic star duo of *To Have and Have Not*, Humphrey Bogart and Lauren Bacall, for his 1946 noir immortal, *The Big Sleep*. The story, adapted from the Raymond Chandler novel, contained so many twists and turns that even Hawks could not completely figure it out, but he knew that the film's greatness lay in its fascinating blend of characters.

cerning Hawks's reason for deciding to adapt the adventure novel to the screen. Perhaps at least partially because Hawks in his late twenties ran the story department of Famous Players under Jesse Lasky, which later became Paramount Studios, and was subsequently invited by William Fox to direct scripts he had developed, the director became close friends with two future Nobel Prize–winning authors. According to legend, Hawks bet his friend Ernest Hemingway that he could tailor a movie from what he termed the author's "worst novel," *To Have and Have Not.* It has not been recorded what the prideful Hemingway had to say about Hawks's "worst novel" description, nor is it in any way clear that such a bet was made or the alleged discussion occurred. What is evident is that in Hollywood, a good story is treasured above all else. Consequently, when in doubt between fact and legend, believe the legend.

To Have and Have Not deserves a unique place in the *Guinness Book of World Records* since it is the only film to combine the writing efforts of two future Nobel laureates. Hemingway wrote the novel; co-authoring the scenario along with seasoned Hollywood professional Jules Furthman was the sage of Oxford, Mississippi, William Faulkner. Hawks was a close personal friend as well as hunting and drinking crony of both Hemingway and Faulkner. Another colorful Hawks story relating to the period when the *To Have and Have Not* screenplay was being written involves Faulkner. The temperamental Mississippi author, following in the tradition of serious novelists of the period, F. Scott Fitzgerald and Nathanael West, detested screenwriting, as the talented trio disdained all but the money that Hollywood supplied for their efforts. Another detestation they shared as creative free spirits was the expectation that they punch time clocks at the studios where they were employed, accustomed as they were as freelance novelists to working at locations of their choosing with no one scrutinizing their activities. The story that has been told and retold had a disenchanted Faulkner telephoning his friend Hawks, lamenting the discomfort and constraints of working in a studio environment and asking permission to work at home. Hawks was said to have assented to Faulkner's request. After several days had passed, he telephoned the author's Hollywood residence, learning that Faulkner had returned to the serenity of Rowan Oaks, his large, tree-lined estate in Oxford. According to legend, when a befuddled Hawks reached Faulkner by telephone at Rowan Oaks, the famous author innocently replied, "Well, you said I could work at home." Faulkner had always referred to Mississippi as home and had assumed that Hawks understood his meaning. This anecdote deserves to be scrutinized with unbridled skepticism. It is highly unlikely that a shrewd director such as Hawks, who knew Faulkner well, would ever have involved himself in such a serious misunderstanding with a project involving a major studio and a large budget hanging in the balance. All the same, the account is a whole lot more colorful and fascinating than the truth, resulting again in the perpetuation of Hollywood legend at the expense of fact.

To appreciate the classic status attained by *The Big Sleep* necessitates an analysis of the team process initiated with *To Have and Have Not.* Hawks raised eyebrows at Warners by discovering model Bacall and propelling her into a major film role at the age of 19 in the same way that Columbia's Harry Cohn had declared Rouben Mamoulian to be "crazy" because he selected unknown Paramount contract player William Holden to star in *Golden Boy*. Hawks screen-tested Bacall, studio head Warner liked what he saw, and so did Bogart, who told her so at their first meeting outside Hawks's office at the studio. It was only natural, however, for a young lady with no previous acting background to become exceedingly nervous over being thrust into the limelight and forced to assume such awesome responsibility, but she was given solid support from both her co-star Bogart as well as director Hawks.

Talented directors have an amazing ability to reap success from unpromising seeds. A nervous and youthful Bacall spoke in a voice that was high and lacking in the kind of confident certainty and power her screen character, pickpocket and seductive flirt Slim Browning, required. Hawks coached her to develop an entirely different voice, which he felt comported with her character, someone who spoke in low, throaty tones. The ploy proved such a spectacular success that the breathy Bacall tone has become a symbolic element accenting her sexy demeanor. In her refreshingly candid autobiography, *Lauren Bacall: By Myself*, the actress recounted how her nervousness resulted in the camera's sensitive eye recording a mannerism that became memorably etched in film arcana. To combat her trembling, Bacall, in scenes with Bogart, tucked her chin resolutely against her neck. The technique was filmed with brilliant effectiveness by cinematographer Sidney Hickox in close-ups in which Harry Morgan, called Steve by Slim, portrayed by Bogart, would be standing and looking down at Bacall. The combination of chin locked against neck and accompanying upward look by the actress conveyed with stunning believability her flirtatious manner toward the cynical loner she was determined to snare.

The film combined the magnificent chemistry between Bogart and Bacall—particularly manifested in their first scene together, when her husky intonations in seeking to get him to give her a match embody a shrewd come-on—with elements that made a just-released Bogart classic, *Casablanca*, an artistic and box office winner. As in *Casablanca*, Bogart is cast as a tough loner who professes to believe in nothing more than looking after himself. As Rick, the nightclub owner in *Casablanca*, Bogart ultimately releases his hold on the woman he loves, played by Ingrid Bergman, so that she remains with French resistance leader Paul Henreid, who is pursuing the cause of world freedom, an objective bigger than the personal romantic aspirations of any of them. He makes the painful sacrifice in the tough, characteristically Bogart "It's no big deal" manner. As skipper Steve Morgan of the *Queen Conch*, Bogart expresses comparable indifference in helping French resistance operatives by ferrying them to safety in wartime Martinique on his boat in *To Have and Have Not*, all the while looking out for his friend Slim, played by Bacall, booking her passage for America.

As in *Casablanca*, the conflict is vividly presented between the idealistic French resistance figures and the Martinique Vichy police in *To Have and Have Not*.

THE HAWKS PENCHANT FOR CONFLICT

As Hawks moved from one mystery adventure on the Warners lot to another, putting Hollywood's hottest new screen team, Bogart and Bacall, back before the cameras, he utilized two-thirds of his writing team from the earlier film, Faulkner and Furthman, while adding a woman's touch, as supplied by scenarist and novelist Leigh Brackett. The astute veteran Hawks retained the element he parlayed to consummate screen effectiveness, that of conflict between two principal characters. This was a penchant he exemplified in both the comedic and dramatic spheres, shifting emphasis when needed.

Howard Hawks was a man with a reverence for machines. A product of the American Middle West, Hawks was born on May 30, 1896, in Goshen, Indiana. The son of a wealthy paper manufacturer and grandson of a rich lumberman, young Howard and family made the trek west to southern California in 1906, settling in Pasadena, where his mother's asthma problems could be relieved by the warm and dry climate. He divided his time between east and west during his school days, attending prestigious Philip Exeter Academy in the East, then graduating from Pasadena High School. He then returned east once more to study engineering and ultimately earn a degree at Cornell University, a top Ivy League school located in Ithaca, New York.

His engineering education was destined to be put to work in the field that commanded young Howard's attention, the blossoming film industry. As Hollywood was quickly being turned into a film company town with frequent arrivals of determined individuals seeking to make a living in the exciting new world of cinema, Hawks by 1917 was working as a prop boy for Famous Players–Lasky, assisting Marshall Neilan on Mary Pickford films. Later that same year, he joined the Army Air Corps as a flying instructor. It was no accident that the man with the fascination with machines would later achieve one of his greatest film successes with an aviation story, *Only Angels Have Wings* with Cary Grant and Jean Arthur.

Hawks was a young man with a fixed objective, succeeding in the rapidly expanding Hollywood film scene, and as the Twenties beckoned, he shared a Hollywood house with several young men with the same objective, two of whom were destined for greatness, Allan Dwan and Irving Thalberg. Dwan was a fellow Hoosier who had served as an assistant football coach at his alma mater, Notre Dame, and discovered Hawks's cousin, Carole Lombard. Thalberg in his short life would achieve greatness as resident production genius at MGM under L.B. Mayer.

After Hawks was provided with his earlier-mentioned major opportunity to head the Famous Players story department, then to write scripts and direct films at Fox, he developed in the comedy field a pattern for friendship interspersed with conflict. His films reflected the saga of two male friends who often vied for the affections of the same girl. Often the friends would engage in lengthy travel, the films documenting their extensive adventures. In the famous Hawks hit of the fifties, *Gentlemen Prefer Blondes*, the sexes were reversed as the wandering friends were Marilyn Monroe and Jane Russell finding adventure on a cruise ship.

While conflict involving friends was one important thematic concern of Hawks, another was his penchant for adventure. He scored a magnificent breakthrough with his electrifying look at the gangland world of Al Capone, as Paul Muni scored one of his greatest screen triumphs in *Scarface*. This was the film in which a young George Raft introduced his enduring characteristic of tossing a coin into the air. Just as the adventurer Hawks had transmitted his interest in flying into the early 1939 Cary Grant success about the world of professional aviators, *Only Angels Have Wings*, another of his passions, auto racing, resulted in two films in the early and latter stages of his prolific career. The 1932 Warners production, *The Crowd Roars*, dealt with the world of auto racing, as did the 1965 release, *Red Line 7000*. A fondness for fast cars was understandable in view of Hawks's mechanical propensities along with his Hoosier background. The interest was so intense, in fact, that the versatile man of many interests designed the racecar that won the 1936 Indianapolis 500. A Hawks 1941 effort, *Sergeant York*, resulted in the only Best Actor Academy Award nomination in the career of Gary Cooper. The film traced the fascinating life of York from his pacifist roots to military heroism in World War I.

A master of adventure, it was only natural for Hawks to team up with America's symbol of action, John Wayne. Their first collaboration proved to be the best, the 1948 release *Red River*, which marked the spectacular film debut of Montgomery Clift in a Western remake of *Mutiny on the Bounty*. Clift usurps Wayne's leadership in the midst of a cattle drive. Wayne starred in three more Hawks westerns: *Rio Bravo* (1959), *El Dorado* (1967) and *Rio Lobo* (1970).

An analysis of Hawks's vehicles reveals a steady pattern of adventure and conflict involving individuals who feel for each other. The reason why *Red River* is perpetually cited for definitive dramatic efforts by both Wayne and Clift and heralded by fans of each leading man is that the story element of the younger actor playing the older performer's surrogate son provided enriching opportunities for each individual to stretch his talents. The dramatic tension woven into the story through the conflict that temporarily separates the two men enhanced the challenge involved for Wayne and Clift to pour every nuance into a relationship supercharged with feeling and emotion. Hawks learned his lessons well as a young man in his late twenties during his period as Jesse Lasky's story editor. Combine the elements of adventure and dramatic tension evolving from relationships that bear true meaning to the individuals involved, and you have a surefire formula for engaging audiences.

When examining the techniques and execution of Howard Hawks as a director, it becomes even easier to see why *The Big Sleep* became a gigantic success, as well as one of the principal films with which his name was associated. The story was a perfect blend of adventure combined with a fascinating conflict involving two characters very much in love, detective Philip Marlowe, case-hardened by the tough side of life, and his social opposite, Vivian Sternwood Rutledge, the daughter of a man of immense wealth, spoiled and accustomed to getting her way. When Marlowe resists, she finds him a challenge, which makes loving him all the more fascinating. It certainly did not hurt the character chemistry of the film that Bogart, rendering an unforgettable performance as Marlowe, and Bacall, the young actress 25 years his junior, were head over heels in love at the time. Their relationship took on even greater fascination in that Bogart was ending his stormy relationship with his combative wife, actress Mayo Methot. During the filming of *The Big Sleep*, Bogart moved out on Methot and took up quarters at the Beverly Hills Hotel, where co-star Bacall went for clandestine meetings.

If a hall of fame were ever established for film noir contributions, Humphrey Bogart would be credited with notable efforts on many fronts. It was Bogart who, portraying Dashiell Hammett's detective, Sam Spade, helped launch the film noir genre in John Huston's 1941 epic, *The Maltese Falcon*. He played the two most famous detectives in American fiction with his Spade portrayal in *Falcon* and as Raymond Chandler's Philip Marlowe in *The Big Sleep*. The two truly convincing Marlowe portraits most frequently mentioned in film annals were etched in the prolific mid-forties noir period with Dick Powell in *Murder, My Sweet* and Bogart in *The Big Sleep*. Each played Marlowe with convincing gusto. Each handled his role with distinctive characteristics extending back to earlier periods when their dramatic personas were being shaped. As will be later revealed, Bogart scored a major triumph in Nicholas Ray's moody noir drama about Hollywood, *In a Lonely Place*, a 1950 film in which he starred opposite the director's then-wife, Gloria Grahame. One year after the release of *The Big Sleep*, Bogart triumphed again opposite Bacall in the noir realm in Delmer Daves's *Dark Passage*, in which he plays an escaped convict attempting, with Bacall's help, to vindicate himself for a murder for which he was framed. He teamed up with Bacall once more in 1948 in *Key Largo*, a noir adaptation of a Maxwell Anderson play, in which he plays a returning World War II veteran who engages in a survival duel with ruthless mobster Edward G. Robinson.

Powell's performance as Marlowe in *Murder, My Sweet* marked a departure from his earlier song and dance roles. All the same, the Powell dramatic persona that evolved after he made the switch highlighted a breezy nonchalance, part of the earlier shaping process. His rendering of Marlowe was, in the mold of Chandler, reflective of the "I don't give a damn" insouciance of a detective who has adopted, as a result of extended experience in the nocturnal underbelly of Los Angeles life, a carefree shrug to it all.

Bogart made his early mark in Warner Bros. gangster films of the thirties. His scowling visage endowed many criminal tough guy roles, a villain to be tracked down and eventually stopped by the likes of James Cagney or George Raft. He played his roles with such consummate skill that he was consistently moved up in the cast, and to be elevated often enough eventuates in being recast as a hero. All the same, that scowling, no-nonsense visage was so convincingly portrayed that his lead roles were shaped to take advantage of Bogart's unique talents. Powell and Bogart, in the Marlowe tradition, both demonstrated the "I don't give a damn" demeanor reflective of the famous detective; but in the case of Powell, the feeling was conveyed with a shrug and a grin, while with Bogart, it was done with a stern stare. While Powell would laugh you off, Bogart would challenge you. Each performer delivered a convincing Marlowe portrait, but within the framework of each actor's individualized style.

Two More Hawks Stories

Howard Hawks became a one-man Hollywood folklore repository. Stories revolved around him in the manner that dogs are surrounded by fleas on a hot summer afternoon. One of the most frequently recounted Hawks stories involved two of the most prominent creative artists of the century, one an eminently famous film actor who was called "The King" long before Elvis Presley was accorded that distinction, the other a premiere novelist lionized throughout the world. As earlier revealed, William Faulkner was a close friend of director Hawks. He worked initially on *To Have and Have Not*, then on *The Big Sleep* for Hawks. Being a traditionalistic Southerner, it was not surprising that Faulkner shared Hawks's passion for hunting. During the period of their collaboration, Faulkner once arrived at Hawks's home early one morning to leave on a hunting trip. Not long before Hawks and Faulkner were ready to depart, the director received a telephone call from another hunting compatriot, Clark Gable, who asked if he could join the party. Gable promised to arrive immediately and not delay the anxious hunters.

The notable threesome left Hawks's home for their Imperial Valley hunting destination. As they were driving through Palm Springs, as Hawks later recalled, the talk turned to writing. Gable idly asked his new gray-haired hunting companion, Faulkner, for his opinion of the notable current writers. The Mississippian immediately responded with his choices: "Thomas Mann, Willa Cather, John Dos Passos, Ernest Hemingway, and myself."

"Oh, do you write, Mr. Faulkner?" a surprised Gable asked.

After a brief pause, Faulkner responded, "Yeah. What do you do, Mr. Gable?"

The story has been frequently recounted as a humorous example of a shrewd Faulkner letting the world's most famous film star know that he was every bit as notable in his field as was Gable. Hawks was not so certain that Faulkner intended his reply as a retort. "I don't think Gable ever read a book, and I don't think Faulkner ever went to see a movie," Hawks reflected. "So they might have been on the same level."

The final Hawks story to be recounted also relates to Faulkner, but to a lesser extent than its principal subject, the perpetually fascinating and enigmatic Raymond Chandler. Hawks, as earlier noted, assigned to write the screenplay for *The Big Sleep* the successful *To Have and Have Not* tandem of Faulkner and Hollywood scripting veteran Jules Furthman. They were joined this time by Leigh Brackett, who provided a female perspective. Brackett, a talented writer who worked sporadically in films and distinguished herself as a novelist specializing in science fiction and mystery, worked under Hawks in scripting the later John Wayne films *Hatari!*, *El Dorado* and *Rio Lobo*. Chandler enthusiasts are aware that she also provided the script for Robert Altman's 1973 film adaptation of the author's last detective novel, *The Long Goodbye.*

What transpired up the road, during filming, was the discovery that the script, following faithfully the plot developments of the Chandler novel, failed to explain who had killed the Sternwood chauffeur, Owen Taylor. In the Hollywood tradition, the basic story has several versions. In one, an angry Chandler, allegedly disgusted over not being asked to adapt his own material to the screen, curtly told Hawks that he did not know the answer, and to provide his own conclusion, then hung up the phone. All accounts indicate that Chandler expressed ignorance on the subject. Lauren Bacall, an eyewitness, revealed in her autobiography that Bogart, a shrewd and perceptive man, arrived on the Warner Bros. set one morning and asked director Hawks, "Who pushed (chauffeur Owen) Taylor off the pier?" According to Bacall, "Everything stopped. Howard, no one, had the answer. Taylor was the mystery chauffeur in the film. His disappearance was what brought Marlowe (Bogie) on the case originally. Howard sent a cable to Raymond Chandler asking him. He didn't know. *The Big Sleep* was a whodunit's whodunit. Intricate, intriguing, mysterious, filled with colorful characters, many of whom made one-scene appearances. Everything added to the aura of the film. And no one ever bothered to figure it out. It was a great detective movie and great fun to watch. Still is."

Bacall's account of the incident rings with plausibility, in addition to the fact that she was an on-the-scene principal during the filming. The dramatic account of a conference call involving one of filmdom's greatest directors, one of the top novelists America produced, along with its most prominent mystery writer, is, to quote Sam Spade from *The Maltese Falcon,* "the stuff dreams are made of." Given the frantic schedule of a director during filming, it is likely that Hawks, rather than attempting to reach Chandler by telephone, would send a cable seeking advice, as Bacall indicates. Her view is also supported by Chandler biographer Frank MacShane, who indicated that Chandler had wired Hawks back with a brief message, "I don't know." According to another Chandler biographer, Tom Hiney, the response was "No idea"—slightly different wording from MacShane's account yet an identical substantive viewpoint. In the Hollywood tradition, however, if a film were ever to be made recounting the event, it is virtually certain that a lengthy and dramatic conversation would be depicted involving Hawks, Faulkner and Chandler. Again, when in doubt between fact and legend, in Hollywood, accept the legend.

A SERIOUS PROBLEM?

Howard Hawks was confronted with a potential dilemma on how and where to proceed in the face of the exposure of a plot hole in the screenplay of *The Big Sleep.* His response demonstrates the difference between an instinctual genius of the craft and lesser talents geared more toward playing by the book. As a former story editor and director noted for not only working closely with writers, but also forming

Humphrey Bogart, cast as Detective Philip Marlowe, is primed for action in a scene from Howard Hawks's adaptation of Raymond Chandler's novel *The Big Sleep*. Nobel Prize–winning author William Faulkner was one of the film's scenarists.

alliances and hunting and drinking with them, Hawks was aware of the difference between a novel, where everything is governed by the printed page and what appears within its confines, and a film, in which, as Rouben Mamoulian had always pointed out, the distinguishing characteristic between the cinema and other creative art forms is the camera.

Hawks made a shrewd decision. Rather than express concern over the plot hole regarding Owen Taylor's unexplained death, the director, noted for his movies' dynamic blend of rapidly paced adventure and personal conflict, never attempted to resolve the point. Instead he let the action, along with the fascinating conflict between lovers Bogart and Bacall, portraying a cynical detective making his living by working the wrong side of the tracks and the spoiled daughter of an old and ill financial titan, carry the day. After the project was completed, a smugly satisfied Hawks could reflect, "Neither the author, the writer, nor myself knew who had killed whom."

As mentioned, *The Big Sleep* was Chandler's first novel. In the tradition of first-time authors, and especially hungry ones, such as the mystery novelist was at that bleak stage of his life, Chandler pulled out all stops. Everything he either experienced or read about the underbelly of Los Angeles life during the Depression-riddled thirties was recorded on paper, creating a lively and endless ensemble of characters marching in and out of action. As Pauline Kael wrote, "The characters are a collection of sophisticated monsters—blackmailers, pornographers, apathetic society girls (Lauren Bacall and Martha Vickers are a baffling pair of spoiled sisters; the latter sucks her thumb), drug addicts, nymphomaniacs (a brunette Dorothy Malone seduces the hero in what must surely be record time), murderers. All of them talk in innuendoes, as if that were a new stylization of the American language, but how reassuring it is to know what the second layer of meaning refers to."

Rather than be concerned about whether the audience comprehended every plot nuance, Hawks realized he had a winner as long as he graphically depicted the two fascinating leads, immersed in love and conflict, played with appropriate conviction by Bogart and Bacall, alongside the fascinating ensemble of characters assembled. Along with the aforementioned stars, Martha Vickers convincingly portrayed Carmen Sternwood, Bacall's sister, a thumb-sucking little girl type with a big girl's sexual appetites, as evidenced by her banter with Bogart. She is into dope as well as nymphomania. Elisha Cook Jr., who had performed so memorably opposite Bogart in *The Maltese Falcon*, is manipulated by his girlfriend in a blackmail scheme, ultimately being sadistically poisoned to death by cold-blooded killer Canino, played by former western star Bob Steele. The sadistic killer Steele is, in turn, killed by Marlowe. Dorothy Malone, in an early role, is the girl of relaxed virtue working in a bookshop who, in the words of Pauline Kael, seduced Marlowe "in record time." John Ridgely plays ruthless criminal boss Eddie Mars, with Bob Steele as his ruthless strongman and, when needed, assassin. Charles Waldron portrays the wealthy widower General Sternwood, whose exceptionally bad health has him confined to his humid, hot greenhouse, which is filled with orchids. Sternwood leads a drab life in the temperature-controlled greenhouse as he awaits death, which is referred to as "the big sleep," reflective of the book's and film's title.

Chandler biographer Tom Hiney pointed out that the author was contractually forbidden by Paramount from any serious involvement in the film, but that he did meet Hawks on numerous occasions and the men got along well. Using the conundrum relating to the identity of the person who killed chauffeur Owen Taylor, Hiney summarized the issue in reference to Chandler's writing strengths and Hawks's perception of the situation: "It was the characters, the style and the atmosphere that were engaging about Chandler's writing, and Hawks eventually understood that."

"I never figured out what was going on," Hawks conceded afterwards, "but I thought that the basic thing had great scenes and it was good entertainment. After that I said, 'I'm never going to worry about being logical again.'"

It is significant to note that, while both *To Have and Have Not* and *The Big Sleep* were big audience favorites and have sustained their popularity through repeated television showings, neither reviewers nor viewers reflect on the plots of either film. What made each a hit was the crisp, stylized dialogue delivered by one of Hollywood's most charismatic love duos, Humphrey Bogart and Lauren Bacall. *The Big Sleep* finds Bogart engaging in bitingly witty dialogue with both Sternwood sisters on his first visit to the giant family mansion owned by the General. Carmen, played by Martha Vickers, is slated to be sent to an asylum at the film's close. As Carmen flirts with him on their first meeting, his brisk responses are designed to tease:

CARMEN: What are you? A prizefighter?
MARLOWE: No, I'm a shamus.
CARMEN: What's a shamus?
MARLOWE: It's a private detective.
CARMEN: You're making fun of me.
MARLOWE: Uh, uh.
CARMEN (leaning back into his arms): You're cute.

Chandler indulges in a nose tweaking exercise on the idle rich through alter ego Marlowe. After his conversation with Carmen ends, Bogart tells Norris the butler, "Wean her, she's old enough." When he is received by General Sternwood, the irreverent detective is asked by his wealthy host how he likes his brandy, to which he replies, "In a glass." He saves his most curt barbs, however, for the spoiled and aloof older Sternwood daughter, Vivian, who tells him she does not like his manners. This leads to one of the memorable ripostes in film noir annals:

MARLOWE: Well, I'm not crazy about yours. I didn't ask to see you. I don't mind if you don't like my manners. I don't like them myself. They're pretty bad. I grieve over them long winter evenings. And I don't mind your ritzing me, or drinking your lunch out of a bottle, but don't waste your time trying to cross-examine me.

Master detective author Chandler invests his famous shamus with a smug air of superiority on occasions when he feels that the sinister forces with whom he deals are demonstrating all muscle and no brainpower. When one of the many racketeers moving on and off camera during the film, Joe Brody, portrayed by Louis Jean Heydt, pulls a gun on him, Marlowe's response is one of condescending pity:

MARLOWE: My, my, my! Such a lot of guns around town and so few brains. You know, you're the second guy I've met today that seems to think a gat in the hand means the world with the tail. Ha, ha, ha. Put it down, Joe. The other guy's name was Eddie Mars.

One inaccuracy persists regarding *The Big Sleep*. It is frequently stated that Bogart and Bacall were married during its filming. The error relates to the fact that *The Big Sleep* was not finally released until 1946, by which time Bacall was Mrs. Bogart, but the movie was actually completed in 1944.

TWO

Lancaster Noir

I never wanted the money. I just wanted you.

Criss Cross (1948)

Toward the end of *Criss Cross*, approaching death, Burt Lancaster stares soulfully at Yvonne De Carlo with funereal resignation and exclaims, "I never wanted the money. I just wanted you."

The cornerstone of powerful drama is truth. In successful film noir, the truth contains an indelible link to the raw emotions of lead characters shrouded in conflict. As noted, the fact that Howard Hawks's dramas and comedies frequently showcased continual conflict between his leading characters made him a natural for film noir, as his jackpot success with Raymond Chandler's *The Big Sleep* richly attested. The Lancaster–De Carlo romance in the shrewdly conceived 1948 Universal International mood piece, brilliantly shaped by Czech cinematographer Franz Planer in richly evocative black and white hues, contained the same stark tug of war of emotional conflict reminiscent of some other leading forties noir epics. One classic instance is James Cain's *Double Indemnity*, with a screenplay co-authored by none other than Chandler with the film's director, Billy Wilder. The bitingly cynical, always crackling dialogue reveals the snare in which hapless Fred MacMurray finds himself. A smarmy, good-time Los Angeles insurance salesman, MacMurray instantly realizes that Barbara Stanwyck constitutes major league trouble. Stanwyck is markedly unsubtle in letting him know that she wants her husband dead, but only after he has been enriched by a generous life insurance policy. MacMurray is drawn in nonetheless by her raw sexuality, making him a pawn in her hands despite his keen awareness of what she represents.

Burt Lancaster's fate at the hands of Yvonne De Carlo is another closely on-point illustration of male victimization. The situation bears a strongly analogous ring to *Out of the Past*—released in 1947, just one year before *Criss* Cross—in which a predatory Jane Greer delivers the performance of her career opposite Robert Mitchum. The same dramatic concept that made the film a classic was used one year later in *Criss Cross*. It also bears a strong creative resemblance to the film which ultimately made Lancaster a star, as will be noted later.

MACHO VICTIMIZATION

Some critics have lamented that, while *Criss Cross* is a well-drawn drama with a finely etched script, the problem lay in the casting. Burt Lancaster was just too macho and clean cut to be the victim of De Carlo. He was no more a victim than was Robert Mitchum, one of Hollywood's prime examples of machismo in motion, as was Lancaster throughout his long and highly successful career. Both roles, that of Lancaster as victimized armored truck driver Steve Thompson and Mitchum as ensnared detective Jeff Markham-Bailey in *Out of the Past*, involve strong men who handle themselves well even in brutal elements, but fall prey to beautiful brunettes.

Cinema macho victimization reaches its zenith with the portraits dramatically sculpted by Mitchum and Lancaster in *Out of the Past* and *Criss Cross*, respectively. Rather than have a weak, vacillating leading man fall victim to a *femme fatale* such as Jane Greer or Yvonne De Carlo, a story can be dramatically enriched by a sharp contrast of emotion. This can be more successfully accomplished if the male lead contains inner and outer strength, creating additional conflict and affording a more formidable challenge to a De Carlo or Greer. In each case, the *femme fatale* is a brunette, her dark beauty accented in shadowy hues of black and white richly evocative photography. Both actresses are up to the task of creating the proper level of temptation with an expectation of lasting romance to throw their macho victims off of their game. In any other instance, the macho male's native intelligence would hold sway, but trapped in the octopus-like clutches of desirable women for whom they hunger, they become victims.

Lancaster received grooming for his *Criss Cross* role through an earlier Universal triumph which made him a star and displayed the same effective noir story technique as *Criss Cross*. Lancaster received the benefit of good timing as well, avoiding what could have been a fatal derailment to his movie career.

LUCKY LANCASTER

Burt Lancaster was spotted on an elevator by Jack Mahor, a scout for Broadway producer Irving Jacobs. Invited to a reading at Manhattan's Warwick Hotel, he impressed enough to land a role in *A Sound of Hunting*, which played at New York's Lyceum Theater. While the play lasted only two weeks, Lancaster's masculine dynamism impressed audiences, including film scouts. Citing the newcomer's potential, fellow cast member Sam Levene knew just the person to handle him, steering Lancaster to the office of Harold Hecht, who managed his career and would later become a partner with him in the highly successful independent production company of Hecht-Hill-Lancaster.

East Harlem native Lancaster was ripe for the opportunity. He had been a USO entertainer in the Army's European theater during WWII. David Selznick almost signed Lancaster, declining since he believed the blonde New Yorker too closely resembled Guy Madison, an actor he had under contract. It was Hal Wallis, studio chief of Paramount who provided Lancaster with a round-trip first-class ticket to Hollywood and $100 a week for a one-month option. If he did not like the results of the screen test, Wallis would depart from the scene and Lancaster could utilize his return ticket back to New York.

The ironic element was that, had it not been for an assist in timing, Lancaster's initial film could have resulted in his demise. After a major buildup by Wallis, the ruggedly handsome former prep basketball star and professional acrobat was cast opposite Paramount's top leading lady, Lizabeth Scott, with whom he had screen-tested, and John Hodiak in *Desert Fury*. The film was greeted by the public with a resounding thud. Potentially faced with a box office failure in his first film, the luck of the Irish reigned on the son of Erin who hailed from East Harlem.

Universal was seeking a male lead for a film which producer Mark Hellinger was readying for production. German émigré Robert Siodmak was slated to direct an adaptation of the Ernest Hemingway short story, *The Killers*. Hellinger was reportedly interested in burly leading man Wayne Morris for the lead role of the ex-professional boxer who is gunned down mysteriously by hired killers in his rooming house residence in a small New Jersey town. Morris was seen as an ideal choice since he achieved initial fame playing a bellboy-turned-boxer under the guidance of manager Edward G. Robinson in the 1937 Warners drama, *Kid Galahad*, but the asking price for a loan-out was reportedly too steep. At that point, eastern newcomer Lancaster, fresh from his Paramount debut in *Desert Fury*, sparked attention. The physically commanding presence of the blonde, tousle-haired former acrobat drew Hellinger's interest. One nagging fear emerged: Would it be a mistake to cast two newcomers as leads in a major film?

Under normal circumstances, an up-and-coming producer like Hellinger would hedge his bets and cast at least one provable box office commodity in a leading man–lady tandem. These, however, were far from normal circumstances, as the leading lady proved to be a youthful North Carolinian with finely chiseled features and a curvaceous, stop-traffic figure named Ava Gardner. When Hellinger viewed the test he ordered of Lancaster with Gardner, he spotted the magic a legion of cinemagoers would later observe after the film debuted in 1946. Fortunately for Lancaster, *Desert Fury* would not reach the theaters until 1947. By that time, he was a red-hot commodity.

STORY SIMILARITIES

The Killers bore two striking similarities to *Criss Cross*: 1) the macho victimization of Lancaster, who is caught in the clutches of a thoroughly ruthless Gard-

Burt Lancaster plays a decent man who falls hard for *femme fatale* Yvonne De Carlo in *Criss Cross*, directed by German emigre Robert Siodmak. One of the 1948 film's most memorable lines is when Lancaster's mother, played by screen veteran Edna Holland, asks her son, "Of all the girls in Los Angeles, why did you have to pick her?" Lancaster made his film debut two years earlier as a victim to *femme fatale* Ava Gardner in another stirring Siodmak epic, *The Killers*, adapted from an Ernest Hemingway short story.

ner in the same manner that he is later eviscerated by De Carlo, and 2) each woman operates under the astutely rapacious guidance of a crime boss—Albert Dekker in *The Killers* and Dan Duryea in *Criss Cross*—using Lancaster to execute a game plan.

Anthony Veiller shrewdly adapted the Hemingway short story, which needed significant embellishment from its original form. Veiller had secured an Oscar nomination in the Best Adapted Screenplay category for *Stage Door* in 1937 and was nominated for his work in *The Killers* as well. During the war, he distinguished himself by co-scripting some of the episodes of Frank Capra's *Why We Fight* series, while John Huston later put him to work adapting the Tennessee Williams drama, *Night of the Iguana*. That 1964 release had as one of its stars Ava Gardner, along with Richard Burton and Deborah Kerr.

The Hemingway story was a challenge for a shrewd screen adapter. *The Killers*, one of the Nick Adams stories in which the famous author is thought to be the narrator in his early manhood, contains two powerful scenes. Two obvious hired killer types descend at early dinner hour on a diner in a sleepy New Jersey town and ask about Ole Anderson, a regular patron who works at a local gas station with Adams. They take Adams captive, along with the establishment's owner and chef, waiting for their intended victim to arrive. When he fails to show up, Adams takes a short cut to the rooming house where the former professional boxer lives, warning him about his impending fate. Anderson thanks Adams, but explains that running would be futile and he is ready to accept his fate.

The first two scenes are faithful to Hemingway's story as William Conrad and Charles McGraw arrive, big-city tough guys who enjoy ridiculing what they consider to be a hick town and the people who inhabit it. Lancaster, who in the film is known at that point as Pete Lund, a name he assumes to bury his past, is lying in bed when Adams, played by Phil Brown, warns him of the impending visit of Conrad and McGraw. Lancaster's face is shrouded in terror as the camera closes in and he thanks the young man for warning him. He explains in a tone leaden with fatalism that it is too late to do anything. Moments after Adams leaves, Lancaster is gunned down in a fusillade of bullets by his experienced executioners.

At that point, Veiller takes over, building his scenario around an insurance investigator, who serves as the bulldog tracking down the mystery to its conclusion. Edmond O'Brien, who spent much of his career seesawing between leads and character roles, plays the insurance investigator who doggedly pursues the case to his boss' chagrin, until the entire story is revealed. He walks through a minefield of activity surrounding a ruthless criminal syndicate and almost loses his life at the hands of one of the thugs in the process.

The O'Brien role is reminiscent of one he would portray in another noir classic four years later in *D.O.A.*, in which, playing an accountant from a small California desert town, he has just one day to learn the identity of his killer before a deadly poison causes his demise. In each case, O'Brien is a thorough, doggedly determined investigator eager to crack a case. In the latter instance, he seeks to solve his own murder, while in *The Killers*, his curiosity is aroused by the story of hard-luck loner, ex-boxer Lancaster, and what prompted him to enter a life of crime which resulted in death by syndicate execution.

O'Brien tracks Lancaster to his hometown of Philadelphia, where Pete Lund took the name of Ole Anderson and achieved a successful career as a light heavyweight fighter until a broken right hand prematurely ended it. O'Brien's contact into Lancaster's world is Philadelphia plainclothes officer Sam Levene, the actor who steered Lancaster to Harold Hecht, who plays an old boyhood chum of the exfighter. He learns that after Lancaster's career ended, he fell head over heels in love with Ava Gardner, the gun moll love interest of Big Jim Colfax, a local mob boss played by Albert Dekker. Levene then falls into the awkward position of arresting Gardner when she is spotted by him wearing an expensive piece of jewelry that had been stolen in a robbery. When Lancaster arrives in the midst of the contretemps, he initially seeks to talk his old neighborhood friend out of arresting the woman with whom he is totally infatuated. Levene plays by the book and Lancaster eventually sucker punches him, escaping in the commotion. When the smoke clears, Lancaster has taken the rap for Gardner and does a stretch in the penitentiary for armed robbery.

The story moves to a new level after Dekker as Big Jim Colfax and Lancaster are both released from prison and the mobster recruits manpower for the robbery of a hat factory. As the plot is hatched, Gardner looks seductive sitting in a far corner. Lancaster's eyes are mountains of unyielding desire as he stares at her, longing to replace Dekker as the man in her life, the mob boss who supplanted him when he finished his prison stretch. Deeply felt anxieties over Gardner prompt tension between Dekker and Lancaster, as a disagreement over a hand of cards ultimately leads Lancaster to punch the mob boss, knocking him down. Dekker assures them that they will have business to settle after the robbery is completed. An equally determined Lancaster declares himself to be ready.

Lancaster a Sting Victim

After the robbery is completed, a distraught Gardner arrives at Lancaster's motel, explaining that Dekker is attempting to do him out of his rightful share. She plays on his always sharp-edged romantic emotions toward her, enlisting his support and convincing him that they will be together for good. He pledges unswerving devotion toward her and she reciprocates by taking all of the robbery proceeds, vanishing without a trace.

The robbery gang, believing that Lancaster is the culprit, seeks to find him. He also vanishes without an apparent trace. As O'Brien and Levene pounce on any potential lead they encounter, an array of fascinating character performers surface. The film is marked with brilliant portrayals at all levels, beginning with O'Brien and Levene as determined investigators and Dekker as a rugged, no-nonsense mob boss. Two gangsters etched with gripping realism follow divergent paths. Vince Barnett, whose show business career began as a party wise guy paid to insult guests with a thick German accent, then confess that it was all in fun, impresses as Charleston, Lancaster's prison cellmate who reads about astronomy and tells his friend about the stars as they stare out the window during long evenings. Barnett is provided with an opportunity to become a part of the robbery team. He decides that he is too old for that sort of thing and tries unsuccessfully to talk Lancaster out of any involvement.

Jeff Corey has one of the memorable scenes of the film, one of the most gripping in noir annals, as a dying man who has been killed by one of his fellow armed robbers, erroneously convinced that Blinky, the character Corey portrays, is the culprit. Tipped off by police, O'Brien and Levene arrive just in time to hear Corey hallucinate about the robbery, trembling and covered with sweat. It reveals the ultimate tragedy of a man of crime believing that he was on the verge of the big score, the one that would change his life. Corey would appear with Lancaster one year later, playing the role of a stool pigeon in *Brute Force*. A veteran of stage and screen, Jeff Corey was one of the best-known dramatic instructors in Hollywood. At one point in the sixties, his famous workshop had as students Jack Nicholson, Robert Towne, Roger Corman and Sally Kellerman.

O'Brien's perseverance finally pays off, but not until he has almost lost his life after being waylaid by Jack Lambert as Dum Dum, Corey's killer, at the motel where Lancaster had gone after the holdup, and where his rendezvous with Gardner occurred. Lambert continues to believe that he will find the elusive cash and pursues his quest to an ultimate meeting with Dekker at the film's end.

LYING YOUR SOUL INTO HELL

Two other memorable character performers who went on to fame in major television roles, Lancaster's executioners from the beginning of the film, Charles McGraw and William Conrad, surface at the end. Determined to wipe out O'Brien after he has made contact with Gardner, they engage in a shootout with O'Brien, Levene and police in a nightspot, losing their lives. The battle was given a dramatic prelude as O'Brien meets Gardner, then travels by cab with her to the nightclub. The music of prolific film composer Miklos Rozsa, who won an Oscar for his haunting *Spellbound* score, accents the mounting drama and the electric tension preceding a showdown. The famous dum-du-dum-dum cadence from the popular *Dragnet* television series for which Rozsa wrote the score is heard during this period, as the cold-blooded mercenaries size up their prospective prey.

McGraw and Conrad were patient performers who ultimately made the grade in a big way. McGraw was under contract to Howard Hughes at RKO and was compelled to wait until getting his break. He appeared as a tough, uncompromisingly honest police detective in a film that many critics believe to be the best low budget noir film ever, *Narrow Margin*, which Richard Fleischer directed at RKO. McGraw played the father of killer Robert Blake in Richard Brooks's pulsating adaptation of Truman Capote's best seller *In Cold Blood* while Jeff Corey portrayed the father of Blake's accomplice killer, Scott Wilson. McGraw is best known in Hollywood circles for playing the legendary Rick in the television series *Casablanca*, modeled on the classic film and role of Humphrey Bogart.

As for Conrad, he looked older and mature even as a younger performer, and as a result never appeared to age. He looked as old as time itself as the boxing manager who steers John Garfield toward success in the 1947 ring classic, *Body and Soul*, only to be dealt out of the scene by corrupt mobster Lloyd Gough. After playing a variety of character roles through the years, Conrad became one of the most popular actors of the seventies in his starring role as the smooth, unflappable detective Cannon in the series of the same name.

The film ends with O'Brien and Levene arriving at Dekker's home after the mob boss and former underling Lambert have inflicted fatal gunshot wounds on one another. The determined investigator and his steady accomplice are able to piece together the final details of the mystery as a dying Dekker provides valuable details. Lancaster was victimized by a sting perpetrated by Dekker with the woman who was actually his wife, Gardner. The ex-fighter was perceived as the individual who absconded with the funds, which were actually shared in their entirety by Dekker and Gardner.

At a climactic high point, a desperate Gardner implores her husband to tell the authorities that she was innocent of any wrongdoing. Levene tartly responds with his most memorable line of the film, "You're asking a dying man to lie his soul into hell." The curt dialogue summarizes the opportunistic treachery of Gardner, who looks after herself first, last and always.

The demise of mob boss Dekker marked the end of the criminal enterprise, as each of the robbery operatives tasted death in the ongoing saga of locating the missing cash. Fall guy Lancaster's link in the unfolding mystery was so fatalistic that Albert Camus the great existentialist could well have written the details. Having been double-crossed by Gardner, the woman he passionately loved, Lancaster disappeared, assuming a new name and persona as a solitary figure in a small New Jersey town. Fate stared him in the face one afternoon, however, when Dekker pulled into the gas station where Lancaster worked. They exchange a few words and Dekker leaves. Immediately Lancaster as Pete Lund tells compatriot Nick Adams that he is not feeling well and asks to leave, with the younger man agreeing to cover for him. He awaits his appointment with death, which comes soon. Dekker realizes how important it is to silence him, since other members of the mob might locate him, thrusting into the open the question of what happened to the robbery money. By then Dekker has taken a new name and is a respectable local figure with a contracting business in Pennsylvania.

Lancaster combines strength and vulnerability in his role, a strong man taken down by a woman for whom he hungers and ultimately cannot have. When he first sees Gardner singing and playing the piano at a party in Dekker's apartment while the mob chieftain is still in prison, his long stare is one of total envelopment, of a man who will never be able to let go. He never does and Gardner proves to be his downfall, as his cellmate Vince Barnett futilely warned.

A clever script ploy by Veiller cast Lancaster as the boyfriend of Virginia Christine. He takes her to a party at the Dekker apartment, then meets Gardner and is never the same again. Christine, who became prominent late in her career as Mrs. Olson in the popular Folgers Coffee commercials of the sixties and seventies, resignedly fades into the background. When we next see her, it is as O'Brien is meeting Levene for the first time. We learn that she is Levene's wife, at which point she reveals that things turned out well and that she and Lancaster were never that serious about one another.

Levene proves the perfect complement to O'Brien, particularly when the insurance investigator, unaccustomed to the brutalities of the mob world, supplies the needed hand of the experienced big city policeman. One year later Levene appeared in another noir classic, RKO's overpowering look at anti-Semitic hatred in Edward Dmytryk's *Crossfire.* In the latter film Levene played a kindly Jewish man who seeks to befriend returning soldier Robert Ryan and some of his WWII companions in his comfortable Washington, D.C., apartment. Sadistic East St. Louis cop Ryan responds by beating Levene to death because he is Jewish.

OVERCOMING A MAJOR OBSTACLE

With *The Killers* achieving critical and box office success for Lancaster and Universal, making a second film on the created impetus for the same studio two years later would appear to be a relatively simple proposition. Such was not the case as the fickle finger of fate intervened, almost dooming the *Criss Cross* project.

Dynamic producer Mark Hellinger followed his success with *The Killers* with another winner, a taut police drama focusing on New York City and the teamwork of its law enforcement officers. *The Naked City* starred Barry Fitzgerald as a wily veteran detective showing the ropes to ambitious Don Taylor as they successfully pursue and arrest killer Ted de Corsia. Directed with a deft touch for detail by Jules Dassin, the film gives a capsulized look to New York's busy streets in the swirl surrounding a murder case. The film proved a catalyst for Jack Webb, who adapted the film's police-oriented big city approach to Los Angeles in launching his major television series hit of the fifties, *Dragnet.*

During the filming of *The Naked City*, workaholic Hellinger, a macho, two-fisted former New York columnist friend of Walter Winchell's before entering the ranks of film producers, died of a heart attack at 44. With *Criss Cross* on the drawing boards, the question emerged as to whether the film would be made. The maxim of "the show must go on" applied as a team fell into place, but albeit after much reluctance. Lancaster, who referred to the project as "celluloid trash," was fearful that continuing in a venture that formed the third and last of a contracted series with Hellinger, would end his career. He sought to convince Twentieth Century Fox to pay off Hellinger's widow, a former Ziegfeld showgirl, so that he could undertake a film project for the Beverly Hills studio, but the asking price of $253,000 was deemed too steep. As a result, Lancaster was once more dealt a lucky hand, albeit this time almost over his dead body.

German émigré Robert Siodmak, who had directed *The Killers*, reemerged to place his stamp on another black and white noir thriller which captured through evocative close-ups the torture of a man suffering the torment of a love for which he hungered, but could not ultimately have. Lancaster, the anguished star of *The Killers*, was the perfect lead, displaying once more the persona of a virile young male whose craving for the wrong woman dooms him ultimately.

Michael Kraike stepped into the late Hellinger's shoes and headed the production, while Daniel Fuchs, a skilled pro who ultimately won a Best Original Story Oscar for the 1955 biography of singer Ruth Etting, *Love Me or Leave Me* with James Cagney and Doris Day, crafted a screenplay with punch, one that focused on two important thematic areas: 1) the overpowering emotion Lancaster displayed for the woman who victimized him, and 2) how the triangle involving the woman he loves and the mobster with whom he competes for her affections leads to a clever double cross, which results in the descriptive title, *Criss Cross*, the story of how a man's powerful sexual hunger renders him vulnerable to criminal activity and eventually costs him his life. Fuchs adapted the screenplay from a novel by Don Tracy.

The immediate post-war scene at Universal saw a beautiful, shapely brunette dancer surface as the studio's new glamorous leading lady. At a time when lovely Canadian songstress Deanna Durbin's career was fading out, British Columbian Peggy Yvonne Middleton assumed the name of Yvonne De Carlo, and screen magic emerged. The Vancouver-born De Carlo was plucked for the lead role in *Salome, Where She Danced* (1945) following a contest organized by studio publicists to find "the most beautiful girl in the world." While far from an impressive opening vehicle, De Carlo's beauty impressed viewers, along with her spirited dancing form. The next studio vehicle for the former dancer, whose talent in her earlier career would be exhibited on screen throughout her career as Columbia did with Rita Hayworth, was a spectacular technicolor musical which achieved great commercial success. Before becoming a film star, Yvonne had become a celebrity in Hollywood as lead dancer at the Florentine Gardens, run by her early show business mentor, N.T. Granlund. *Song of Scheherezade* was a thinly based autobiography on the early life of composer Nikolai Rimsky-Korsakov, which provided a vehicle for his great music and an opportunity for De Carlo to dance amid the glitz of numbers choreographed by Tilly Loesch in spectacular technicolor. French heartthrob Jean-Pierre Aumont starred as the great Russian composer while New York Metropolitan opera star Charles Kullman was recruited to sing some of the composer's memorable numbers.

Robert Kendall left his hometown of Battle Creek, Michigan, after winning a talent contest sponsored by local merchants, with the top prize being a trip to Hollywood and a promised screen test. When the Hollywood production company instead went out of business, Kendall persevered, receiving his big break when prominent agent Christian Hofeld was served a hamburger by the aspiring actor at McDonnells and noticed that the young man waiting on him fit the part of Hassan in the film Universal was casting, *Song of Scheherezade*. After a meeting with the film's director, Walter Reisch, Kendall was given the role, playing the young servant of Eve Arden, the mother of De Carlo.

"I had the same makeup man as Yvonne De Carlo and I sat a short distance from her while her makeup was being applied and I was waiting my turn," Kendall recalls. "I couldn't help but observe that Yvonne De Carlo had beautiful, expressive, large blue eyes, with raven black hair falling about her shoulders. She had very smooth skin. Yvonne said very little as her makeup was being applied. She often stayed in her dressing room until called to act in a scene. Apparently she was concentrating on the character she was portraying in the picture."

Kendall remembers one memorable day during the filming when Maria Montez, the other exotically beautiful brunette leading lady at Universal, appeared on the set to watch her husband Jean-Pierre Aumont perform a tender love scene with De Carlo. "Carefully she watched them, her face becoming a mask displaying no emotion," Kendall relates. "When the scene was over Yvonne walked over and greeted Maria Montez, who smiled in a friendly manner and assured her husband that he had done a good job of acting. One could not help but wonder if she meant too good."

The success of De Carlo in the 1947 release *Scheherezade* prompted Universal to star her opposite crooner Tony Martin in a musical remake of *Algiers* called *Casbah*, which was released one year after the earlier musical. While blazing a trail to success, with her sensuous dancing showing off her sveltely sexy dancer's figure, De Carlo received an opportunity to play a vastly different role in *Criss Cross*. The opportunity arose at a time when she was almost convinced that it had passed her by.

While achieving success, De Carlo longed to stretch her wings and appear in a solid drama, something beyond what she termed "rock candy." While Hellinger had promised her the role opposite Lancaster, the brunette actress believed that his untimely death had perhaps destroyed her opportunity to secure a role she coveted. "As I went about my studio routines I heard that it would be either Ava (Gardner) or Shelley Winters for the female lead," De Carlo noted in her autobiography. "There was some doubt that the project would go at all without Mark but suddenly it was all go, and surprise of surprises, I got the role of Anna. I was told that producer Michael Kraike and director Robert Siodmak had done battle with the high brass to see that they honored Hellinger's promise to me."

The Naked City as a Model

In Hellinger's journalistic days, his famous *New York Mirror* column had a readership of 22 million. He considered himself a man with the people's touch, like his good friend Damon Runyon, but with one difference. Whereas Runyon, the author of the famous musical *Guys and Dolls*, had a sensitive ear attuned to some of New York society's colorful characters among racetrack touts, punchy prizefighters, mobsters and zany drunks, Hellinger concentrated on the common folk, the regular citizenry, people with stories to tell behind often superficially ordinary veneers. As a producer, he exerted influence on the development of *The Naked City* as a New York story revealing the people of the city. The focal point was pitching together through teamwork to catch ruthless killer Ted de Corsia. Barry Fitzgerald is a father figure as an older police detective to Don Taylor, who talks about his young family. Fitzgerald epitomizes a policeman with what in doctor's terminology constitutes "good bedside manner." He knows how to relate to the common folk. They pitch together through teamwork to snare a killer on New York's busy streets.

One of the appealing elements of the *Criss Cross* project to Hellinger was the opportunity to produce the same result for Los Angeles that *The Naked City* evoked with New York. The increasingly sprawling West Coast metropolis was to be examined with the camera's probing eye. Whereas the large city to the east was a symbol of stability, Los Angeles was increasingly burgeoning with fresh faces flocking steadily into the city, in many instances the families of returning veterans who were previously stationed in bases in southern California.

Hellinger had something in common with city of the angels laureate Raymond Chandler, who also, despite his critical comments about the city which became his home, was fascinated as an always-curious creative artist by the sprawling metropolis' collection of grafters, drifters, and just plain folks seeking a better life. While New York furnished a traditional stability, Los Angeles was in transition.

The film opens with an overhead shot of Los Angeles City Hall, situated in the heart of downtown. Fuchs then shifts the action to the period immediately preceding the pivotal moment of Steve Thompson's life, as he transports an armored truck toward the factory 45 minutes from the city where the big payoff is to be secured. Thompson has arranged for the designated third member of the team to be absent to make it easier for the upcoming heist to be accomplished through a call to the driver revealing that his wife is ill and he is needed immediately at home. Thompson drives while his compatriot is none other than his surrogate father, his widow mother's boyfriend Pop, played by Griff Barnett, who spends a great deal of time at the Thompson home. Crafty veteran Pop is initially suspicious about the call and the fact that regulations are being broken by having only two drivers secure the large payload, but Thompson is able to convince him that there is nothing to worry about.

The mainspring of dramatic tension is revealed as a tense young man attempts to appear calm and prepares to meet his fate in a daring make-or-break holdup. At that point, Fuchs shrewdly alters his focus and takes the story back to the critical developments leading to the holdup.

KIDDING ONLY HIMSELF

The timeless saying that "men wear their hearts on their sleeves" could have been written for armored truck driver Steve Thompson, portrayed with a rich and restless fidelity by Burt Lancaster. Lancaster's restless virility is on display from the outset as the film focuses on his arrival from a self-imposed one-year-and-three-month hiatus, in which he roamed through the southwest and Midwest of America, taking odd jobs. Nine months earlier, he had married Anna, the woman who stirred his blood to vaporous levels. The marriage lasted seven months. Following two painful months attempting to adjust to the change, he decides that an alteration of scenery might finally cool his burning passions for Anna.

Lancaster is observed exiting the red car, the streetcar line that for years ran through the city. The sign over the front window reveals "Hollywood" as its ultimate destination, but Lancaster disembarks in the old section of the city hovering just above an area of downtown Los Angeles known as Bunker Hill, which can be seen below. This is an area about which L.A. chronicler Chandler wrote a great deal, and with good reason. An area containing older residences, it gave the impression of having been lived in, a sharp contrast from the new tract homes springing up in the San Fernando Valley and other suburban sections outside Los Angeles proper. Criminal elements down on their luck frequented the area. Chandler's detective, Philip Marlowe, visited Bunker Hill to meet down-and-outers with valuable information to assist him on cases.

After Lancaster exits the red car, he walks up a hill and arrives at an old white-framed house. It is typical of many in the area, built in the twenties. This is a bread-and-butter community consisting of people who work hard to make a living. The area and homestead establish Lancaster's social status.

Lancaster's restlessness becomes immediately clear. His younger brother, played by Richard Long, tries to convince him to go ice skating his first evening home. He explains that he would rather stay home, read the paper, and spend some time with his best girl, his mother, played by silent screen veteran Edna Holland, all the while kidding himself. His hot blood rushing, Lancaster is eager to relocate the woman he left Los Angeles to forget. He fails to fool his shrewd mother however, and from the outset of their reunion, we see the look of concern on the face of Holland concerning the oppressive torch her son carries for his ex-wife.

FATEFUL MEETING

Pretending that he just wants to revisit his old haunt, a nightclub-bar near home, Lancaster leaves his home and adventures. The tension is revealed in his eyes as he walks into the nightclub section and observes the woman of his dreams, the one he has vowed to forget, dancing with another man. The dancing partner of the young woman who initially earned her show business spurs dancing at Florentine Gardens is a New York newcomer making his film debut, Tony Curtis, to the tune of "Brazilian Rhapsody." Curtis's sole function is dancing and when the number ends so does Tony, without a line.

De Carlo observes her former husband, and they sit down at a table. She asks him why he never answered the letter she wrote to him. "I didn't have anything to say," he replies, far from the truth, as they both know. Immediately tension is discernible, the emotional mix of two people who cannot seem to get along when they are together and think constantly of one another when they are apart.

The tension accelerates some more when De Carlo's date for the evening, Dan Duryea, arrives at the table, informing Lancaster that he is sitting in his chair. Lancaster's expression and body language reveal his distaste for Duryea. The brief meeting establishes the major clash of the film, the dangerous triangle that will ultimately destroy each individual.

The casting of Duryea as local mob boss Slim Dundee was a stroke of perfection. Duryea's sneering manner made him one of the definitive slimy villains of postwar Hollywood. Like Lancaster, Duryea was a New Yorker, growing up in the comfortable Big Apple suburb of White Plains. His pedigree was thoroughly disjointed from the persona in which he made his mark. An Ivy Leaguer who attended Cornell, Duryea inherited the president's position of the Cornell Drama Society after future cinema leading man Franchot Tone graduated. Duryea's slim, brooding, frequently sneering manner made him a natural for black and white noir drama. He impressed with his believable sleaziness as the "bodyguard" of Joan Bennett in the Fritz Lang noir gem, *Scarlet Street*, as he orchestrates her shakedown of lovelorn Edward G. Robinson, and in Lang's *The Woman in the Window*, when as a corrupt ex-policeman, he shakes down Bennett. Both films will be explored later in detail.

In his next meeting with De Carlo, an angry Lancaster excoriates her for going with mobster Duryea. She responds with the assurance that their meeting was no more than a date and that Duryea meant nothing to her. This statement is De Carlo at her most duplicitous, a manner which keeps Lancaster perpetually off balance as he continues aching for her.

One fateful evening when he visits the old haunt, where they spent so much of their time together, Lancaster is told by the bartender that the head waiter has given away the table he has reserved. Lancaster demands to know why, and the bartender haltingly explains that De Carlo, the girl of his dreams, has gone to Yuma to marry Duryea.

An Existential Result

The best of film noir frequently resembles the existentialism of Jean Paul Sartre and Albert Camus. Characters become pawns of fate as intervening events take charge of their lives. The narrative of Lancaster contains this ring when he is seen standing at a counter at expansive Union Station in downtown Los Angeles. He explains that things would have been different had he left moments earlier and not ordered a pack of cigarettes. His eyes capture a departing Duryea and his new wife Anna, who is seeing him off.

They meet outside Union Station. She tells him that Duryea has gone to Detroit on business. It marks the beginning of a reunion as the old flames are rekindled within Lancaster. As always, the sparks fly in two directions as the strong-willed couple battles as well. Eventually Duryea returns and the plot spins into its key phase, when the fate of the distrustful triangle is decided following a daring gambit.

A Shrewd Criss Cross

The criss cross of the film's title occurs after Duryea's return. Lancaster, seething over sharing a woman he believes rightly belongs to him, becomes so agitated at one point over her marrying a man he feels is well beneath her that he calls her a "tramp," repeating the name with more sorrow than ferocity. De Carlo complains about her mistreatment at his hands, at one point showing him her back, which bears marks from Duryea attacks. She also complains about the terrible treatment she has received from Stephen McNally, a boyhood neighborhood friend of Lancaster's who is now a police detective. For the first time in his life, Lancaster and McNally find themselves on different sides.

The clash with McNally, his old Los Angeles boyhood friend, is reminiscent of Lancaster's eventual confrontation with old Philadelphia lifelong friend Sam Levene, the detective who is belted by Lancaster when he is prepared to run his girlfriend Ava Gardner in on a theft charge for stealing an expensive pin, only to see the ex-fighter take the rap for her.

An angry Lancaster confronts McNally in a drunken stupor at his favorite haunt. McNally admits to taking her to the station and threatening to run her out of town. He concedes that this step was taken after Lancaster's mother, Edna Holland, implored him to do something about her son's infatuation with a woman she is convinced will bring him nothing but trouble. At one point, she asks her older son with deep frustration, "Out of all the girls in Los Angeles, why did you have to pick her?" After McNally admits to having attempted to run De Carlo out of town, the inebriated Lancaster takes a furious and wild swing, connecting with air and falling to the ground.

At that critical moment in the drama, when Lancaster burns with desire for De Carlo, Duryea catches Lancaster at home with his wife. Members of his gang accompany him. Lancaster believes that De Carlo's life is at stake as well as his. After some quick thinking, he tells Duryea why he has been speaking to De Carlo, explaining that he has conveyed his interest in using Duryea's gang to execute an armored truck holdup.

"It can't be done!" experienced mobster Duryea snaps, expressing conventional wisdom.

"Yes it can," Lancaster responds with conviction, "if you have an inside man."

With that statement, made in the heat of the moment to cover for the woman he loves and the fact she is seeing him while married to a feared gang leader, seals the fate of all of them. From that point the enterprise moves into high gear. Duryea's henchmen express delight at the prospect of a large payoff, one that can set them all on easy street. The well-nigh impossible can be accomplished with the aid of armored truck operative Lancaster.

ENLISTING AN OLD PRO

The pivotal planning meeting for the heist involves as its centerpiece a character who could have come directly from the pen of Raymond Chandler immersed in a setting familiar to the hard-boiled mystery writer. Duryea and his operatives along with Lancaster meet in a dilapidated rooming house in the heart of Bunker Hill. Chandler knew it to be an area inhabited by the down-and-outers, the derelicts and small timers of crime hoping to climb the ladder and achieve the ultimate big payday that proves as elusive as the perfect wave a surfer seeks to capture. As the Duryea entourage climbs the hill to the rooming house, word circulates as to who will be at the meeting.

"Finchley's coming," one of the men exclaims with the boyish reverence of a New York youngster waiting for the appearance and, hopefully, the autograph of Joe Dimaggio.

Finchley is one of those fascinating noir figures that captures the imagination. He walks in, slender and bespectacled, assuming the manner of a tenured Oxford professor preparing to lecture a class of respectful acolytes. Alan Napier's background was classically theatrical in the definitive British sense. Two of his fellow classmates were John Gielgud and Robert Morley. Doubt concerning why this distinguished-looking man has taken a position as consultant to underworld figures such as Duryea is quickly resolved as one of the mobster's operatives carries two bottles of whiskey with him, then informs the adviser to the lawless that his effort will be rewarded by a one-week supply at the local liquor store. Finchley disdains the offer of a drink before he commences, explaining that he will imbibe only after he finishes his work, conveying the distinct impression that otherwise the work would not be completed.

"It can't be done!" Finchley crisply responds when being told of the group's objective.

"Yes it can," Lancaster bounds forth, supplying the same explanation that had earlier intrigued Duryea. Finchley's eyes light up and his agile subterranean creative mind begins clicking.

The setting for the meeting is textbook noir. Shadows fill the room, and the periodic clang of the passing Angels Flight streetcar can be heard. The train can also be seen passing in the shadowy darkness of approaching evening through a window. Meanwhile Finchley goes to work, explaining the use of an ice cream truck on the scene as a helpful tool and diversionary tactic. De Carlo sits idly in a corner of the room during the meeting. Lancaster occasionally shoots a hungry stare her way. The audience is reminded that she is the reason why this otherwise decent man is cavorting with such questionable company. This scene is comparable to the one in *The Killers* where a lusty Lancaster cannot keep his eyes off of Ava Gardner as he is asked by mob boss Albert Dekker if he wants to participate in the hat box factory robbery. Yearning to be near Gardner, hoping to eventually rekindle old flames, he consents, spurning the warning of his old cellmate Vince Barnett. In *Criss Cross*, it is Lancaster's desire to shield De Carlo from danger vis-a-vis Duryea and his henchmen which prompts him to suggest the daring armored truck robbery.

As the meeting ends, Finchley, believing an award is then justified, hungrily wolfs down whiskey in the manner of a youngster devouring soda pop on a hot summer afternoon. With the end of the meeting, the plan spins from its formulative to active stage. At one point, however, what was supposed to be a clever ploy to divert suspicion turns into something else.

The gang decides to meet in a private room at their favorite nightclub haunt, at which Duryea and Lancaster, who hold no love for one another, are supposed to clash. This coupled with the announcement that Duryea would be taking another one of his business trips to Detroit represents diversionary strategy.

In *The Killers*, Lancaster clashes with a mob boss who is also his rival for the woman for whom he hungers. On the eve of the hat factory robbery, Dekker and Lancaster clash over the ex-fighter's erroneous conviction that the mob boss is cheating him out of a hand of cards. The misunderstanding stems from Lancaster not getting a chance to see Dekker's hand. Lancaster punches Dekker, who falls to the floor and begins to make a move for his gun. An angry Lancaster threatens to kick his teeth in if he moves for the gun. Dekker rises from the floor as Lancaster is restrained by gang members, telling his armed robbery subordinate that once the job has been accomplished, "We'll have business together." Lancaster declares himself ready.

All the while the burning image of himself alone with the woman of his dreams resounds in his mind. He longs for the days of being the man in Kitty Collins's life, as he was when Big Jim Colfax was in prison.

In the case of hated rivals Lancaster and Duryea, the previously arranged fight for strategic show proves to be "too good" in the estimation of concerned gang members, who fear that tomorrow's important job will be compromised. As a concerned Stephen McNally bursts into the room, he finds Duryea lying on the floor with a knife resting next to him. Lieutenant Pete Ramirez can barely contain his joy, telling mobster Slim Dundee that he has been looking for an opportunity for some time to arrest the mobster. Lancaster immediately shuts the door on his old friend McNally's intention, explaining that his difference of opinion with Duryea was personal, refusing to make a complaint. A dejected McNally leaves and the gang disperses shortly thereafter, avoiding a close call and preparing for the next day.

It has been agreed by mutual antagonists Lancaster and Duryea that De Carlo should be the individual hanging on to the money secured from the robbery. Duryea is scheduled to take a trip to Detroit to cover his activity. Lancaster believes that not only has he protected De Carlo by hatching the robbery idea to cover for her infidelity, but also that the executed heist will free her from her criminal husband and bring her back into his arms. She has assured him repeatedly that this is her desire. They have planned post-robbery activities. He will meet her at the small house in Palos Verdes, which has served as their private hideaway retreat.

HERO OR PRIME SUCKER?

The holdup scene is shot at a factory on Terminal Island. As Lancaster drives the armored truck onto the premises, the ice cream truck, around which the mob figures hover, the brainchild of criminal mastermind Finchley, is observable. The fireworks begin when mob members fire tear gas bombs. Lancaster's surrogate father Pop, played by Griff Barnett, jumps from the truck, beginning to shoot. The mob members place gas masks over their face and begin firing relentlessly. Lancaster had obtained a promise from Duryea beforehand that Pop would not be harmed, but the relentless mobster immediately shoots him. He then goes after Lancaster in the ensuing double cross.

As his mother's boyfriend, the lovable Pop, drops to the ground, fury overtakes Lancaster. He fights Duryea initially with his fists, then shoots him. The armored truck driver finally falls into a haze and collapses.

When Lancaster awakens in the hospital, his right arm hangs on an upraised sling. His family is with him. Prideful younger brother, Richard Long, smiles as he brandishes the morning's newspaper. Lancaster is the headline subject. The article extols his heroism in the line of duty, revealing that he has saved half of the armored truck's payroll and fought off a mob of dangerous criminals.

"What about Pop?" Lancaster asks with apprehensive concern.

He learns that Pop was killed in the robbery assault. Lancaster is crushed, painfully aware of his own involvement in the robbery, which cost the life of the man he loved like a father.

An important element of film drama is the skillful use of contrasts. After Lancaster's proud family leaves his room, convinced as is the media that he is a hero, a sharply contrasting figure arrives, his boyhood pal and recent nemesis Lieutenant Pete Ramirez, played by Stephen McNally. Ramirez occupies the role of the conscience, which his old friend Steve Thompson abandoned in pursuit of mob girl Anna. A former lawyer, McNally gained film prominence playing hateful villains opposite Jane Wyman in *Johnny Belinda* (1948) and *Winchester 73* (1950) opposite Jimmy Stewart. This time he emerges straight and true, a shrewd police officer who seeks to help Lancaster and his mother by seeking to banish De Carlo from Los Angeles before she can do his old friend irreparable harm.

Lancaster's family might have been fooled concerning his alleged heroic status, but the wily police lieutenant knows otherwise and lashes out immediately against his old friend. His reasoning, paralleling that of Slim Dundee and Finchley, is that the only way an armored truck robbery can succeed is with inside help. Lancaster quickly realizes that it is futile to mount a defense. The shrewd McNally has it all figured out.

"Didn't they work you as the prize sucker of all time?" McNally's voice booms.

The resolute detective is more furious with himself over circumstances than he is at Lancaster. "I should have been a better friend," McNally sadly exclaims. "I should have kicked your teeth in."

McNally's shrewd detective's brain not only has the past scenario figured out, but future developments as well. Lancaster's eyes become as large as saucers as McNally spells out his future for him. For one thing, he did not kill Dundee; he only wounded him in the leg. McNally warns that, if Anna has not gone to Duryea following the robbery, the mobster will send a man to capture Lancaster, then take him directly to him. Lancaster is aware of the arrangement he has made to meet De Carlo at the Palos Verdes retreat.

Lancaster, with an expression of painful realization openly tormenting him, now understands the wily machinations of De Carlo working in tandem with Duryea. He believed that the proposal for the armored truck robbery to Duryea was his own, made to protect De Carlo from the appearance of infidelity. Instead the armored truck employee was, as McNally succinctly noted, being played for a prize sucker by the husband and wife team. Duryea, while being able to afford jewelry for De Carlo, and busy enough to take periodic trips on business to Detroit, was still basically an operative on the climb. What he needed to extend his wings and provide financial muscle was a big payoff, the kind for which Lancaster's help was vital. He would even later agree to a fifty-fifty split after initial balking, finally growling, "Okay, you're the boss man." Meanwhile, inside man Lancaster followed the plan of Duryea and De Carlo.

When McNally leaves, Lancaster's attention is riveted by a man sitting on a bench outside his room. He asks the nurse about him. While he holds deep inner concern about his very survival, worried by McNally's disclosures, the nurse is in a contrasting situation. Glowing over Lancaster's hero status, she reveals her own mundane life, telling him that she is due to leave and is compelled to go to a barbecue with her husband to a friend's house in Monrovia, which she considers an unwanted chore. The nurse reveals that the man is from Bakersfield. His wife was injured in an automobile accident, and his concern will not permit him to leave the hospital, where he has sat for hours. Lancaster asks the nurse to request that the man come and see him. The nurse leaves after telling the visitor about Lancaster's hero status. The man explains that he is a salesman from Bakersfield, showing Lancaster his ledger. He expresses guilt since he was driving the car in which the accident occurred and his wife was injured. Just when Lancaster begins to believe in the man's authenticity, asking him to stay in his room and keep him company, fearful of an intruder in Duryea's employ, the man reveals the true nature of his business, cutting the cast and removing Lancaster from his room. He is an operative of the mobster, who remains alive and a lurking presence.

Motives Clearly Displayed

Determined to get back to the woman he loves, and whom he is convinced reciprocates, Lancaster, sitting painfully in the backseat of his captor's car, attempts to make a deal. He offers his abductor $10,000 of the money De Carlo is holding if he will drive him to the Palos Verdes hideout where she is staying. The man does so, and the injured Lancaster tells her to pay him off. He leaves grinning, holding a thick wad of bills.

"Who was that man?" De Carlo asks after Lancaster's abductor has exited. His explanation further enhances her legitimate suspicions. "Don't you see?" she exclaims with alarm. "He'll go right back to Slim!"

As Lancaster lies in a painful stupor, belonging back in the hospital bed from which Duryea's paid thug had abducted him, De Carlo leaves no doubt as to where her loyalty lies, preparing to vacate the premises before the anticipated visit from her vengeful husband. A crestfallen Lancaster is quickly told that there is no place for him. He will prove a burden. "You'll need doctors," she explains.

"I never wanted the money," he honestly declares. "I only wanted you."

De Carlo makes a declaration of her own, assuring him of where she stands. "You have to watch out for yourself," she explains with cool resolve, expressing the determination of an icy *femme fatale* to look after herself.

Before she can make her exit, fate intervenes in the person of a wounded Dan Duryea, limping with the aid of a crutch, having been shot by Lancaster during the holdup. His right hand brandishes a gun. He declares that since De Carlo wanted to be with Lancaster, together they would be.

De Carlo lets out an anguished scream and throws herself on top of Lancaster, hoping that somehow he can protect her. The armored car driver sits with a painful, tired stare, awaiting the inevitable. It comes with fatal shots from Duryea's gun.

As for the mob boss, his fate is sealed. As he prepares to make his exit, the shrill sounds of sirens are heard. In masterful noir fashion, light blends with darkness as the illumination of approaching police cars beam into the house. A final close-up on Duryea's face reveals a blend of anguish amid resignation. His hectic journey has also come to an end, as have the journeys of Lancaster and De Carlo.

THEMATIC THREADS

Criss Cross was one of a Universal duo of film noir projects Lancaster undertook for producer Mark Hellinger, its predecessor being *The Killers*, which propelled him to stardom two years earlier in 1946. Focused sequentially between those two films was RKO's brilliant noir epic, *Out of the Past*. Thematic threads abound regarding these three electrifying films:

1) A tough, street-wise macho victim whose better judgment is overruled in the clutches of the woman he seems ordained by fate to pursue no matter what the ultimate cost.

In both *The Killers* and *Criss Cross*, Lancaster is plunged into crime by beautiful women with ice water in their veins, Ava Gardner and Yvonne De Carlo, respectively. In *Out of the Past*, wily detective Robert Mitchum succumbs to the brunette beauty of the always-resourceful, permanently self-centered Jane Greer.

2) The presence of a ruthless mob boss, through which an explosive environment emerges wherein the macho victim is plunged into a triangle as he competes for the affections of the resourceful *femme fatale*.

Lancaster clashes physically with Albert Dekker as Big Jim Colfax in *The*

Killers and Dan Duryea as Slim Dundee in *Criss Cross*, while Robert Mitchum comes close to blows after angering Kirk Douglas, cast as syndicate boss Whit Sterling, in *Out of the Past*. The objects of conflict in all three films were the women for whose affections the strong-willed men in question vied. A tension pervades all relationships involving the men due to the passions they hold, and do not wish to share, concerning the calculating *femmes fatale.*

3) A pivotal double cross initiated against the victim, which propels the action into its most dramatic phase. Overwhelmed by passion, the victim becomes the object of a double cross employed by a calculating mob boss and an equally cunning *femme fatale.*

In *The Killers*, it is not revealed that Albert Dekker and Ava Gardner are married until the end of the picture. In *Criss Cross*, unlike Lancaster's role of the Swede, Ole Anderson, in the earlier film, where the passion-hungry ex-boxer spends much of his time hungering for a woman with whom he dealt firsthand only when her husband was in prison, Steve Thompson longs for another lasting commitment with De Carlo such as he experienced during the seven months when they were married. Both men pine for the woman of their dreams, but Thompson, with Duryea agreeing to cooperate for strategic reasons, sees more of De Carlo in a romantic context than the long-suffering Swede of *The Killers.*

Mitchum, in *Out of the Past*, has actually developed a new relationship with Virginia Houston in Bridgeport, the small town where he launches his filling station business. This comes after Jane Greer has left him following her murder of his former partner, Steve Brodie. He is lured back, however, by Paul Valentine, lieutenant to mob boss Kirk Douglas. He then is drawn once more into the lair of the treacherous Greer.

4) The dramatic centerpiece of the film occurs when the victim is lured through a double cross into a critical situation, from which the affected triangle members cannot draw back, and which ultimately results in the destruction of all concerned.

The Swede of *The Killers* is the least sophisticated of the three macho victims. Albert Dekker, who combines toughness with native intelligence, uses wife Gardner as the honey to draw a prospective bee for use as a convenient victim. When she visits Lancaster at the seedy hotel where he is staying, Gardner convinces him that he is being undercut by Dekker and other members of the gang. This prompts him to surprise them at gunpoint at the altered meeting place after the robbery. Dekker only pretends to be surprised, leaving Lancaster ignorant. Lancaster grabs the money and leaves, with Dekker, who has prompted the visit, swearing vengeance. On the pretext of reemerging in his life as his woman, Gardner then steals the robbery money at Lancaster's hotel and leaves. He is ready to commit suicide by jumping through the window until a compassionate Irish chambermaid talks him out of it. As a result, he leaves her as beneficiary of his life insurance policy.

Duryea and De Carlo place Lancaster in an awkward situation where he must conceive of an explanation for her being seen with him at his home. He suggests, under the pressure of the moment, the armored truck robbery which they are eager to carry out, and for which they need his assistance.

Mitchum agrees to perform one last job for Douglas, hoping this will put him out of the mobster's life for good. In reality, he is being set up for the murder of the San Francisco attorney who holds incriminating evidence which could result in a 10-year sentence for Douglas for income tax evasion. In addition, Greer has signed an affidavit linking Mitchum to the earlier murder of Brodie, which she committed. The one-two punch is familiar. The pattern which resonates from film to film is Dekker-Gardner and Duryea-De Carlo against victim Lancaster in *The Killers* and *Criss Cross*, respectively, and Douglas-Greer opposite victim Mitchum in *Out of the Past*.

APPRAISING THE TALENT

It is instructive to evaluate the talent for double cross evidenced by the participants in the three pictures being evaluated, along with the vulnerabilities of the victims. Lancaster's Swede in *The Killers* is the most vulnerable of the three victims. His image extending to his days as a successful Philadelphia light heavyweight fighter is that of tough and durable, with an ability to withstand punishment. He falls like putty into the hands of Kitty Collins, played with impressive credibility by Gardner in her first starring role.

Gardner demonstrates a toughness which impresses the tough yet suave Dekker. On one occasion Lancaster eagerly jumps to her defense after Dekker has threatened to strike her. She brusquely tells Lancaster to keep out of the squabble, indicating she is capable of fending for herself. Gardner then tells the man, whom viewers will learn much later is her husband, that if he lays so much as a hand on her, she will kill him. Dekker's response is fascinating. The tough mobster reacts to a threat made in front of his gang members by conveying a "that's my girl" prideful smile. The impression conveyed throughout the film is that Dekker is the brains while Gardner as Kitty succeeds due to her amoral iciness. That quality coupled with her exceptional beauty makes her the perfect vehicle to assist Dekker in hoodwinking the Swede and, in the process, his criminal consorts.

Lancaster as Steve Thompson constitutes a considerable step up the intelligence ladder from the compliant, highly vulnerable, far-from-brainy Swede. The fire in his loins for the brutally self-centered Anna, played with the proper nonchalance by De Carlo, ultimately triumphs over his better judgment. He pretends to listen to his mother and his old friend, uncompromisingly honest police lieutenant Stephen McNally, but ultimately tunes them out when they register concerns. The wily Duryea knows that Lancaster's love for De Carlo, and concern about protecting her, leaves him vulnerable. Duryea picks at that vulnerability in the manner of a sadist attacking a scab, making Lancaster his victim by appearing to be fooled when the armored truck operative explains why De Carlo is alone with him. De Carlo is a

As this picture makes clear, the characters played by Burt Lancaster, right, and Dan Duryea do not like each other. To help out his ex-wife and the woman he still loves, Yvonne De Carlo, who watches the action in the background, Lancaster agrees to help gang boss Dan Duryea, De Carlo's current husband, to stage an armored truck robbery in *Criss Cross*. Duryea henchman Tom Pedi also watches in the background. A Hollywood irony is that Dan Duryea, who built a reputation by playing sleazy gangsters, was a polished Ivy Leaguer from Cornell.

cold opportunist in the manner of Gardner in *The Killers*. She is willing to leave a badly wounded Lancaster, faced with prospective death, by himself at their Palos Verdes hideaway because "You have to look out for yourself." Between De Carlo's opportunistic coldness and the fires raging in Lancaster's loins for her, Duryea sees an opportunity to score with a major armored truck heist and seeks to take advantage.

If *femmes fatale* were invested with intelligence tests, Jane Greer as the predatory Kathie Moffet in *Out of the Past* would be the criminal world's equivalent of the highest-level Mensa member. She constantly sets two intelligent men on their heels. Despite their recognition of her treachery, Douglas and Lancaster both refuse to let her go. Once she bares her fangs, her vulnerable victims follow. Even as he is being double-crossed, Mitchum lauds her skills, saying, "You change sides so

smoothly." Mitchum, whose intelligence is lavishly praised by Douglas, who com-
pares him favorably to his lieutenant in crime, Paul Valentine, constantly sees where
Greer is heading, but is so entranced by her brunette beauty that he succumbs repeatedly.

Of the three females in the great forties films analyzed, Greer looms as the
most treacherous, intelligent, and sociopathic. When Mitchum arrives at Douglas's
Lake Tahoe mansion for what proves to be his final meeting, as well as last few minutes alive, he discovers the syndicate boss' body lying lifeless on the floor. Greer is
nonchalant throughout. She tells Mitchum that he has nobody left with whom to
make deals anymore other than her, reminding him unsubtly that she has information that could send him to prison. All the while, he is aware that she has made a
previous unsuccessful attempt on his life. Greer coolly concludes that they have had
a run of bad luck and deserve a break, which she hopes they will obtain by starting
a new chapter and driving together to Mexico. Realizing there is no way out,
Mitchum calls and tips off police when she walks upstairs to finish packing. Shortly
thereafter, she will bring him down by gunfire upon realizing that he has summoned
the police, after which Greer, in turn, will have her criminal life snuffed out in a
volley of police bullets.

A CAREER MARKED BY VERSATILITY

Her starring role in *Criss Cross* provided Yvonne De Carlo with just the kind
of exposure she sought, a solid achievement to prove her dramatic credentials. Her
exotic French Canadian brunette beauty was perfect in the black and white mood
settings which enhanced the film's artistic appeal. This film would rank as one of
her dramatic milestones alongside her role opposite box office giant Clark Gable in
Raoul Walsh's nineteenth-century American post-Civil War period piece, *Band of
Angels* (1955), which also starred Sidney Poitier.

During the fifties, De Carlo starred in two British films which enabled her to
combine her finest comedic instincts alongside a flair for drama. The 1951 release,
Hotel Sahara, directed by Ken Annakin, revealed her as a crafty woman who could
use her feminine charms in the midst of invasions by military forces during WWII
to hang onto the Sahara desert hotel she ran with husband Peter Ustinov. In *The
Captain's Paradise* (1954), directed by Anthony Kimmins, De Carlo played the exotic
dancer who is the "girl in the port" wife of ship captain Alec Guinness when he was
away from his other spouse, played by Celia Johnson. This was a period when De
Carlo put her musical talent to good use, making records and performing at con-
certs, including an impressive appearance at the Hollywood Bowl.

"I remember Yvonne with very warm and positive feelings," Ken Annakin, De
Carlo's director of *Hotel Sahara*, enthused. "There was a warmth and sexiness which
came out in everything she did, and that is what was irresistible to audiences. Like
most top actresses, she needed direction and support, but her objective was always

to be equal to the stars around her, especially the males. To my mind, both in *Hotel Sahara* and *Criss Cross*, she achieved this. I am sure Robert Siodmak would tell you the same thing about her if he was alive."

In 1964 De Carlo, always known for her beauty, made a daring move into the ranks of television comedy. She starred for four years in the successful series, *The Munsters*, playing a century-old vampire with a floor-length black wig. The television series resulted in a film, *Munster, Go Home* (1966).

De Carlo displayed her versatility by starring on Broadway in 1971 in *Follies* at the Wintergarden Theatre. She played a glamorous showgirl returning to the Broadway she had abandoned years before along with Alexis Smith and Dorothy Collins. Stephen Sondheim did the musical lyrics, Michael Bennett choreographed, and Hal Prince directed, a veritable all-star team which helped assure the show's success. Her face, figure, and voice all impressed as she looked every bit the part of a dazzling showgirl returning to the scene of earlier Broadway performances. She wowed audiences with her show-stopping number "I'm Still Here," a testament to surviving the rigors of show business, as she certainly had in her own career.

Robert Kendall, who had worked with De Carlo in the forties at Universal in *Song of Scheherezade* and *Casbah*, was assigned by a southern California magazine to interview her and do a story about *Follies*.

"Yvonne agreed to meet me at a popular show business bar," Kendall recalls. "When I arrived a message awaited me that she would not be able to make it, and that I could have drinks on her before the show. I had a great seat near the front row of the packed theater and enjoyed the show immensely. After the show I interviewed her in her dressing room. We had a nice chat. She explained she couldn't meet me earlier because she had to take her children, who had been visiting her, to the airport. She graciously insisted on driving me back to my hotel, the St. Moritz across the street from Central Park. It was evident that Yvonne was an incredible human being. She had begun her career as a dancer and after some small roles at Paramount moved up the ladder and appeared opposite some of the cinema's top leading men. She also had done a lot of nightclub work, starring with Donald O'Connor in Las Vegas. Then she made her bow on Broadway and was a big hit."

LANCASTER'S THIRD NOIR TRIUMPH

Burt Lancaster's career was propelled by two early noir successes, in which his sensitively attuned dramatic instincts enabled him to walk the fine line between virile strength and helpless vulnerability at the hands of beauties Gardner and De Carlo. By the late fifties, the production team of Hecht-Hill-Lancaster was garnering more than its share of Hollywood attention. It gained prominence by copping the first-ever Best Picture Oscar by an independent production company, leapfrogging over stern studio competition in triumphing with the 1954 drama *Marty*, in which the film's male lead, Ernest Borgnine, also secured a statuette. The production team combined not long thereafter with British director Alexander MacKendrick in *Sweet Smell of Success*, with Lancaster starring opposite Tony Curtis.

The 1957 release, written by Ernest Lehman and Clifford Odets, was ahead of its time and initially a box office flop, so much so that director MacKendrick was ridiculously fired from his next film for being a presumed failure after directing one of the most bitingly corrosive and psychologically witty films of the post-war era. It was a unique noir experience, in which in many ways, the film's big star was New York City itself, which was revealed in all its hustle and glitter, emphasizing the rapacious competition to get ahead. The pungent dialogue of Odets, who took over after Lehman became ill and wrote such great American Depression plays as *Waiting for Lefty*, *Golden Boy* and *Awake and Sing*, resonated when applied to Manhattan and the hustlers of show business and journalism. The violent competition of the Manhattan big-time media and show business worlds were never presented more graphically, an achievement made all the more impressive in view of director MacKendrick being British.

"Alexander MacKendrick made some wonderful movies for producer Michael Balcon at Ealing Studios in the early fifties," exclaimed Ken Annakin, who was directing and living in London at the time. "I met him several times and found him to be pleasant, but retiring. But he clearly had great strength and inner determination."

Lancaster, sporting glasses and conveying a stern look rather than the handsome, all-American demeanor he displayed when he broke into films, played the role of avaricious and egomaniacal columnist J.J. Hunsecker, said by many to be modeled after Walter Winchell. The closeness of the name Hunsecker to bloodsucker was surely more than coincidental. He walks the streets of New York like a prowling lion set to leap on helpless prey. Lancaster inhabits the glitzy clubs as a solitary figure, no matter how large the crowd of which he might be a part, forever locked into his own suffocated world, devoid of humanity. He uses words from his typewriter as tenacious bulldozers to crush numerous enemies in his path. Those words reach thirty million people in his daily column in New York's *Globe*, a figure he is only too eager to brandish.

The story's complexities are immersed in the way that Lancaster and Curtis operate as hatchet men, the columnist through his poison pen and his so-called public relations emissary Sidney Falco in the relentlessly amoral manner in which he follows his orders. As for the story's plot, it is simple. Lancaster, incapable of love, instead seeks to suffocate his young sister, played by newcomer Susan Harrison, thoroughly dominating every aspect of her life. Curtis, as the thoroughly opportunistic Falco, needs the columnist's cooperation to obtain for clients valuable space in Hunsecker's widely read column. The major project Lancaster assigns to Curtis is to destroy his sister's romance with Marty Milner, a jazz guitarist with his own quintet.

The roles of Curtis and Lancaster in their relationship are spelled out early in the film. When Curtis's secretary, played by Jeff Donnell, expresses concern over his boss' unswerving fealty toward Lancaster, he replies crisply, "Watch me run a fifty yard dash with my legs cut off."

When Curtis meets with Lancaster, the bespectacled columnist coldly glowers at him, delivering another of the many acid-etched one-liners in the film, "You're dead, son. Get yourself buried." He reflects the brutal restlessness of one who expects his orders to be immediately executed. In this case, Curtis has run into problems accomplishing Lancaster's mandate to destroy his sister's romance with the doggedly determined Milner, who lets him know that he will not lie down and become the latest victim of the remorseless columnist who is perpetually used to getting his own way. By Milner's side during tense discussions with Curtis and Lancaster is Lancaster's old stage friend Sam Levene, who is Curtis's nephew and, as an agent and surrogate father to young Milner, seeks to inject common sense and reason into an atmosphere boiling over with bile.

Curtis's groveling subservience toward Lancaster disgusts both Harrison and the columnist. Harrison tells him that her brother has him "jumping through hoops like a trained poodle." Lancaster stares at Curtis with a mixture of pity and disbelief, asking him at one point just how low it is possible for one man to stoop.

The unsavory public relations hatchet man answers Lancaster's question with his actions. At a pivotal point, he seeks to take Milner out of Harrison's life by planting a newspaper story that he is a drug user and a Communist. Curtis vehemently denies being the story's source when confronted by a livid Milner. The story results in the musician being fired at the club where he and his group regularly perform.

THE SHIFTING TIDES OF LANCASTER

After the damage is done and Milner is fired, Lancaster has second thoughts. He gets him back his job and requests that he visit him at his apartment to talk about his relationship with his sister. When the young musician demonstrates he has a mind of his own and courageously berates the bullying columnist for his vulturine ways, constantly aware of the perpetual domination he seeks over Harrison, the egomaniacal columnist huffs in disbelief after Milner leaves. "Did you hear how he talked to me?" Lancaster says to Curtis in disbelief.

Ruffling the feathers of New York's proud peacock columnist J.J. Hunsecker necessitates revenge. The plan comes in the form of a piece of paper with the name "Kello" written on it. Lancaster hands it to Curtis, who blanches, but still finds himself incapable of resisting another highly distasteful order. Harry Kello is a muscular police officer bully whom the columnist calls upon periodically as an enforcer. Playing Kello is Emile G. Meyer, memorable in the solid feature role of Ryker, the frustrated landowner in *Shane* (1953) who hires gunslinger Jack Palance to force homesteaders off of his property. Not only does the sadistic Meyer enjoy his enforcer work, in Lancaster's case, he has another reason, since the columnist spared him from a terrible scandal after he brutalized a young man in custody.

Previously Curtis planted an untrue newspaper smear against Milner. This time he plants marijuana in his overcoat, after which Meyer is summoned and an arrest is made. The cop supplies some of his sadistic rough treatment to Milner, which results in a dramatic showdown with Harrison.

Curtis, who by then appears as incapable of good as Lancaster, performs his one positive deed in the film when a thoroughly despondent Harrison attempts to jump out of her bedroom window. Curtis barely saves her from a suicide leap. Shortly thereafter, Lancaster arrives. He sees Curtis caressing a still badly rattled Harrison, at which point he flies into a rage. "Don't you dare touch my sister!" the columnist shrieks possessively, racing toward Curtis, whom he begins pummeling.

Someone is always caught within the busy crosshairs of Lancaster, and now Curtis becomes his convenient target. As a new day beckons, Curtis is approached by the sadistic Meyer, who laughs with boyish delight at the prospect of having the public relations operative as his next victim. Curtis has previously insulted him, referring to him as fat and relating that he does not like him. Meyer laughed off his remarks at the time, but now that he has an opportunity to use his bulk to bully Curtis, he is immersed in heaven.

Meanwhile Harrison has summoned the courage to leave her domineering brother. As she walks down an almost deserted street while day breaks, a forlorn, totally defeated Lancaster looks down that same street after she has left. The empty street symbolizes his own existence, despite his power and bravado. He is without emotion, a man who seeks to utilize total control over his young sister as an unsatisfactory substitute for love. Lancaster realizes that he grovels every bit as much as Curtis, but in a different manner, using his column to debase and demoralize, projecting misery rather than joy. At one point in the film, he enters a deserted street and exclaims, "I love this dirty town." One concludes that any town would be dirty provided he had the opportunity to establish an imprint.

Sweet Smell of Success moves at a rapid pace. Enhancing the beat and flow of a large metropolis in which predators such as Lancaster and Curtis live by night, moving from nightclubs, bars and theaters at a devastating pace, is the musical score of Elmer Bernstein. Its surging syncopation matches the acting. Curtis moves with the quickness of a jungle cat as he makes deals. On the spur of the moment, he uses cigarette girl Barbara Nichols, who entertains genuine feelings for him, as a prostitute, setting up a rendezvous in his office with a local columnist from whom he seeks publicity for a client. It is later revealed that she had met the columnist before in Palm Springs.

As for the Svengali hold which Lancaster seeks to perpetuate on his sister, his persona is reminiscent of another destructive, egomaniacal New York columnist from a famous film of better than one decade earlier. The character was Waldo Lydecker played by New York theater veteran and film newcomer Clifton Webb in *Laura* (1944). In that film, Webb destroyed in print the reputation of an artist wooing the woman he felt he created, Madison Avenue advertising executive Laura Hunt, played by Gene Tierney. He then sets his sights on her fiancé Shelby Carpenter, played by Vincent Price. Ultimately, when he realizes he cannot control her, Webb tries to kill someone he viewed as a creation rather than a flesh and blood human being. His ego matches Lancaster's. On one occasion, when his self-absorption is discussed, he states crisply, "In my case it is totally justified."

In many respects, Lancaster's hugely successful career as one of filmdom's leading superstars displays shifting tides pertaining to his own life. *Sweet Smell of Success* marked a return to his New York roots for the East Harlem native. The same applied to Brooklyn-born Tony Curtis. When Lancaster won a highly deserved Best Actor Oscar for the 1960 adaptation of the Sinclair Lewis novel *Elmer Gantry*, directed by Richard Brooks, he began receiving letters from boyhood friends from his neighborhood. They marveled at the likeness on the screen of the fast-talking preacher with the penchant for effective gab combined with an air of bravado. These traits were said to resemble those of the Burt Lancaster of East Harlem.

In addition to his Oscar triumph in *Elmer Gantry*, Lancaster also secured Best Actor nominations for *From Here to Eternity* (1953) and *Birdman of Alcatraz* (1962). His final Academy nomination was secured in his final major triumph, *Atlantic City*.

RETURNING TO ATLANTIC CITY

Atlantic City marks a creative return of Lancaster to the city where his life is changed forever by the sting perpetrated by the husband and wife team of Ava Gardner and Albert Dekker, culminating with the woman he loves taking the money from the hat factory robbery and leaving him brokenhearted and suicidal in a seedy Atlantic City hotel. In *Atlantic City*, a brilliant 1980 mood piece directed by Frenchman Louis Malle and written by John Guare, the accomplished playwright who authored *House of Blue Leaves* and *Six Degrees of Separation*, an older Lancaster is victimized by another woman, but under completely changed circumstances from his bitter and ultimately futile pursuit of Gardner.

The Atlantic City that Lancaster revisits after the long gap between the immediate post-war period and the advent of the eighties finds the legendary boardwalk, the most notable site of the city, being torn down to accommodate the building of new hotels with lucrative gambling casinos. He is once more victimized by a woman, in this case Kate Reid, but his status is completely different than it was during his association with the tempestuous gun moll Gardner. One link remains, however, between Reid and Gardner, their association with criminal elements. The early Lancaster was deemed capable of performing rugged physical functions. His virility was more than capable of pleasing Gardner, but hovering nearby was Dekker. Lancaster's unswerving passion for her, exemplified by clinging to a silk handkerchief she once owned, which he even holds with reverence during his prison stretch, is used against him by a wily mob boss to make him a fall guy.

Kate Reid, like Gardner, was married to a materially successful mob boss. Also, as in the earlier film, Lancaster worked for the woman's husband. The similarities end here, however, as in the case of Reid's husband, we learn through her constant negative barbs that he was a low-level functionary. When Reid's husband dies, Lancaster assumes the job of taking care of Reid in her residence at a boardwalk hotel. He fulfills her sexual desires as well as performing other tasks for her as she is incapacitated and confined to her hotel room. Her cutting remarks frequently focus on the superiority of her late husband in every regard to Lancaster, who accepts the criticism and continues silently soldiering on.

Lancaster develops a crush on the sensuous Susan Sarandon, cast in a brilliant breakthrough role as a woman trying to start a new life after a bad marriage by training to become a dealer at one of the many gambling casinos opening up in the new Atlantic City. He exaggerates his gangster career by boasting that he was once a cellmate of the noted Bugsy Siegel, later conceding that it was a brief experience as the famous Las Vegas mobster was kept in a holding cell on his way to a stretch at Leavenworth.

Lancaster's friendship with Sarandon develops into more as he seeks to move her through the rough edges as her trouble-laden husband returns. The husband, played by Robert Joy, becomes a marked man as syndicate executioners kill him over drugs in his possession, which then end up in Lancaster's hands as they seek to locate the missing booty. When they rough up Sarandon, treating Lancaster as a helpless old man, he whips out a revolver and kills them.

After the taunting insults of Reid and self-doubts, Lancaster is ecstatic over his accomplishment as he drives Sarandon to a nearby motel, where he orders champagne and snacks in celebratory style. When the news concerning the deaths of the mob executioners is shown on television, he points proudly to the set and exclaims to Sarandon, "That's me!"

Another similarity then emerges between Lancaster's experience at the seedy Atlantic City hotel and his experience with Sarandon. After he makes arrangements to start a new life with Sarandon and leaves the motel room briefly, he then returns to find her and the money gone. He is left behind as he was 34 years earlier by Ava Gardner.

The drama ends with Lancaster back in the same situation he occupied at the beginning of the film. Stumped local police continue to look for the assailants of the mob hoodlums, and Lancaster returns to his duties of attending to the needs of Kate Reid.

Atlantic City resulted in Lancaster's final Best Actor Oscar nomination. It was befitting that it thematically resembled the vulnerable figures he played, the Swede and Steve Thompson, in the two great noir dramas which helped propel him to superstar status, *The Killers* and *Criss Cross*, where solid dramatic tension was created in his relationships with women for whom he hungered but could not ultimately have.

THREE

Solving Your Own Murder

All I did was notarize one little paper. One little paper out of hundreds.
D.O.A. (1950)

It was an existential story that could have come fresh from the pen of Albert Camus. A man is doomed as a victim of circumstance. At a peak dramatic moment, Edmond O'Brien, in his last meeting with the woman he loves, lovely blonde Pamela Britton, speaks with sad conviction as a man doomed by the hand of a deadly fate. "All I did was notarize one little paper," he exclaims mournfully. "One little paper out of hundreds."

D.O.A. was an early effort from the collaborative writing team of Russell Rouse and Clarence Greene. *Laura* began as a production with a B movie tag. The same applied to *D.O.A.* Its budget might have been frugal, but the product continued to impress, reaching classic status over the course of time as filmgoers and critics alike thrilled to its fast pacing, snappy dialogue, ingenious plotting, excellent photography and consummate acting. A low budget film can often hold an advantage over a large-scale major studio product. This advantage was evident in *D.O.A.*—casting. Whereas major films were made to feature key performers often working at robust salary levels, with major casting decisions dictated by the front office for commercial reasons, in a low budget effort such as *D.O.A.*, there are no such mandates or strictures. The right people are found for every part, irrespective of how well or little known they happen to be. This is a film which included many performers starting out, who would achieve numerous credits as their careers developed.

The film's dramatic opening intersects with its unique story line. A brightly illuminated Los Angeles City Hall is shown in the darkness of evening. A stocky man in a dark suit is observed walking toward the Hall of Justice. The camera follows him from behind, and we cannot see his face. The haunting sounds of the film's theme, written by Dimitri Tiomkin, are dramatically heard. After entering the building, the man asks a uniformed police officer a question. The officer points and the

49

man walks to his left. He enters the Homicide Division and asks to speak with the man in charge. As the Captain, played by George Lynn, flashes him a curious look, the man speaks solemnly. The expression on Edmond O'Brien's face matches his solemnity of speech.

"I'd like to report a murder," he begins.

"Who was murdered?" the Captain asks.

There is a long, painful pause. The impression is clear. Here is a man under some form of physical duress. The words do not come easily.

"I was," he finally exclaims.

This marks one of the memorable openings in film history. The audience is taken on a roller-coaster suspense ride until O'Brien, playing a man cursed by fate, accountant Frank Bigelow from Banning, a small town near Palm Springs in the California desert, is ultimately able to piece together the crazy quilt fabric of criminal double-dealings which results in his demise. Racing against time, he is able to resolve the mystery and avenge his death with precious few minutes to spare.

The incredible staying power of this great film was revealed to me once more on a recent visit to Canada. On May 31, 2002, I visited the downtown Vancouver Museum of Art as part of a delightful trip to the beautiful western Canada city. When I walked to the third floor, I heard sounds emanating from a nearby gallery. They appeared to be from a motion picture. The sounds were strangely familiar, and my curiosity increased as I moved toward the exhibit room from which the sounds emanated.

I looked up and observed a spectacular three-screen simultaneous showing of *D.O.A.* A further inquiry revealed that the exhibit was the artistic vision of Gordon Douglas, who was deeply affected by the haunting, poetic beauty of the cult classic as a young man in his native Glasgow. I stood and watched the breathtakingly dramatic scenes unfold on the right of the regular 35-mm theater screen. This marked the first time I had seen three screens showing scenes from the same film as the various scenes were transposed, moving from one screen to the other. As I watched the action unfold on three screens simultaneously, I was once more impressed by the raw power and poetic beauty of the noir classic, realizing why it would hold such impact for budding young Scottish artist Gordon Douglas in his early years, resulting in his tribute.

D.O.A. received a standing ovation when it was shown recently at a Palm Springs film festival. The festival site revealed a poetic consistency in that this long-popular affluent retreat for Hollywood's cinema community was located no more than half an hour south of Frank Bigelow's Banning accounting office, where the fateful bill of sale was notarized, which would ultimately cost him his life. Actress Beverly Garland, the honored guest who viewed the film with the audience, provided more than a little touch of *déjà vu*; after appearing in D.O.A., she eventually became one of the most prolific and popular leading ladies in the history of television drama and comedy. Garland, then billed as Beverly Campbell, was involved in perhaps the key pivotal scene of the entire film, when an angry O'Brien, realizing he is dying of a slow-acting poison and determined to find out why before it is too late, descends on secretary Campbell in the Phillips Exports office and demands answers. At one point, he furiously bellows, "This thing is gonna break wide open!" Thanks to his determined sleuthing, time proves him correct.

GARLAND'S BIG BREAK

Beverly Garland will always remember the film with fondness, in that it launched her film career. While later appearing with Academy Award-winning actors such as Humphrey Bogart in *The Desperate Hours* (1955) and Frank Sinatra in *The Joker is Wild* (1957) in a prolific film career, Garland established a major reputation as well in television, playing the wives of the male stars of the *Bing Crosby Show* and Fred MacMurray in *My Three Sons*. She broke new ground as the first female detective in the television genre in *Decoy*. The then-Beverly Campbell was waiting tables at a Newport Beach restaurant by day and acting in plays at a Laguna Beach playhouse by night. One day, she found herself waiting on Bette Davis, who told her, "I saw your performance and I thought you were marvelous!"

"That was the biggest compliment I ever got," Beverly related. "Her kind and thoughtful words were a real inspiration as I pursued my theatrical career."

Not long after her memorable meeting with Davis, Beverly was spotted in a Laguna Beach production by a talent scout, who suggested that she do a screen test, relating that he had a specific role in mind.

"Of course I took the screen test," Beverly reminisced, "and the role was *D.O.A.* That is how my motion picture career began."

Beverly had an inkling from the outset that the film was something special. "We knew it was a 'sleeper' from the excellent reviews," she acknowledged. "There was talk about *D.O.A.* winning some Academy Awards. When it was originally released it was recognized as a unique motion picture, with some tremendous talent."

One of the fascinating aspects of *D.O.A.* is the excellent location scouting. Some of the most interesting locations and buildings of mid-century Los Angeles are depicted in the film. Frank Bigelow begins in Banning, travels to San Francisco, then flies to Los Angeles with a mission tied to a rapidly ticking time capsule, that of uncovering the answer concerning why he has been singled out for murder.

TOLD IN FLASHBACK

An eager-eyed homicide captain is as interested in hearing Bigelow's account as he is to tell it during the closing minutes of his life. He begins his riveting story, told in flashback. It has its origin in the small desert town of Banning, California, about 100 miles from Los Angeles. Banning for many years was on the only main

Pamela Britton, left, is plainly unhappy as client Carolyn Hughes flirts with her accountant, Edmond O'Brien, in *D.O.A.*, a 1950 low budget sleeper directed by former cinematographer Rudolph Maté, which attained the rank of classic. Britton, O'Brien's loyal secretary, regrets the trip he will shortly make to San Francisco, which will prove fatal to the man she loves. Four years later O'Brien would win a Best Supporting Actor Oscar in Joseph Mankiewicz's *The Barefoot Contessa*, starring Humphrey Bogart and Ava Gardner.

highway leading from L.A. to Palm Springs. Eventually a freeway was built, whizzing sun worshipers from L.A. to the star-studded desert oasis of Palm Springs, framed by a picturesque mountain backdrop.

The action-laden drama proved a superb dramatic challenge for Edmond O'Brien, who appears in every scene. He would four years later win an Academy Award for Best Supporting Actor as perpetually nervous, sweaty-palmed publicity man Oscar Muldoon in Joseph Mankiewicz's classic film about Hollywood, *The Barefoot Contessa* (1954), starring Ava Gardner and Humphrey Bogart. In the sixties, the New York-born actor starred in the highly successful television series *Sam Benedict*, in which he played a criminal defense attorney.

O'Brien as Frank Bigelow is complemented in *D.O.A.* by Pamela Britton, who plays his faithful secretary, Paula Gibson. O'Brien and Britton work out of public accountant Bigelow's nondescript office in Banning. O'Brien confides to his secretary that he needs to go to San Francisco alone. She recognizes the implications, fearing that the trip may ultimately involve another woman and a breakup. Over cold beers on an intensely hot desert afternoon in the air-conditioned comfort of a nearby bar, after Britton tearfully begs O'Brien to let her accompany him, he explains with requisite sensitivity his need for privacy. He is haunted by the memory of an earlier unsuccessful romance. O'Brien loves his blonde secretary too much to expose her to anything other than the solid prospect of enduring success. The trip is an experiment to see if he is ready for such a permanent commitment. Pamela listens patiently, but one senses a psychic premonition on her part, an apprehension that something could go wrong on O'Brien's trip.

The story quickly moves from Banning to a long shot overview of San Francisco by night, as O'Brien checks into the St. Francis Hotel, a city landmark located across the street from Union Square in the heart of the bustling downtown area.

As O'Brien approaches the front desk, he is greeted by Bill Baldwin, a prominent Los Angeles radio announcer appearing in his only scene of the film. Baldwin's lone scene is short but memorable, enhanced by humor as he remarks to O'Brien that the hotel is crowded with women, which the currently footloose accountant observes. When an interested O'Brien inquires as to the large presence of the fairer sex, Baldwin explains that it is Market Week, with female buyers interacting with male traveling salesmen. O'Brien's wandering eye immediately begins checking out some of the buyers scampering around the lobby. Baldwin delivers a memorable line loaded with innuendo as he hands O'Brien a booklet, adding grinningly, "This is all about how to have fun in San Francisco."

The rapidly paced action continues once O'Brien reaches his hotel room. The bellhop who assists him is Jerry Paris in one of his earliest roles. Paris later became a comedy mainstay on television, playing a regular on *The Dick Van Dyke Show*. He was also a prominent television director, moving between comedy and drama. Paris's one memorable line is, "Why does everybody come to San Francisco to have fun?" He observes a party in full swing across the hall.

O'Brien watches the party's unfolding action after telling Paris not to close the door. As he returns a call to loyal secretary Britton, who assures him that the call is "strictly business," the contrast is evident between the woman he has at least temporarily left behind in Banning and the slice of life he intends to experimentally experience in fun-loving San Francisco. She tells him about a series of calls from an exporter from Los Angeles named Eugene Philips, who is willing to tell her nothing, stressing the need of talking to Bigelow about an "urgent" matter. Never having heard of him, O'Brien shrugs the matter off. An important story thread has been dropped, a link to important events that will begin transpiring the following day with Philips's problem becoming the accountant's as well.

After the call ends, the occupant of the suite across the way where the party is in progress, salesman Sam Haskell, played by Jeff Kirkpatrick, asks to borrow O'Brien's phone to order more whiskey and ice. O'Brien agrees, after which the salesman invites the Banning accountant to join the party. Awkwardness arises when

O'Brien meets Haskell's flirtatious wife, who has had too much to drink. She dances very close to an embarrassed Bigelow while her concerned husband watches carefully.

"My wife, she's a good dancer, isn't she, Bigelow?" an increasingly wary Haskell reminds the accountant subtly about his married status while the accountant is being pursued by a fully absorbed, sufficiently inebriated Sadie Hawkins type.

Eventually the flirtatious housewife suggests that they go out for a night on the town, since it is the last evening of Market Week and she will be resuming her regular housewife duties shortly thereafter. O'Brien accompanies the reveling salesmen and female buyers to a red-hot San Francisco Wharf jazz spot called The Fisherman. The jazz sequence is one of the hottest ever filmed, as the African American musicians accelerate their pace to dizzying levels. A drummer pounds frenziedly, a trumpet players blasts away on his instrument, a saxophonist gives his all, and close-ups reveal the intense sweating of performers investing every ounce of their collective energies. A young Hugh O'Brian can be seen and heard clapping his hands and calling out jive talk encouragement to the musicians. A few years later, he would, like Beverly Garland, become a television mainstay by starring as famous frontier marshal Wyatt Earp in the popular series of the same name.

The camera of Ernest Laszlo is used to create interest through a series of images who pass like the twinkling of an eye. There are the musicians performing with exhausting fury. There are the patrons, who are caught up in the frenzy of the jive movement which was popular during the period, and are happy to lose themselves in a deliriously exciting, engrossingly liberating environment. There is also the flirtatious wife of Kirkpatrick, who seeks to cuddle O'Brien until he is able to break away and move to the opposite end of the bar. She observes his departure and continues looking for him until her husband places a restraining hand on her shoulder, stating succinctly his disgust. "I think you've had enough," he admonishes.

O'Brien's interest level noticeably rises as he observes a beautiful, elegantly dressed blonde sit down at the other side of the bar and order a drink. His distraction enables the pivotal event of the film, around which the entire story is structured, to occur. A tall, slender man enters The Fisherman, wearing an overcoat turned up menacingly at the collar along with a scarf. His face cannot be seen. The stranger watches closely as O'Brien concentrates his attentions on the blonde, next to whom he occupies a barstool. Seizing the moment, the mysterious man switches O'Brien's drink with one he has fatally doctored with luminous toxic poison.

Playing the role of the bartender who serves O'Brien is Peter Leeds, who later became a prominent movie and television character actor. O'Brien makes a face when he takes his first sip of the poisoned drink.

"This isn't my drink," O'Brien complains. "I ordered bourbon."

His statement perplexes bartender Leeds, who crisply replies, "Sure it is. You saw me pour it."

O'Brien shrugs the matter off, orders a fresh drink, and is totally unaware that his life has been snuffed out by one drink switch conducted by a man he does not even see. He makes some small talk with the blonde, who tells him her name is Jeanie. She is played by Virginia Lindley. He is able to secure the phone number from her of the next jazz club she will visit. Leeds previously explained to O'Brien that Jeanie is "jive crazy," as are so many of The Fisherman's patrons. The sequence provides a slice of life from the late forties, early fifties period when jazz, bee bop and jive were popular.

When O'Brien returns to his room at the St. Francis, an element of irony is reached. He has flown to San Francisco to conduct an experiment, to determine if he should follow through and marry his faithful secretary. At the point where it appears he is prepared to determine how much wild oats he is prepared to sow, an event occurs which stops him in his tracks. Britton has sent him a bouquet of flowers, along with a note reading, "I'll keep a light burning." Recognizing he is committed to Britton, O'Brien tears up the piece of paper where the jive-crazy blonde has written the number of her next jazz club, tossing it symbolically into a wastepaper basket. The symbolism is extended as he makes a tip-of-the-hat gesture as he tosses the paper into the receptacle, an impromptu adios to his bachelor life on the prowl, a quick conclusion to his experiment as he realizes that Britton is the only woman for him.

The following morning, O'Brien awakens with a strange headache-type sensation. After ordering a soothing soda combination from room service, he feels revulsion at the prospect of drinking it. Once more, a possible psychic element enters the story. Could it be that O'Brien realizes he had digested a harmful substance the preceding evening?

A troubled O'Brien is next seen jumping onto a cable car in front of the hotel. He gets off shortly thereafter and enters a medical building. It soon appears that all is well, as the examining doctor tells O'Brien with a chuckle that if everyone were as healthy as the Banning accountant, doctors such as himself would be put out of business. A major story shock occurs when the medical group's specialist in toxicology, Dr. Schaeffer, surfaces. He grimly tells O'Brien that he has ingested a fatal dose of luminous toxic poison, which has attacked his vital organs to the point where nothing can save him. He may have as little as one day to live, depending upon how much of the deadly poison he ingested. The bespectacled Dr. Schaeffer, bearing a smooth, well-modulated voice, is Lawrence Dobkin, who was a prominent radio actor during the forties and fifties.

O'Brien is so stunned that he reacts in disbelief, then becomes rattled, bellowing a loud and angry response to the fatal verdict. He storms out of the office after telling Dobkin and his colleague, "You're crazy!" We soon learn, however, that he is far from convinced of the accuracy of his accusation. He storms into a hospital, making such a commotion with the nurses that the doctor storms into the room, grabbing O'Brien's arms and demanding to know what is wrong. The even-featured, muscular Dr. MacDonald is Frank Gerstle, recognized by baby boomers as a popular television commercial actor from the sixties. When O'Brien, speaking with desperation, reveals that he wants Gerstle to treat him for luminous toxic poison, the doctor immediately recognizes the gravity of the situation. Moments later, Gerstle turns off the lights and reveals his results to O'Brien. The luminous toxic specimen, which the doctor holds up for the victim to see, glows in the dark, an excellent film noir technique with the glowing white light contrasted by an otherwise all-enveloping darkness, dramatically symbolizing the fate of O'Brien.

When Gerstle picks up the phone to call the Homicide Bureau of the San Francisco Police Department and expresses his intention of admitting O'Brien to a hospital, the victim reacts by asking Gerstle why he is telephoning Homicide. Gerstle eyes him sternly.

"I don't think you get it, Bigelow," Gerstle explains. "You've been murdered!"

A thoroughly shocked O'Brien darts out of the hospital. He runs down a busy Market Street, bumping into startled pedestrians. The contrast between the formality of mid-century attire and the casual present is revealed in the number of suits and hats being worn by both men and women.

GRIPPING SYMBOLISM AND DEEP RESOLVE

As an exhausted O'Brien stops running, catching his breath in front of a newspaper rack, a scene of gripping symbolism occurs. He stoops over and picks up a ball belonging to a young girl, who walks away with her mother. O'Brien next observes a slender young woman wave to a trimly fit young man. They kiss, then walk away arm-in-arm accompanied by a few bars from Johann Strauss's *The Blue Danube*. Youth, young love, and glowing, optimistic promise are starkly contrasted with the death sentence handed O'Brien with a sudden jolt.

More symbolism sans dialogue is observed as a thoroughly deflated O'Brien begins walking in the direction of Fisherman's Wharf. Suddenly the defeated facial expression and slow, doomed walk disappear as a resolute spring surfaces in O'Brien's every step. A determined fire emerges in his eyes. The change is acknowledged with the almost militaristic music from the score of Dimitri Tiomkin, renowned Oscar-winning composer. Its pacing dovetails with the steady determination in his brisk walk.

At that critical moment, O'Brien has decided that, rather than accepting defeat and preparing for his impending death, he will go down fighting. He is filled with an overpowering mission to find his killer and obtain revenge before the final curtain is swiftly rung down on his life. This critical moment is handled with finesse by director Rudolph Maté. There is no dialogue of any kind in which O'Brien makes a declaration to someone that he is now dedicated to finding his killer. This critical moment of resolution instead occurs during a walk along a San Francisco street, as O'Brien adjusts to his death sentence after Frank Gerstle has provided a second opinion to the verdict which was earlier rendered with sad empathy by Lawrence Dobkin.

The movie surges forward at a breakneck pace as O'Brien realizes he may have less than twenty-four hours to live. He walks immediately to The Fisherman, which is closed. On his return to the St. Francis Hotel, he pounds with angry determination on the door of the room occupied by the salesman, Sam Haskell. A terrified elderly woman answers the door as a chambermaid tells O'Brien that the salesman and his wife, along with the rest of the salesmen, checked out early that morning. O'Brien apologizes, then rushes to his room as he hears the telephone ring. The eruption in the hallway interrupted by the ring of the telephone provides another instance of fast pacing.

When a still-stunned O'Brien recognizes his secretary's voice and responds despondently, Pamela Britton reprimands him for showing so little enthusiasm. The conversation is an excellent illustration of dramatic contrast as the faithful secretary is totally unaware of O'Brien's current emotional state and, importantly, what has prompted it. She tells him matter-of-factly that he need not worry about why Eugene Philips of Los Angeles was so eager to talk to him. She reveals that he died. Britton is stunned over O'Brien's concern to know about what happened to Philips. After all, Philips is someone he earlier told her he had never met. He quickly pries out of her the downtown Los Angeles address of Philips Exports. Britton is left sputtering in confusion as O'Brien reveals that he is departing immediately for Los Angeles and will be staying at the Allison Hotel.

A FINAL RENDEZVOUS IN LOS ANGELES

A genuine appreciation for this film requires constant attention. A quick move to grab a bag of popcorn can disrupt the rhythm and flow of a story that weaves, builds, and continues to generate steam until its finale. The Rouse-Greene writing team, recognizing the gravity of the story's central plot, makes certain to not weight the story down with too much gravity. Some levity is attached, such as the pursuit of O'Brien by the aggressive, drunken salesman's wife. There is also the fast-paced entertainment of the African American jazz performers. Rouse and Greene give us a great overall mix. Rudolph Maté, making his directorial debut after a highly successful career as a choreographer at Columbia, where his deft photographic touch enhanced Rita Hayworth's beauty in her two greatest hits, *Cover Girl* and *Gilda*, worked with stellar cameraman Laszlo to keep the action busy and the camera in frequent movement:

1) When the lobby of the St. Francis Hotel is photographed, we see the busy atmosphere of Market Week with the nubile female buyers darting back and forth, interesting O'Brien.

2) When the salesmen and buyers go out for their final howl in San Francisco before flying back to their respective home bases, we see the stirring jive activity at The Fisherman, with the camera moving from musicians, then back and forth to reveal the responses at tables and at the bar.

3) We see the glow in the eyes of the lovely blonde, Jeanie, who responds to

the lively sounds with, "I dig The Fisherman. That's silk." We see the corresponding glow in O'Brien's eyes as he observes the blonde. Now is the time to see if he really needs to adventure, or if his heart belongs solely to Pamela Britton.

4) We see the brilliant dramatic maneuver and use of action devoid of dialogue when the mystery man wearing the overcoat, hat and scarf, enters The Fisherman and unobtrusively sits down at the bar near O'Brien. The use of distraction is deftly employed as he, seeking to flap his bachelor wings and get quickly acquainted with Jeanie, is totally unaware of how his life is being snuffed out by the quick switch of a glass of liquor after it has been swiftly doctored. As O'Brien takes the fatal gulp of liquor that will ultimately cost him his life, the unobtrusive and peripatetic mystery man leaves, the same unnoticed figure who arrived moments earlier and ordered a drink. O'Brien never sees him. The only tangible sign arising from his quick visit occurs when O'Brien makes a face and expresses surprise over taking a sip from a glass which does not contain the bourbon he ordered. He shrugs off the incident by ordering another drink and going back to concentrating on the blonde.

5) With camera magic, a change of mood is registered by an initially crestfallen O'Brien in the wake of confirmation of the earlier revealed death verdict. The determined sudden jauntiness of step displays the passing of gloom to instant resolve over cracking his own murder case, of learning just who killed him and why. He recognizes that if he is to solve his own murder, he has no time to brood. After all, he might have as little as one day to live. As events later reveal, he has less than one full day at his disposal.

O'Brien flies to Los Angeles after his phone conversation with a thoroughly perplexed Britton. The Allison Hotel, which he checks into, was then situated near Pershing Square and the Los Angeles Public Library. A Bank of America branch was located directly across the street. The hotel was located behind the Biltmore Bowl, long gone but once a top theater venue for prominent Los Angeles stage productions, as well as the Biltmore Hotel, which still exists. The Biltmore Hotel gained fame as the headquarters of presidential candidates, including then-senators John F. Kennedy and Lyndon Johnson at the 1960 Democratic National Convention held in L.A.

Philips Exports was located in the Bradbury Building, situated in The Arcade. It was a notable building for years, which served as office headquarters for many prominent local law and accounting firms.

When O'Brien arrives at Philips Exports, he is greeted by Miss Foster, secretary to the company's auditor, Halliday, played by William Ching. The attractive, dark-haired Miss Foster was played by Beverly Campbell. As earlier mentioned, she would later change her last name to Garland and enjoy a productive acting career. The name Beverly Garland rings a distinctive bell in current film nostalgia circles. Her establishment, the Beverly Garland Hotel at 4222 Vineland Avenue in North Hollywood, located just off the 101 Freeway, serves as headquarters for scores of movie nostalgia conventions and collectors' meetings.

During O'Brien's first face-to-face meeting with Ching, with great reluctance the auditor provides him with the address of the widow of the recently deceased Philips. He cautions the determined O'Brien to be respectful of her grief.

Mrs. Philips lives in a fashionable Hollywood apartment. Playing the role of Mrs. Philips is Lynne Baggett, who was better known for being the wife of one of Hollywood's producing immortals rather than as a performer. From 1948 to 1955, she was married to Sam Spiegel, producer of such cinema epics as *The African Queen*, *On the Waterfront*, *The Bridge on the River Kwai* and *Lawrence of Arabia*. After the death of a nine-year-old youngster following a hit-and-run accident in which Baggett was driving, she was sentenced to 50 days in Los Angeles County Jail. A major point of irony concerning her role in *D.O.A.* surrounds her tragic death in 1960 at the age of 36. The cause of death was ruled to be an excess dose of barbiturates. In *D.O.A.*, the leading role of her film career, Edmond O'Brien wastes away as luminous toxic poison attacks his vital organs.

While O'Brien learns nothing from Baggett, who explains that she has no idea why her deceased husband was so frantic to speak to him, he is informed that Philips plunged to his death as an alleged "suicide victim" by the deceased's brother, Stanley, played by Henry Hart. Philips had been arrested for selling a stolen shipment of iridium, a rare metal. Armed with this information, O'Brien returns to see Halliday, who is out. Campbell-Garland is finally compelled by the pressure of O'Brien twisting her arm to tell her who else the deceased exporter Philips was attempting to reach before his death. With great reluctance, she supplies the information. The important tidbit spins the nonstop action in yet another new direction, revealing scandalous information about Campbell-Garland's deceased boss.

COLD, BEAUTIFUL AND DEADLY

At this stage, the drama's *femme fatale* enters the scene. A furious O'Brien storms into the apartment of Marla "Molly" Rakubian, a seductive model who had used her wiles to entice the late exporter Eugene Philips to buy the stolen iridium. O'Brien has been clued in via a phone call from Britton that the deal had been notarized six months earlier by the accountant, who had no inkling that the transaction involved a ruthless mob. The man who had the bill of sale notarized was George Reynolds. O'Brien spots a framed picture of Reynolds in Rakubian's apartment, grabbing it as a possible aid in obtaining information. The scene between temptress Rakubian and O'Brien is a classic as her dark eyes flash hatred for O'Brien, who observes a first-class ticket to Buenos Aires in her name, prompting him to wonder aloud how she could afford it on a model's salary.

Playing the role of Rakubian is Laurette Luez, a dark, exotic Polynesian beauty who came to Hollywood from her native Honolulu. Her recent death prompted an informative obituary in *Classic Images*, revealing a linkage to one of the film industry's most legendary stars. Luez was a member of the same drama class with a beautiful blonde actress with whom she became friends. When the gorgeous blonde contemplated a new professional name to boost her career, Luez helpfully suggested, "Why not Marilyn Monroe?" The exotic brunette appeared in a few other films, including the 1961 hit *Flower Drum Song*, then returned to Honolulu. She established a reputation as one of the island's finest drama coaches and spoke with nostalgic reverence with her students about her Hollywood career. Had she not suffered the misfortune of being in the film industry at a time when producers were less receptive toward giving opportunities to exotic types such as Laurette Luez represented, a longer, more promising career might well have awaited her.

The O'Brien-Luez fireworks represent film noir drama at its best. At one point, she pulls a gun on him, which he wrests away from her, retaining it for later use. It will come in handy almost immediately as well as in one dramatic sequence near the end of the film. Luez's dark eyes flash hate as she stares at O'Brien after he has taken her picture of Reynolds and prepares to leave. A dialogue exchange out of Raymond Chandler emerges.

"If I were a man, I'd punch your dirty face in!" an enraged Luez hisses.

A consummate actor, O'Brien stares at her, then replies in a calm, understated tone, "Now, I really believe you would."

The brief exchange represents the difference between top noir suspense drama and a cheaper imitation. A cheaper imitation might well have had O'Brien and Luez exchanging shrieks. Instead O'Brien, after eyeing the angry, cold-blooded *femme fatale*, speaks in a low, understated tone, which makes the conclusion of a memorable scene all the more impactful. Before departing, O'Brien provides Luez with a blunt warning. Referring to her planned boat excursion to Buenos Aires, he exclaims tartly, "Don't be surprised if I'm there to see you off."

With time quickly ticking by in his dwindling life, O'Brien makes a stop at the photography studio where the picture of George Reynolds that he took from Marla Rakubian was made. Here the story takes a clever turn. With so much pulsating drama and tense, sobering subject matter, it is time for a contrast; and here humor is invoked as a bridge to the breakneck pacing which will continue to Fadeout. Two sleazy photographers shake O'Brien down before supplying the information he needs about George Reynolds. One of the men refers to "privileged information," which prompts O'Brien to sardonically deadpan, "I know. You're a couple of high-classed guys." The photographer responds with an immediate "Thank you." The photographer indicates that he is revealing personal information, but that he is making an exception because O'Brien has declared himself to be a personal friend of Reynolds's. O'Brien quips, "I know. Honesty is the best policy."

The information O'Brien receives after paying off the photographers prompts him to see things in a new light. They reveal to him that the man he refers to as George Reynolds is actually named Raymond Rakubian. He had used a false name when having the important bill of sale of the stolen iridium notarized. It becomes obvious why Marla Rakubian had a framed photograph of the so-called Reynolds in her apartment. Raymond Rakubian was the model's husband, tightening the web some more in revealing the machinations surrounding the iridium transaction and the victimization of the luckless Eugene Philips, who was used as a tragic pawn of fate in the same way as Banning accountant Frank Bigelow.

O'Brien no sooner leaves the photography studio armed with his important new information than an attempt is made on his life. Gunshots are fired and his unseen prospective assassin retreats to a dusty, abandoned warehouse, where shots are exchanged. The gun taken from Molly Rakubian has become immediately helpful. Before the shooter escapes, he leaves a matchbook which O'Brien picks up. It contains a symbolic link to where the accountant was swiftly and effectively murdered the previous evening in San Francisco. The matchbook bears the name of The Fisherman.

Meeting the Mob

After a brief stop at Philips Exports and a heated discussion with Ching, who threatens to throw him out for being an abusive pest, O'Brien returns to his room at the Allison Hotel, where a guest convoy is there to receive him in hostile fashion. Molly Rabukian has placed a call, and the mob is there to take charge. Neville Brand makes his initial appearance as Chester, a depraved killer who delights in the sight of other people's blood.

Brand's portrayal of Chester, a brutal psycho, is poles removed from his pre-film image as the U.S. Army's fourth most decorated hero of WWII. He rubbed out a German 50-caliber machine gun nest. His unforgettable screen debut role as Chester, played with a chilling vehemence, is reminiscent of Richard Widmark's film bow three years earlier in 1947 in *Kiss of Death*, when he played psychopathic sadist Tommy Udo. Widmark's psychotic laugh along with the scene where he pushes Mildred Dunnock down a flight of stairs in her wheelchair have made the Twentieth Century Fox film directed by Henry Hathaway a landmark in the realm of psychotic criminal behavior. Brand warns O'Brien early on, "Don't get cute! I'm itching to work you over!" As in the case of many psychologically disturbed persons, the deranged mob enforcer refers to himself frequently in the third person as Chester.

O'Brien's appearance in his room and first meeting with Brand and his cohorts reveal another clever story concept of contrasts as, before the hoodlums can escort their victim away, the telephone rings and a thoroughly melancholy O'Brien, seeing his life ebbing away, speaks with his loyal secretary and lover. Pamela Britton becomes aware that something is terribly wrong due to her boss' deflated tone, along with his responses. He tells her to draw all of the funds out of their business account and use some of the money to buy herself a coat she has long wanted. "You're drunk!" she gasps at one point, but the viewer gets the feeling that the superficial comment masks her troubled feelings, as the woman in O'Brien's life attempts to resolve the dark mystery of his sudden behavioral change.

Brand and entourage drive O'Brien to a private residence, where the Banning accountant has his first meeting with mob kingpin Majak, played by New York stage

Tiring of the bullying he is receiving from psychotic hoodlum Neville Brand, Edmond O'Brien lashes back with a hard right to the jaw in a tense scene from *D.O.A.* Watching from the sofa are mob boss Luther Adler and Laurette Luez, the film's *femme fatale*. Adler was a noted stage actor and brother of famous drama coach Stella Adler. His *D.O.A.* starring role opposite O'Brien was one of the New Yorker's rare film roles.

great Luther Adler. Beginning as a youngster in Yiddish theater in New York City, Adler played the lead role of violinist-boxer Joe Bonaparte in the Clifford Odets Depression hit, *Golden Boy*. In his few cinema appearances, Hollywood honored his presence with special billings.

Adler's role as the ruthless Majak is reminiscent of another memorable performance as a heavy in the 1945 RKO noir gem, *Cornered*, starring Dick Powell and directed by Edward Dmytryk. The plot is similar to *D.O.A.* in one important respect in that Powell, at the close of the war, seeks revenge by trying to locate the man who killed his wife. In the film's powerful final scene, Adler surfaces as an unrepentant Nazi who is killed by the furious fists of the vengeance-seeking Powell. In *D.O.A.*, O'Brien seeks vengeance by finding and killing his own killer before the clock runs out on his life. Adler was the brother of Stella Adler, one of New York's famous drama coaches. Between 1938 and 1947, he was married to film great Sylvia Sidney. His brother Jay appeared in films and had roles in three notable noir entries from the fifties, Stanley Kubrick's *The Killing*, to be discussed later, the previously analyzed *Sweet Smell of Success*, and Joseph Lewis's *The Big Combo* (1955).

Whereas Neville Brand is the personification of enraged violence, Luther Adler as mob boss Majak is the personification of control and coolness under fire. With Marla Rakubian sitting next to him, a puzzled Adler seeks to learn why O'Brien has made it a point to "pry into my affairs." O'Brien can tell him only a few basic facts since he is trying to piece together the mystery. Adler quickly squelches the O'Brien suspicion that Raymond Rakubian, previously known to the accountant as George Reynolds, was his killer. Adler shows him the indoor crypt within the house which contains the ashes of Rakubian, who died five months earlier, just one month after the important bill of sale for iridium was notarized by accountant-notary Frank Bigelow in his Banning office. The meeting is made increasingly uncomfortable by Brand periodically punching O'Brien in the stomach. "Soft in the belly," he delivers a macabre mantra. "He can't take it. Soft in the belly." At one juncture, an enraged O'Brien punches him, with Brand pulling a gun and threatening to blow his adversary's brains out. When a colleague seeks to intervene, an enraged Brand slams his partner with the butt of his gun.

Adler expresses sympathy for O'Brien's plight, explaining that Brand is "a poor, unfortunate boy. He is psychopathic. He loves the sight of blood." O'Brien begs the mob boss to let him go, explaining that the only person he is interested in finding was the one who poisoned him. Adler refuses, explaining that with what O'Brien knows about the iridium sting on victim Philips, he could go to prison for ten years. "At my age that is my life, my entire life," Adler explains. "With my life I do not take chances."

When Brand is assigned the responsibility of disposing of O'Brien, he smiles with ghoulish delight and exclaims, "Just Bigelow and me and Baby makes three." The "Baby" referred to is the revolver he draws.

As O'Brien heads for the door with Brand for what has been planned as his ultimate exit, Luez, the embittered *femme fatale* who has remained previously silent, exclaims tartly, "I guess you won't be there to see me off." Her reference is to O'Brien's threat to be at the dock to stop her from going to Argentina.

The scene marks Luez's final appearance. In film noir, *femmes fatale* generally play leads. In this case, the script by Rouse and Greene incorporates a *femme fatale* into a feature role. While Laurette Luez is on screen but a short time, and has only one line in her second of two scenes, a superlative command of facts and dialogue make her a central and always-memorable figure with an economy of effort. Here is the woman who enticed the hapless victim Eugene Philips, whom we never see, to make a sale of stolen iridium through her husband Raymond, who uses the fictitious name of George Reynolds. When the iridium is sold to Majak, the hapless Philips becomes a victim. This provides O'Brien with the knowledge that Philips did not commit suicide since, as he notes, "Innocent men don't need to jump out of windows." A wily Majak then seeks to send manipulator Luez to Buenos Aires until the coast is clear.

The important sequences beginning with Campbell-Garland's disclosure of her former boss' clandestine relationship with Luez, to the fiery meeting between the film's *femme fatale*, to the forced confrontation with syndicate boss Adler reveal a great deal of information in a brief period of time, the hallmark of excellent story plotting and execution. After the meeting with Adler, O'Brien realizes that he knows a great deal more than before and is eager to explore more. He can see that he is closing in on solving the mystery surrounding his own murder. The gripping problem confronting him is whether any of this new information will help him since he is now in the hands of psychopathic syndicate hit man Brand.

Brand takes O'Brien for a ride in his convertible down Broadway in downtown Los Angeles. They pass the Million Dollar Theater at one point. The Million Dollar was Los Angeles's answer to New York's Radio City Music Hall in that a first-run film would be shown along with a stage show. Radio City Music Hall features its precision dancing group, the Rockettes, while the Million Dollar built shows around pianists such as Carmen Caballero and Jose Iturbi. Brand then drives by the Orpheum Theater, also a memorable part of the city's cinema firmament.

While Brand drives, he lustily contemplates the moment when he will shoot O'Brien. He promises to make his death "nice and slow." The psychotic killer adds the chilling mantra he states periodically with frightening repetition, "Soft in the belly." As Brand contemplates the delicious delight of watching O'Brien slowly bleed to death, his intended victim makes a move, shoving his foot atop Brand's, as the killer's foot is on the gas pedal. This causes the convertible to veer off course as O'Brien jumps out.

SUPERB EDITING

What worked with superb editing and location shooting was far from accurate geographically, which was no impediment to the film's breakneck pacing. O'Brien runs into Lee's Drugstore, located on the northwest corner of Hollywood and Highland. At that time, the Hollywood Hotel was located directly across the street on Hollywood Boulevard and situated on the southwest corner. A musical starring Dick Powell was made called *Hollywood Hotel*, but it probably gained even greater recognition throughout the rest of the nation as the location of Louella Parsons's nationally syndicated radio program which aired on Sunday nights. Situated now where the Hollywood Hotel once stood is the Kodak Theater, scene of the Oscar presentations.

Located just a half block east on the same side of the street as Lee's was the Paramount Theater. Grauman's Chinese Theater and its famous forecourt, where movie fans from all over the world have flocked to see the footprints and handprints of the film industry's stars, was situated directly across the street from the Paramount.

The man with more lives than a cat, whose life is ironically moving ever closer to death by poison, survives another immediate brush with the grim reaper. Brand pursues O'Brien into the drugstore. One of the best camera sequences occurs when, amid shrieks from women and customers darting for the door, a pharmacist turns the tables on the gun-wielding executioner. The pharmacist takes dead aim and, in the manner of an accomplished major league pitcher, hurls a bottle containing a medical formula at Brand's head. He scores a bulls-eye, and as Brand staggers, a uniformed police officer enters the drugstore and fires on the crazed killer, the bullets finding their mark. O'Brien staggers out of the drugstore as the officer stares down at the lifeless body of Brand.

ONE FINAL MEETING

A contrast is needed at that point, a breather for viewers since the action has been moving at such a feverish clip. It is provided in the most tender scene of the film. When O'Brien steps out of a cab in front of the Allison Hotel, having escaped another attempt on his life, Pamela Britton rushes into the street and throws her arms around him. She has come to see him amid great concern after having received a telephone call at the Banning office from a police detective in San Francisco who is looking for her boss. While nothing is said, it becomes increasingly obvious that secretary and loyal lover Paula Gibson knows that this will be her last meeting with Frank Bigelow. His vulnerable role as an innocent pawn of fate, an existentialist victim, is revealed when he says with great pathos, "I know, all I did was notarize one little paper. One little paper out of hundreds." The pathos and sensitivity reach their zenith when Bigelow, walking toward his car, turns and waves to Paula for the last time.

Working on another hunch, an angry Bigelow darts into the apartment of Miss Foster, finding her with her boyfriend, Stanley Philips. As he excitedly tells her that Stanley is the person who is out to kill him, and that he had the knowledge and opportunity to fit the profile, Stanley staggers into the living room. He tells Bigelow that he has been sidetracked, but not by him, and that Halliday is his man. Philips shows Bigelow a letter just found, which implicates Halliday in a romantic relationship with none other than Mrs. Eugene Philips. Bigelow becomes concerned about Philips's condition. He learns that the stricken man had dinner with Halliday earlier that evening and drank some wine with his meal. Before darting out of the apartment for his next stop, Bigelow grabs Miss Foster by the arm and implores her to telephone emergency, summoning a team to provide the victim with an immediate stomach wash for luminous toxic poison. "Quick!" he implores. "There might be time to save his life!"

Yet another new element surfaces in a script replete with surprises and numerous plot twists. Frank Bigelow stands on the brink of death because he was unaware of any physical problem until it was too late. As Bigelow's life moves to a rapid close, he hopes to save the life of someone who has been victimized in the identical manner as himself one night earlier. The sinister Halliday has struck another victim through the intercession of luminous toxic poison.

The Final Showdown

The film next moves swiftly toward a final conclusion filled with action, as a determined Majak seeks to prevent Bigelow from accomplishing his goal. O'Brien drives next to the apartment of Lynne Baggett. He pushes her out onto the balcony, grabbing her and threatening to hurl her to her death if she does not tell him the truth. She explains that Eugene Philips, aware of her affair with Halliday, confronted him, after which they fought and the company auditor pushed him off of the same balcony on which they are standing. At that point, he observes Majak and his remaining troops, minus the departed Chester, pulling to a stop at the curb in front of the apartment.

D.O.A. is a film utilizing some of the most famous locations in the Los Angeles area. So many are utilized, in fact, that it would be possible to put together a *D.O.A.* tour showing interesting locations used in the film. Some of the most fascinating are shown during the final chase, when O'Brien seeks to elude Luther Adler and his criminal operatives to confront his hated adversary who has poisoned him, played by William Ching.

As soon as O'Brien exits the widow's apartment, the chase commences across the street at the Laurel Arms. In 1940, author F. Scott Fitzgerald sustained a fatal heart attack in his apartment there. Years later, a famous name from film noir annals, Jacques Tourneur, who directed RKO's celebrated *Out of the Past*, also lived at Laurel Arms.

Adler's operatives begin chasing O'Brien at the Laurel Arms, but the pursuit soon extends north toward Sunset Boulevard and the famous Garden of Allah, residence of some of America's famous writers. During wealthier times, Fitzgerald lived there. His move to the nearby Laurel Arms was an effort to remain close to a residence where he felt at home.

The Garden of Allah was the creation of silent film star Alla Nazimova. Its tropical fruit trees and whitewashed bungalows were set around a pool shaped like the Black Sea. It resembled a Moroccan village, or at least a movie version of one. The greats of the New York literary scene stayed there, interacting with Hollywood creative counterparts. From George S. Kaufman, Clifford Odets, Dorothy Parker and Robert Benchley from the East to movie personalities such as Humphrey Bogart and Lauren Bacall, Groucho Marx, John Carradine, Louis Calhern and Dorothy Gish, they came and alternately worked or meditated in their private bungalows or partied together. During WWII, when rationing was in vogue, Gloria Stuart, a noted resident, actress, social hostess and gourmet cook, would visit the Farmers Market on Fairfax Avenue nearby and shop meticulously for items which would serve as her current version of *nouveau cuisine*.

As O'Brien seeks to elude Adler's gang, he steps into the dark labyrinth of the Garden of Allah complex, weaving around pillars, moving toward Sunset Boulevard, and what he hopes will be freedom. It is an ideal location for a chase sequence, and ultimately O'Brien is able to run to Sunset, entering a Hollywood bus proceeding east. No more than a half block from where O'Brien enters the bus, on the same side of the street, was the location of Schwabs Drugstore, which became famous for the erroneous claim that Lana Turner was discovered there sipping a soda. She was actually discovered at an ice cream parlor across the street from Hollywood High, which she was then attending. Schwabs, which no longer exists, remained for years a hangout for aspirants to careers in the film industry. This side of Schwabs was revealed in Andrew Lloyd Weber's musical, *Sunset Boulevard.*

On the opposite side of the street, just across from Schwabs, was Ah Fong's Restaurant. Specializing in Chinese cuisine at a reasonable price, the popular establishment was owned by Benson Fong, who played Tommy "Number Three Son" in scores of Charlie Chan films. Encouraged early in his career by his friend Gregory Peck to develop a successful enterprise for economic security amid the uncertainties of the film industry, Fong paid heed and opened the Sunset Boulevard restaurant. He was so successful that he opened another Ah Fong's in Anaheim, near Disneyland, continuing to prosper until his death in 1987.

As O'Brien sits nervously in the bus, he observes Adler and group following side by side. At one point, the bus is seen on Wilshire Boulevard. Observable from the distance is a bright sign with the word "Gaylord," a prominent local hotel named after wealthy property magnate Gaylord Wilshire, after whom the street was named. Directly across the street from the Gaylord was the Ambassador Hotel. The Ambassador's famous Cocoanut Grove was the site of Oscar ceremonies in early years of the event. It was used as the site of the Oscar award scenes from two versions of *A Star is Born*—in 1937 with Janet Gaynor and Fredric March and 1954 featuring Judy Garland and James Mason. The Cocoanut Grove was frequented by Hollywood's greatest stars for years. They danced and listened to great musical talent such as Artie Shaw, Nat "King" Cole and a steady constellation of other greats. On a more solemn note, the Ambassador was where Senator Robert Kennedy was gunned down after making his victory speech in the 1968 California Democratic Presidential Primary.

When an Adler operative seeks to enter the bus after it stops, O'Brien makes a quick exit. Adler and his group watch helplessly from their automobile as a uniformed traffic officer implores them to "Get moving." Two other patrolmen sit on motorcycles nearby, creating an impossible atmosphere for the criminals to do anything other than comply with the officer's request, and so they move on after repeated urgings.

The stage is now set for an anticipated showdown. O'Brien observes a light burning in Halliday's office at Philips Exports. As O'Brien moves up the stairs, Ching makes his exit. As symbolically befitting, he is wearing the same hat, overcoat and scarf in which he was attired one evening earlier at The Fisherman on San Francisco's Wharf, where he cut O'Brien's life tragically short by poisoning him. They move in a combination of shadow and light in the historic old Bradbury Building settings replete with black iron railings. Ching seeks to make a quick retreat down the stairs. O'Brien's cold-eyed expression informs the shrewd, cold-blooded killer that his victim now knows everything and is there to obtain vengeance. A retreating Ching suddenly pivots and fires as O'Brien steps away from the line of bullets. O'Brien fires repeatedly and Ching slinks to the ground, his life snuffed away in one violent exchange as O'Brien's existence moves into its final few minutes.

His incredible story completed, the action swings back to where the film began, with O'Brien talking to the homicide captain, who has listened attentively. Once more, he mentions with sad irony, "So you see, all I did was notarize one document. One document out of hundreds." The Captain nods sympathetically, after which O'Brien stands up and, with great effort, barely manages to speak his last word, "Paula!"

The tragedy of Banning accountant Frank Bigelow ends abruptly as he drops to the floor. An officer takes his pulse and shakes his head, silently revealing the victim's status. "How should I make out the report, Captain?" the officer asks.

"Make it out as Dead on Arrival," the Captain concludes.

The last image on the screen prior to Fadeout is the official police document concerning Frank Bigelow, which is stamped in stark black lettering—"D.O.A."

A European Influence

One element of the movie that becomes evident after repeated viewings is that its dramatic development and enriching symbolism convey the feel of a European film. *D.O.A.* was adapted from a 1931 German film, *Der Mann, Der Seinen Morden Gucht.* The director was Robert Siodmak who, after emigrating to America with his screenwriter brother Curt to escape Nazi Germany, directed three of the most memorable noir classics ever produced in Hollywood, all for Universal. The first was the 1944 release, *Phantom Lady*, based on a Cornell Woolrich story, in which Franchot Tone plays a brilliant, thoroughly twisted serial killer. *The Killers* and *Criss Cross* were each covered earlier in detail in the preceding chapter. Siodmak had an affinity for the dark and brooding, bearing a linkage to four of the greatest noir films ever made.

Another important link and similarity between *The Killers* and *D.O.A.* relates to Edmond O'Brien, who also played a prominent role in the earlier film. O'Brien actually emerges with more screen time than Lancaster or Gardner. His role contains story similarities to *D.O.A.* In *The Killers*, he is an insurance investigator probing into the death of former prizefighter and later ex-convict Burt Lancaster. As with Frank Bigelow in *D.O.A.*, he suspects foul play. In *D.O.A.*, his suspicions surround his own poisoning, while in *The Killers*, his investigative instincts prompt him to doggedly research Lancaster's life. He encounters criminal gangland elements out to kill him. These elements on several occasions almost do him in, as with Frank Bigelow in *D.O.A.* The earlier role in *The Killers*, with O'Brien cast as a dogged investigator risking death from mob elements, could have been a factor in him being chosen for the similar role he played in *D.O.A.* What gave the 1950 film a compelling uniqueness was that O'Brien was tracking down his own killer.

"Edmond O'Brien poured his all into this role," Beverly Garland acknowledged. "He had the most screen time of anyone in the cast, of course, and top billing. He knew this was a tremendous opportunity for an actor to put his talent on display. This was a man who experiences the shock of discovering that he has been poisoned, there is no cure, and he has only 24 or 48 hours to live. This would be a challenging role for any star. The only way it could work would be to have a tightly knit script, excellent direction, a cast that was always on target, and music to match the mood of the scene. Fortunately *D.O.A.* had all of those elements working together, creating a harmony that made the unique premise of the picture completely credible."

D.O.A. was filmed in three weeks. Garland recognized the importance of the strategically selected locations, which enhanced film interest and provided additional enjoyment. "A second unit went up to San Francisco with just the performers that appear in the San Francisco scenes," Beverly revealed. "The wonderful locations on Fisherman's Wharf, at the St. Francis Hotel, and on Market Street were vital. Of course, the many location shots in Los Angeles at historic landmark buildings along downtown Broadway, Wilshire Boulevard and on Sunset Boulevard gives movie buffs a tour of the Los Angeles area as it looked long ago."

The direction and camera work were superb. The director, in fact, was launching into a new field after a highly successful career as a cinematographer. Rudolph Maté made his mark by showing Columbia's glamour girl Rita Hayworth in her best light, handling the camera work for her two most notable showcase roles, both directed by Charles Vidor, in *Cover Girl* (1944) and *Gilda* (1946). In 1950, two other films Maté directed debuted in theaters, *Union Station* with William Holden and Nancy Olson and *No Sad Songs for Me* starring Margaret Sullavan and Wendell Corey. The cinematographer for *D.O.A.*, Ernest Laszlo, was Elia Kazan's cameraman for Marlon Brando's Oscar triumph, *On The Waterfront*. Laszlo later became associated with Stanley Kramer. After pleasing Kramer with his work on *Inherit The Wind* (1960), he was invested with cinematography responsibilities for *Ship of Fools*, the spectacular 1965 adaptation of Katherine Ann Porter's best-selling novel featuring Vivien Leigh. Laszlo secured an Oscar for his work on *Ship of Fools*.

The young writing team of Russell Rouse and Clarence Greene, which combined to hammer out the brilliant script for *D.O.A.*, continued to work as a team. While *D.O.A.* was produced by Leo Popkin, the Rouse-Greene team would later collaborate as producers and writers on various projects. Just as *D.O.A.* was known for its unique story element, the Rouse-Greene team united with British Oscar-winning star Ray Milland, who less than a decade earlier collected a Best Actor statuette for his brilliant work in *The Lost Weekend* (1945), an arty project which suffered for being ahead of its time. Milland made his directorial debut and starred while Rouse and Greene wrote the script and produced the 1952 release, *The Thief*. Milland plays a nuclear physicist who sells out to a foreign power. The film's intriguing element is that it is without dialogue, the first such film made in America since fellow Britisher Charlie Chaplin directed and starred in *City Lights* over two decades earlier in 1931. Russell and Greene later combined to form Seven Arts Productions, which ultimately became Warner Bros.-Seven Arts.

The raw dramatic power of *D.O.A.* continues to impress accelerating numbers of film enthusiasts, as we move beyond the half-century mark from its 1950 release. From the unique talent assembled, beginning with the talented Edmond O'Brien, it is obvious that this is a film put together with great precision. Top personnel was employed at each level, with many of the individuals just beginning great careers.

Considering the fact that television was just beginning to achieve popularity when the film was released at the beginning of the fifties, it was understandable that so many members of the cast would click in the new medium, notably O'Brien and Beverly Garland. Director Maté also garnered recognition there. A close friend of Academy Award-winning actress Loretta Young, Maté directed numerous episodes of her highly successful fifties' Sunday night program, *The Loretta Young Show.*

O'Brien handled the challenge of appearing in each scene and maintaining an appropriately high level of energy as befitting a man trying to make the most of the few remaining hours left to him. Pamela Britton performed with brilliant sensitivity as his lover and secretary. The bittersweet theme by Dimitri Tiomkin set just the right tone in establishing a loving relationship which contained much promise, which O'Brien did not ultimately realize until the final day of his life.

The film is a love story between two people seeking to establish a firm relationship as well as a pulsating mystery containing a series of fascinating characters. Luther Adler set the proper tone as the imperious mob boss Majak while Neville Brand, in his film debut, is chilling as the blood-loving homicidal enforcer Chester. Laurette Luez generated fireworks in her scene with O'Brien as the predatory *femme fatale* Marla Rakubian.

Beverly Campbell-Garland, in her film debut, demonstrated pathos as secretary to the deceased Eugene Philips, reluctant to disclose any information that would sully his memory. O'Brien is forced to pry the information out of her about her boss' intimate relationship with the scheming Molly Rakubian, which made the iridium sale sting possible.

D.O.A. was filmed twice after its 1950 version, an indication that others in the industry were aware of its rare power. In 1969, an Australian remake of the film appeared as Tom Tryon starred in *Color Me Dead.* Another version was released in 1988, which bore the name *D.O.A.* and starred Dennis Quaid and Meg Ryan.

FOUR

The Laureates of Night

I was born when you kissed me. I died when you left me. I lived a few weeks while you loved me.

In a Lonely Place (1950)

The night has a poetry all its own. When a talented director from Wisconsin who learned his craft on the New York stage combined his efforts with one of the early creators of film noir, the result was a majesty of darkness and isolation.

Humphrey Bogart was the perfect actor to star in what has been generally billed as the first-ever noir film, the 1941 detective classic, *The Maltese Falcon*, which marked the directing debut of John Huston, who also directed the great star in his Oscar-winning role in *The African Queen* (1952), along with such other classics as *The Treasure of Sierra Madre* (1946), *Key Largo* (1950) and the offbeat cult classic *Beat the Devil* (1954). From that initial noir vehicle, with Bogart cast as author Dashiell Hammett's famous detective Sam Spade, two great careers were launched. While Huston moved from the rank of prominent screenwriter to director, Bogart completed his ascending leap to stardom's frontal ranks. Bogart's Spade was a wily character with a moral code, a man at home in the evening, shadowing characters from the underworld, such as Sydney Greenstreet, Peter Lorre and Elisha Cook Jr.

If success is marked by being in the right place at the right time, stardom results from having the right role and the proper script. The Bogart persona from the outset was that of the loner, the man of experience who one moment is mad at the world, at other times is bored, but is determined to make his unique mark. It summarizes Bogart's private life. Born a son of privilege, with a prominent doctor father and newspaper illustrator mother, Bogart, who grew up on the affluent Upper East Side of Manhattan, tossed away the kinds of opportunities which would have led to a more structured existence as a prominent doctor, lawyer, or corporate executive. A rebel from the beginning marching to the tune of his own drummer, Bogart dismayed his famous parents by being expelled from one prominent prep school after another.

71

When Bogart shunned the world of book learning for acting, he became a man of controversy with his frequent brawling with hot-tempered second wife, Mayo Methot. As a major star, known for his two-fisted drinking bouts, Bogart made the newspapers by being involved in bar brawls at famous Hollywood nightclubs like Ciro's and Mocambo as a participant or instigator.

Hollywood recognized early on that Bogart was a unique talent, a rebel for all to see, someone who looked as if he was carrying the world on his shoulders. He was alternately morose and diffident, violent and uncaring, sympathetic and sadistic. Here was an actor who could run the gamut, but was always better with the running start of a rebel. Clad in a customary dark suit and dark hat, Bogart displayed the demeanor of someone who was never young. Despite the expression he could convey of somebody who had lived forever and had nothing more to learn, Bogart, since he had never been young, developed an essentially unchanged status where, conversely, he would never be old. This was the wily man of experience who, like the young Puck, could laugh about what fools we mortals be. Just about the time that you were convinced, however, that you had him figured out, he would fool you. What made *Casablanca* such a prodigious tearjerker was that Rick, the same self-expressed anarchistic, uncaring nightclub owner, had the kind of sensitive inner core that was admirable. It was a side which his hard-boiled persona felt compelled to deny.

Bogart's ultimate springboard toward the stardom opportunity Huston offered in *The Maltese Falcon* was linked to their directly preceding film, *High Sierra*. Huston co-wrote the script along with the author from whose novel it was adapted, W.R. Burnett, with Raoul Walsh directing. Once again, Bogart is cast as a complex figure split between a tough, anti-social exterior he displays openly and a tender humanitarian interior he is loathe to admit he possesses. A robber linked to the syndicate, he travels from Indiana to California to continue a life of crime after leaving prison. His sympathy toward club-footed Joan Leslie prompts him to pay for an operation to correct the handicap, after which he is repulsed when he finds her with a boyfriend he detests. Bogart, seemingly doomed to extinction, as represented by the antiquated criminal figure he embodies, ultimately succumbs to the charms of the girl from the wrong side of the tracks whom he earlier rejected in pursuit of the ultimately elusive Leslie, played by Ida Lupino. He even consents to keep a dog linked to the deaths of previous criminal owners, despite being superstitious.

BOGART MEETS RAY

Bogart, an actor who thrived on playing characters from stories containing brooding darkness and moral ambiguity, found a kindred spirit in a talented director from Wisconsin who learned his craft on the New York stage, then moved to Hollywood, touching base with a studio noted for well-crafted stories about the world of night, RKO's noir factory. It was not long after the studio's triumphs with such film noir classics as *Out of the Past*, *Crossfire*, and *Murder, My Sweet* that a young director named Nicholas Ray arrived in Hollywood. Born Raymond Nicholas Kienzle, the future director grew up in La Crosse, Wisconsin, going to the same high school with and becoming lifelong friends with fellow director Joseph Losey. In those early days in New York, when they were learning their craft, fellow Wisconsinites Ray and Losey sought to establish a proletariat-oriented theater group consistent with so many of the Communist ideologues groping for answers in the depths of the Great Depression.

During the wave of post-WWII anti-communist zeal dominating Cold War America in that turbulent period, Losey, like other directors, sought refuge across the Atlantic. He found England to his liking and developed a flourishing partnership ultimately with a young playwright-turned-screenwriter, Harold Pinter, the result being critically acclaimed successes, such as *The Servant* (1963), *Accident* (1967) and *The Go-Between* (1971).

While one would think that, by touching down in one of the most provocative nerve centers of the emerging Hollywood ideological conflict, RKO, that young director Ray would run headlong into the investigation that would ultimately lead to the Hollywood Ten and the incumbent controversy surrounding it, Ray dodged that potential career-ending, or at least severely damaging, prospect by putting his beliefs into his work. His friendship with Howard Hughes at RKO also helped.

The dependable way to avail oneself of the rich scenic opportunities available by filming a world of tension and darkness, the hallmark of noir cinema at its best, is to link the elements to disaffected people, troubled individuals immersed in burning psychological trauma. Nicholas Ray's body of cinematic work is indelible proof of his abiding interest in the disaffected, those shaped by internal and external conflict, along with his unique sensitivity in providing his stories with a ringing conviction that holds up, yet is never bogged down by preachiness.

THEY LIVE BY NIGHT (1949)

As was frequently characteristic of post-WWII Hollywood, Ray received the break that launched his directing career through the benefit of a supportive New York theater contact. John Houseman was then in the early stages of a successful career as a producer at RKO. A short time earlier, he had provided the proper measure of support to coax an imbibing Raymond Chandler to bring in a script on time to coincide with the clock-ticking deadline of Paramount Studio's top leading man being recalled into active military duty. Not knowing what the future might hold, Paramount's hierarchy was eager to extract one more film out of tough guy leading man Alan Ladd before he was slated to depart Hollywood with his duffel bag for foreign conflict during the final year of the war. Ladd was a blazing box office commodity, along with his Paramount romantic partner, Veronica Lake, and a script was needed fast to ensure that the film would be made.

Producer Houseman nursed Chandler along, using their common English roots and prep school loyalties to good advantage as he allowed the temperamental writer to work at home with a steady supply of liquor, which the great detective author insisted he needed to meet deadline exigencies. The result was the successful 1946 release, *The Blue Dahlia*, which enhanced studio coffers. Meanwhile studio golden boy Ladd, after finishing a rapid fire shooting schedule, rejoined the Army and was dismissed quickly from active duty, much to Paramount's relief and delight, despite the nervous flurry of studio activity to meet the deadline imposed by Uncle Sam.

Houseman had been a part of Orson Welles's Mercury Theater and in later years would become famous as the oldest Best Supporting Actor Oscar winner in 1974 for playing a Harvard law professor in *The Paper Chase*, while Tatum O'Neal simultaneously became the youngest-ever Best Supporting Actress recipient for *Paper Moon*. Toward the end of his life, he became a familiar American household figure by doing a commercial for the investment firm Smith Barney with his maxim, "They make money the old-fashioned way. They earn it." Houseman also produced one of the greatest films ever done about Hollywood, the 1952 release, *The Bad and the Beautiful*, at MGM.

By then ensconced some two blocks away from Paramount in a producer's office at RKO, Houseman found a Depression novel featuring two young runaways who, while not basically bad, were victimized by fates governed by the period of social instability in which they lived. Written by Edward Anderson, *Thieves Like Us* was published in 1937. Houseman provided his old New York theater confidante Ray with an opportunity to aid him in constructing a treatment of the Anderson novel.

Ray had made his film debut as an assistant director to New York theater crony and enduring friend Elia Kazan in the 1945 smash hit, *A Tree Grows in Brooklyn*. In addition to his New York theater experience, Ray had earlier been associated with the brilliant architect and folklore figure Frank Lloyd Wright during his Wisconsin days. After a radio script had won Ray a scholarship to the University of Chicago, two years later, he secured another endowment, this time to Wright's legendary artists colony at Taliesin. In addition to studying architecture under the great American master, he also studied music, philosophy, sculpture and theater. His formal architectural training would be of later benefit as a director.

Ray was a whiz at spatial design, whether the impression was claustrophobic in the psychologically adapted, darkened, self-imposed constraints of film noir or, later in his career, to encompass the broader use of space in the CinemaScope widescreen world of the fifties. From Taliesin, an idealistic Ray went east to New York, collaborating in left-wing theater projects with the aforementioned Houseman, Kazan and Losey, along with playwright Clifford Odets. He gained notices appearing in Kazan's directorial debut, *The Young Go First*, produced by the Theater of Action in the spring of 1935.

A Vehicle for Social Activism

At the close of the thirties, Ray traveled through the American South and West, collecting folk music and lore for the Library of Congress. His journey through America during the turbulent Depression period along with his political activism gave Ray the proper measure of authority to tackle a project such as *Thieves Like Us*, of which a wily Houseman was certainly aware. Ray was politically active during the thirties and was a daily contributor to the American Communist Party newspaper published in New York, *The Daily Worker*. Rejected for military service during the war by the draft board resulting from a heart ailment, Ray joined Houseman in helping to establish the Voice of America radio network, spending the war years producing propaganda for broadcast in occupied Europe.

It was perhaps poetic justice that Ray would arrive in Hollywood to work under former crony Kazan as assistant director on *A Tree Grows in Brooklyn* in the latter's cinema debut, since he had earlier made his New York theater bow as an actor with him as well. The poetic thread continued with the Houseman involvement in a Depression-rooted sociopolitical drama set in barren stretches of Oklahoma, refamiliarizing Ray with the America he had traveled during the same period depicted in the earthy 1937 Edward Anderson novel, *Thieves Like Us*.

Just when the Houseman-Ray team had become appropriately assimilated into the pre-production process, they were victimized by an obstacle. RKO production chief William Dozier was fired, and the project went into limbo. They filled in the interim period before the project would ultimately be launched by teaming up in a stage musical, *Beggar's Holiday*, an update of *Beggar's Opera* featuring new music by Duke Ellington. Following a disastrous New Haven production, Houseman pulled out while Ray remained as director until the play reached Broadway, where New York reviewers confirmed the antipathy earlier registered in New Haven.

When Dore Schary arrived at RKO as new production head, the project was revived. Despite reservations on Schary's part, Houseman handed the directorial reins of the film that would ultimately become *They Live by Night* to Ray. A great deal of internalizing was generated before the final title was ultimately settled upon. The original U.S. title for the film was to have been *The Twisted Road*, while Schary had originally opted for *Your Red Wagon*, adapted from a song in the film. Charles Schnee, who had just finished scripting the Howard Hawks western classic, *Red River*, honed Ray's 124-page treatment into a finished product.

Open Spaces Claustrophobia

The Ray cinematic strategy of using the dry, barren open spaces of the Depression Southwest while revealing a story involving two young people on the run from the law presents another creative application of what appears on the surface as an oxymoron, but, when explained, is anything but a contradiction. The film noir claustrophobia experienced by people closed in by the forces of fate is presented by Ray's discerning camera through the irony of using expansive areas, often with nothing in sight beyond dust and highways, and with no sounds beyond rustling winds and passing trains. While some see such circumstances in terms of expansiveness, to fugitives perpetually on the run, the open spaces induce the claustrophobia of life's losers with no place to run. With the exploits of bank robbers being constantly written about in local newspapers and discussed on radio, where does one hide? In small communities, people know each other and are suspicious of outsiders. The dusty open spaces of sparsely populated areas make anonymity a far more difficult objective than losing oneself in a large city as part of a lonely crowd.

The superimposed opening title reveals Ray's interest in and identification with society's disaffected: "This boy ... and this girl ... were never properly introduced to the world we live in." The message is immediately impressed into the minds of audience members with the imagery of Ray's camera from the film's outset.

Haunted young lovers Farley Granger and Cathy O'Donnell kiss at the film's opening, after which Ray furnishes a scene demonstrating his ingenuity as a director amid great controversy. After the opening kiss, a getaway car is seen carrying three criminals down a dusty road pursued by police. Ray sought to use something alien to filmmakers at the time, a scene photographed from a helicopter rather than employing a standard camera shot. Such shots are commonly employed today, but Ray was forced to lobby to get his way at the time. Opposition from RKO vanished when the director proved his point, revealing how effective such a shot could be. Once the RKO executives had an opportunity to view the footage, they became believers. The idea of filming from overhead implanted the idea of an ultimately losing struggle against the forces of destiny, three men battling nature in the wide-open spaces. The overhead photography made the sprawling expanses appear that much more vast. As Ephraim Katz wrote, "Not only did it (the overhead scene) open the film with a burst of unharnessed energy, but thematically it conveyed a sense of godlike fate, looking down on Granger and relentlessly pursuing him."

Another shrewd ploy was conveyed early in the film to demonstrate the unyielding forces against which the luckless Farley Granger operated. Injured in the getaway, he is left by partners in crime Howard da Silva and Jay C. Flippen to await help since his limping presence will slow down the pursued in the battle with their pursuers. He cowers in total obscurity beneath a large billboard. The scene reveals the isolation of the young man and the ultimate hopelessness of an existence on the run.

The casting of Farley Granger by Ray as Bowie, the young man cursed by fate, provided the young actor with an opportunity to be seen by Alfred Hitchcock, who promptly put him to work. Hitchcock had viewed a preview of *They Live by Night*, perceiving that Granger would be ideal as the vulnerable member of the duo that also consisted of John Dahl in *Rope* (1948), a story based on the Leopold-Loeb thrill murders in Chicago. James Stewart plays the shrewd lawyer who solves the crime. Hitchcock remained impressed with Granger and his persona of the young, vulnerable victim and cast him also as Guy Haines, the tennis player opposite psychopathic killer Bruno Antony, played with engrossing conviction by Robert Walker in his final completed film, *Strangers on a Train* (1951).

Granger came to the attention of a Samuel Goldwyn talent scout as a teenager. He was spotted in a Los Angeles theater production, and Goldwyn signed him to a film contract. Granger debuted on screen as a Russian youth in the 1943 release, *The North Star*. His sensitivity registered in the part he played as the loving husband of Jeanne Crain in a segment from *O. Henry's Full House* (1952). He played troubled Pittsburgh steel heir Harry K. Thaw in *The Girl in the Red Velvet Swing* (1955), in which he kills famed New York architect Stanford White, portrayed by Ray Milland, over the affections of showgirl Evelyn Nesbitt, played by Joan Collins. The film was based on the most-publicized triangular romance scandal of the early twentieth century and was directed by Richard Fleischer. Granger, as typical of so many performers, became typecast as the vulnerable and sensitive young man, which made it more difficult for him to secure roles as he matured. After acting in films in Italy, he became a regular on the popular television soap opera, *One Life to Live*.

JANE GREER CONSIDERED

With starring roles in *They Won't Believe Me* (1946) and *Out of the Past* (1947), two of the better dramas filmed on the RKO lot in the late forties, it was anything but surprising that Jane Greer would be called in to read for the female lead in a brooding film noir drama such as *They Live by Night*. Ray had her read for the role of Bowie's equally vulnerable, equally naive wife, Keechie.

"I tested for the lead in *They Live by Night* when I was at RKO," Greer recalled. "I did not expect to get the part because they were looking for somebody younger. I understood this. I later became a good friend of Gloria Grahame's when she was married to Nick."

In real terms, Cathy O'Donnell, selected by Ray to play Keechie, was only ten months younger than Jane Greer. The characteristics Greer was referring to really counted, screen presence and the level of experience contrasted with youthful naivete which surfaced on camera. The element that astounded film critics and historians, along with the legions of fans of *Out of the Past*, was the level of cold, calculating intelligence Jane Greer projected as the wily *femme fatale* operator who Robert Mitchum, despite awareness of her dangerous duplicity, could not leave alone.

While only twenty-two when *Out of the Past* was filmed, Greer, from a level of projected worldly experience, conjured up images beyond the age of a young lady who had reached voting age only one year earlier. Greer's cool maturity had surfaced just one film earlier, her first with star billing, *They Won't Believe Me* with Robert Young and Susan Hayward, as she convincingly portrayed a magazine writer who seeks unsuccessfully to convince Young that the jury might well believe his insistent claims that he is innocent.

With the image of a shrewd, mature woman well beyond her actual years, Jane Greer was the opposite of the youthful, tormented Keechie. What was needed was a female counterpart to Granger, a soul mate who stumbles through a youthful existence looking for answers that are seemingly never there. Cathy O'Donnell fit that image perfectly in a brilliant double casting triumph by Ray. O'Donnell, like Granger, was also signed to a contract by Goldwyn Studios after early stage activity. Goldwyn put her immediately to good use in what many consider the finest film the legendary producer ever made, *The Best Years of Our Lives* (1946).

While never on the run from the law as she was opposite Granger in *They Live by Night*, O'Donnell was cast as a sensitive woman providing maximum support to her man in the William Wyler-directed classic. She ultimately convinces her fiancé Harold Russell that she loves him for himself, rather than out of pity over the fact that he has returned from the war after losing both hands. Their wedding at the end of the film brings the drama to a conclusion on a high note, providing hope that Teresa Wright's and Dana Andrews's blossoming romance will realize comparable success. The wide-eyed sensitivity and sweetness displayed by O'Donnell made her perfect for the role opposite fellow Goldwyn contractee Granger in *They Live by Night*.

DEFYING THE ODDS AND THE CHRISTENING OF CATHY

Born Ann Steely in the tiny Alabama town of Siluria, Cathy left her home state after her father's death and spent a brief period living with an aunt in Greensboro, Alabama. After working briefly as a stenographer at the Army induction center of her new home of Oklahoma City, the young woman, hoping to become a movie star, quit her job to study acting at Oklahoma City University. Young Ann finally saved up enough money for a very brief trip to Hollywood. "I only had enough money to last for a couple of weeks," she recalled. "If I didn't break into the movies by then, I was going to have to go back home to Oklahoma City."

To expect to be signed to a contract by a Hollywood studio within two weeks of arrival required surmounting astronomical odds. This was a period when scores of young men and women were descending on the film capital from all over the world hoping to be discovered. The incredible result in this case was that, as naive as the projection was, the young actress achieved her goal within the financially necessary time frame.

Ed Glover, an RKO contract player, was having lunch with his agent in a small Hollywood cafe discussing what qualities it took to interest studios in film talent. He pointed out a sweetly attractive young woman seated at the counter, who was nursing a cup of coffee. Glover asked his agent where he would place the young woman sitting at the counter as a Hollywood type. The hypothetical conversation came to an end as the agent told Glover that she embodied the sweet, innocent type that Samuel Goldwyn liked.

Ann Steely was whisked off by the agent to Goldwyn Studios. The mogul was then reportedly having problems with Teresa Wright, deciding to sign a comparable type as a means of seeking to keep her in line. The same ploy was employed at MGM by Louis B. Mayer when Greer Garson sought to break out of the mold in which she had been cast by the studio to do different roles, whereupon Deborah Kerr was signed. Despite the fact that her screen test revealed a thick southern accent, prompting Goldwyn to turn off the sound track and concentrate solely on her facial image, he signed Steely to a contract and put her in the same film with Wright, the great Goldwyn triumph, *The Best Years of Our Lives*.

Before young Ann went before the cameras, however, there was the accent problem to be overcome. In addition to providing acting and diction lessons for Ann, Goldwyn used his influence to have her cast in local plays, one of which was *Little Women* at Pasadena Playhouse. Dean Goodman, who appeared with her in that play, recalls conversations with the recent arrival from Oklahoma City as they took the bus from Hollywood to their Pasadena rehearsals. She explained how her new professional name of Cathy O'Donnell had been acquired.

"I chose the name Cathy after the character in *Wuthering Heights*," she explained to Goodman, "but Mrs. (Frances) Goldwyn suggested O'Donnell because she said the public loves Irish names."

The chemistry with fellow Goldwynite Granger was so ideal that MGM later re-teamed the young couple who captivated the minds and hearts of moviegoers in *They Live by Night*. The 1950 release, *Side Street*, failed at the box office, and the two stars never appeared together again.

Regrettably, the career of the talented O'Donnell lasted only through the fifties. She was cast with Greer Garson in a major 1950 MGM release, *The Miniver Story*, while the 1954 British film, *Eight O'Clock Walk*, found her rendering a touching performance of the supportive young wife to cab driver Richard Attenborough, who is wrongly accused of molesting and murdering a young girl in London. O'Donnell is steadfastly convinced of his innocence, and ultimately the real killer is found. She married Robert Wyler, the brother of the famous director, William Wyler, who cast her in the 1950 suspense film based on the successful Sidney Kingsley play, *Detective Story*, starring Kirk Douglas and Eleanor Parker. Her final performance was under Wyler's direction as she played Charlton Heston's younger sister in the actor's Academy Award-winning biblical vehicle, *Ben Hur*, in 1959. She died in 1970 at the age of 45 after a long illness.

O'Donnell's open-eyed innocence coupled with Granger's equally innocent expression of naivete proved the perfect ingredients for Ray's use of the contrasting darkness of evening. It is O'Donnell who arrives to rescue him as he lies in the darkness in front of a billboard. As she nurses him back to health, they each concede how little they know of life. They decide that they are better off fighting the cruelties and injustices of a world in which they have been dealt a short hand in each other's arms. Perhaps some measure of protection can be derived through their compact of love and devotion.

It soon becomes apparent how much a victim of circumstances Granger is when he explains that he never received decent legal representation and was convicted routinely on a murder charge. Da Silva and Flippen are career criminals. The only reason Granger is with them is their belief that three make the ideal team in performing bank robberies. For that reason, when they engineer a daring prison break, Granger, the ill-fitting member of the trio, is taken with the hardened criminals.

Paying His Debt

As O'Donnell begins to fall in love with Granger and empathize with his plight, she advocates that he find a good criminal lawyer in Oklahoma City, fight his conviction, and clear his name. This alternative is promptly closed off as da Silva and Flippen, intent upon educating him in the ways of crime, insist that Granger pay back the debt he owes them for securing his freedom by helping them commit bank robberies. While they enter the banks and perform robberies, Granger sits in the getaway car, after which he spirits them to freedom.

At one point, using money from robberies, Granger and O'Donnell decide to flee the area. Granger impulsively suggests that they get off the bus in a small town and get married after observing the residence-office of a justice of the peace across the street from the bus station. One of the most touching scenes of the film is the simple wedding ceremony, with the wedding chapel proprietor, who is used to marrying people on an assembly line basis, using two of his relatives as witnesses. While Granger chooses the cheaper of the two services, his sincerity and commitment are contrasted with the disgust he feels over the blase and routinized manner in which the justice of the peace performs his duties.

The wedding chapel proprietor, played by Ian Wolfe, is an older man of experience who scents that Granger and O'Donnell are on the run. He talks about how he can provide Granger with a car and, once that has been accomplished, he can arrange for them to contact friends of his in Mexico, who will see that their needs are properly met. It is a scene that represents the best of film noir as well as Depression drama: two people in trouble and a man who admits that, at this stage of his life, he is not particular about how he makes money. Granger spurns the offer and decides to go his own way, a decision he will later regret.

Despite Granger's intention to leave the criminal world and embark upon a different life with his new wife, the tugging strings of restless fate continue to plague him. He selects a cabin in an out-of-the-way place, but it is not remote enough to thwart da Silva, who finds him. A later confrontation with da Silva and Flippen, in which Granger states his intention to commence a new life away from crime, results in the two hardened criminals roughing him up and informing him emphatically that this is not a partnership from which he can walk away.

The boyish naivete of Granger is sharply contrasted by the hardened criminals invested with just the right note of embittered anarchy by Howard da Silva and Jay C. Flippen. Da Silva as Chickamaw looms all the more threateningly with his gruesome expression and glass eye. Flippen as T-Dub is more paternalistic, but in a "don't ever cross me" way.

Da Silva, a former steelworker, was a veteran Broadway character performer who, after playing Dub in *Oklahoma*, clicked big with two major character roles. He provided a sympathetic ear as a bartender to alcohol-obsessed Ray Milland in *The Lost Weekend*. The following year, 1946, da Silva received kudos in the role of a Hollywood nightclub owner trying to outrun his past as a New Jersey killer opposite Alan Ladd and Veronica Lake in *The Blue Dahlia*. His career was waylaid at a crucial juncture following his success as Chickamaw by the Hollywood Red Scare. Fingered as a vocal leftist activist, da Silva was among the blacklisted, making a comeback in the sixties as a playwright and actor, starring on Broadway and in the film version of the highly acclaimed historical musical, *1776* (1972).

Flippen specialized in portraying lovable pop figures and raspy-voiced villains. Like da Silva, he started on Broadway in the twenties. Flippen appeared in *Broadway Varieties* and shared billing with such noted talents as Jack Benny and Texas Guinan. The versatile Flippen was also a radio announcer for the New York Yankees. He appeared in the touring version of the Olsen and Johnson comedy hit, *Hellzapoppin*, and, following years of film experience, played C.P.O. Nelson on the 1962 sitcom, *Ensign O'Toole*.

Eventually Flippen is killed in a bank holdup, and da Silva, crazed by alcohol, is gunned down attempting to break into a liquor store. Does this mean that Granger and O'Donnell are now free? Fate is seen in the form of an inevitably tightening noose in the case of the luckless young couple. Their fortunes run in the following manner: 1) Inability to escape from the strong bonds to da Silva and Flippen; 2) After his partners in crime are dead, Granger becomes even more of a marked man as he is earmarked as the lone survivor of the daring holdup team; 3) His marked status is enhanced further by the fact that Granger, a more glamorous figure from a media standpoint than grizzly crime veterans da Silva and Flippen, has been wrongly touted as the daring leader of the gang.

A LIFE ON THE RUN AND A COURTYARD SHOWDOWN

Bowie and Keechie are doomed to a life on the run, living by night, always looking over their shoulders. Keechie reveals to Bowie that she is pregnant, enhancing their plight. Their helplessness is underscored even more when, after stopping in one town and enjoying an evening at a nightclub, Granger steps into the rest room and is immediately confronted by the establishment's proprietor. While it is obvious that the proprietor is involved in organized crime, rather than empathizing with

Granger as a man on the run, he feels threatened. The message is that the club and its proprietor can continue to function as long as undue suspicion is not aroused. To maintain the status quo, it is necessary for people like Granger to stay out of town. The young man on the run is told to leave town in an hour.

All too aware that time is running out and capture increasingly imminent, Granger returns to the wily wedding chapel proprietor, who had been willing to provide help earlier. He provides a sympathetic ear but no more. The unspoken becomes obvious in his words—Granger has become too hot to assist. This is a more polite version of what he had heard from the nightclub owner. Granger watches despondently as the man breaks off their conversation to marry another couple that has arrived in his parlor.

Granger walks slowly and dejectedly from the wedding chapel back to the dismal courtyard setting of the motel run by Mattie, the sister of T-Dub. It is befitting of Bowie's fate that stern opposition awaits him even at the dingy motel where he stays. Mattie, played with appropriate rock-hard toughness by Helen Craig, has always resented Bowie because he was chosen by her brother and Chickamaw for escape while her husband remains behind bars at the same prison.

The young man has made the ultimate decision to part company with his pregnant wife until he can at least get settled. Granger asks Craig to give his wife, who is sound asleep, a note from him along with money to help her. Unknown to him, Craig, desperate for a new life with her husband before, as she put it, "it's too late," has told authorities that she can deliver Granger to them as long as her husband is immediately pardoned and set free. She insists on the bargain being put in writing before delivering. Despite her dislike of Granger, she acknowledges that this is a decision concerning which she will always feel conscience pangs, dictated by self-interest. When Granger explains his desire to leave immediately, a battle of wills ensues. Granger does not wish to disturb his pregnant wife while Craig, becoming increasingly edgier, recommends that, based on her understanding as a woman, he should go see her one more time. Granger finally agrees to do so.

The final scene in the courtyard, showing a contrast between the darkness of late evening and the lights burning brightly, demonstrates Nicholas Ray drama at its best. The slow walk of Granger, the sound of a passing train's whistle, and the feeling of claustrophobic confinement and impoverished small town desolation present the image of a young man doomed by the fates. The authorities promptly surface and Granger is gunned down. A shaken O'Donnell, now left to make her own way for herself and a new child, cradles Granger in her arms and declares her love one last time.

If any dialogue in the film could be said to best represent Ray's viewpoint, coexisting along with his sharply defined images of darkness and confinement, it would be the statement of Commissioner Hubbell, played by Charles Meredith. While agreeing to the terms of Helen Craig to free her husband in exchange for delivering Granger into the law's hands, he sadly exclaims that the system has badly failed a young man who could have turned out much better, and now there is nothing left to do but stop him before he persists in a life of crime made inevitable by the despairing circumstances described. The commissioner has described a vicious and highly painful social cycle. It is noteworthy to view the expression of distaste on the face of Craig's husband, whose freedom is being guaranteed, over the terms of the agreement.

The confining circumstances of the courtyard were used to great advantage in Ray's other noir masterpiece, *In a Lonely Place*. While never becoming an architect, student Ray learned his lessons well from teacher Frank Lloyd Wright about using space to optimum advantage.

This powerful drama sat gathering dust in RKO vaults until receiving a boost from across the Atlantic. England, the land of Shakespeare and Marlowe, appreciated dark, brooding drama. The film was released there under what would become its ultimate U.S. title, *They Live by Night*, enjoying an enthusiastic response. Ray left RKO amid a studio shakeup in which Schary left and Howard Hughes arrived. Despite the fact that *They Live by Night*, filmed in 1947, was Ray's first completed film, by the time it appeared in American theaters in 1949, two subsequently completed Ray films, *A Woman's Secret* and *Knock on Any Door*, had already been seen.

They Live by Night would be later filmed by director Robert Altman. Altman's 1974 release starring Keith Carradine reverted to the original title of the 1937 Edward Anderson novel, *Thieves Like Us*.

On the surface, *A Woman's Secret* (1949), would appear to have had the ingredients for success. Ray's second RKO venture was based on the novel *Mortgage on Life* by Vicki Baum, the celebrated author of *Grand Hotel*. Producing along with adapting Baum's novel to the screen was Herman J. Mankiewicz, scenarist of what many film enthusiasts, including the American Film Institute's panel of experts, regard as the greatest film ever made, *Citizen Kane*. A top cast was recruited, headed by Maureen O'Hara as a singer and singing coach who confesses to killing her protégée, played by Gloria Grahame. Melvyn Douglas, O'Hara's piano player friend, doubts her confession. His skepticism is shared by Jay C. Flippen, cast this time by Ray as a police officer. The film deals with the danger of seeking to live vicariously through someone else, but in a less-than-convincing way. Convoluted flashback sequences also dilute both message and entertainment value, as a project that looked promising on paper lost a whopping $760,000 for the studio. *TV Guide* called the film a "convoluted mess."

RAY JOINS BOGART

At that point, Ray left the RKO noir factory to join forces with another laureate of night, Humphrey Bogart, who was launching his own company, Santana Productions. Bogart's foray into independent production followed his well-publicized departure from Warner Bros. After expressing dissatisfaction for years with Warners studio head Jack Warner over script quality, a complaint shared by Bette

Davis and Errol Flynn, Bogart reportedly gained revenge on Warner, whom he personally detested, by proclaiming interest in signing a new studio contract, only to reportedly tell the studio boss where he could take his offer.

The Bogart name choice of Santana Productions provides a clue about the solitary nature of the man. It was named after his yacht, where he would spend large amounts of time while away from the sound stages.

The first Bogart-Ray film venture, *Knock on Any Door* (1949), was the second of the director's releases before *They Live by Night* was finally made available to American theaters. It failed to presage the classic to be realized in their second collaboration.

The subject matter was to Ray's liking, a study of a disaffected young man, someone with the deck of cards stacked against him in the manner of Farley Granger in *They Live by Night*. Bogart is cast as his defense attorney.

The project was initially the brainchild of producer Mark Hellinger, who interested a young Marlon Brando for the role of troubled young Nick Romano. When Hellinger died, Brando disassociated himself from the project, and John Derek was cast as Romano. The handsome Derek was better suited for the role of a collegian, as he played in the football drama *Saturday's Hero* two years later. The part called for a young rebel in the mold of Brando, a young Bogart, or James Dean. Another problem was that the film preached rather than revealed action, prompting Pauline Kael to conclude, "Bogart is so wearing that you wish he'd stop orating and get out his own rod again." The film's most memorable line was Derek's succinct summary of life: "Live fast. Die young. Have a good looking corpse."

The next time Santana and the Bogart-Ray team united, the result would be markedly better, a film noir classic that gathers additional devotees with every passing year. It was made all the more compelling by the teaming of Bogart with someone who, in the realm of disaffection and vulnerability, matched him stride for stride.

In a Lonely Place (1950)

The script assignment for the new Santana Productions film, *In a Lonely Place*, an adaptation of a novel by Dorothy Hughes, was placed in the hands of longtime Bogart friend Edmund North. The beginning of the screenplay he submitted reveals the film's subject matter and tone along with the intended star:

> EXT. ROMANOFF'S—NIGHT
> A big car pulls up to the curb and unloads a party of well-dressed people. The parking boy takes the car ... Into the scene, headed for Romanoff's, comes Dix Steele. He is a tightly knit man with an air of controlled, spring-steel tension about him. He wears a well cut, but well-worn tweed jacket and slacks. Mr. Steele—God help him—is a motion picture writer.

North had known Bogart since the thirties through good and bad times, as well as three marriages. He was definitely the actor in mind in his projection of Dixon Steele, a role which intrigued Bogart. When North sketched the female lead, struggling actress Laurel Gray, the intended choice was equally certain:

> She's about twenty-six, a striking-looking girl with high cheek bones and tawny hair. Sultry and smooth, she is sexy without being cheap-looking…. She appraises him coolly as he does her.

The best-laid plans of Santana, Bogart and North to cast Lauren Bacall in the role of Laurel were promptly dashed by Bogart's former studio boss and archenemy, Jack Warner. The mogul refused to loan Bacall out to Santana for *In a Lonely Place*. The refusal infuriated Bacall, and her relations with her studio became increasingly hostile. When Bacall was unavailable, the juicy role was given to the wife of director Nicholas Ray, Gloria Grahame. In retrospect, the casting change resulting from Warner's stubborn refusal gave the film an added dimension. Bacall had the presence of a woman of authority, a take-charge personality. Grahame, on the other hand, possessed the level of fragility coupled with a quiet rebelliousness that magnificently blended with the Dix Steele character that was so typical of the real-life Bogart.

BOGART AS A WRITER?

Humphrey Bogart has become so firmly etched on the world cinema firmament that it is well-nigh impossible to conceive of him as anything but an actor, but his friend and drinking companion, drama critic John McClain, felt that Bogart "would much rather have made a more modest living as a writer, where he could have aired his frustrations in print. He was a guy who didn't open up much, but the people he always sought out were writers … and they were the people for whom he had the most affection."

Bogart biographers A.M. Sperber and Eric Lax wrote, "Bogart admired and somewhat envied writers, who fight their battles on paper rather than before the camera." They and others found striking parallels between the Dix Steele character initially revealed on paper by Edmund North. Andrew Solt received final screenplay credit while North was credited with the story. Sperber and Lax noted; "The parallels between Steele and Bogart are striking—the aloofness, the lightning-quick intelligence evident even in hack work, the flashes of humor and warmth, and the unexpected anger." Critic Richard Schickel observed that Steele's "WASPish name implies the possibility of a solid background, as do his manners, dress and literate speech." Humphrey Bogart grew up in a lavish New York Upper East Side apartment building as the son of a doctor and prominent illustrator Maud Humphrey. His rebelliousness soon became evident when he was sent to a series of prominent schools, an anticipated orderly education process from which he openly mutinied. His rocky marriage to actress Mayo Methot, to whom he was married when his asso-

Humphrey Bogart plays a volatile screenwriter with a hair-trigger temper in Nicholas Ray's 1950 noir film about Hollywood, *In a Lonely Place*. Sitting next to Bogart as he speaks on the telephone is girlfriend Gloria Grahame, who would achieve a Best Supporting Actress Oscar two years later in Vincente Minnelli's *The Bad and the Beautiful*. Art Smith plays Bogart's loyal agent. Smith's role was said to be modeled after Bogart's actual agent, Sam Jaffe, while the restaurant where they sit was said to represent Chasens, a popular Beverly Hills eatery frequented by many film notables, including Bogart.

ciation with Bacall began, made good copy for gossip columnists due to the combative nature of the Bogarts. Bogart, along with fellow Warners contractees Bette Davis and Errol Flynn, constantly scrapped with Jack Warner for better scripts. He was very much a solitary man, given to brooding, as was Dix Steele, preferring to spend off-camera hours out of the limelight sailing in his boat, The Santana.

While Bogart had clicked in two film noir classics earlier in his career, *The Maltese Falcon* and *The Big Sleep*, those flashy detective roles more associated with the younger Bogart depicted a different type of character than Dix Steele from *In a Lonely Place*. The Dashiell Hammett character of Sam Spade, which Bogart rode into cinema immortality, was a man who could stay one jump ahead of his rivals in both physical toughness and mental agility. One of the memorable scenes from the film was the tantrum he launched in Sydney Greenstreet's hotel room, following which, after making a deliberately obstreperous exit, he broke into a broad grin. It was an obvious case of a crafty man using his wiles rather than losing his temper. In *The Big Sleep*, Bogart plays Raymond Chandler's wise-cracking detective, Philip Marlowe, as a world-wise one-line artist determined to show Bacall that her rich girl status holds no weight. He displays both physical zest, particularly with the ladies, along with a native intelligence and determination to solve the cases he has been given, no matter how tough they appear to be on the surface.

As Bogart matured, though, as earlier mentioned, he always resembled an experienced oracle; and as lines of care surfaced on his expressive face, he became perfect for an older, more reflective version of the detective characters he formerly played. He has seen more of life and is willing to grin less and frowningly contemplate more. A no-nonsense rebelliousness began to take hold, a more anarchistic bent, somebody snarling inwardly at the absurdities in the world while, if crossed or in a particularly bad mood, displays a willingness to lash out dangerously. This persona was evidenced in varying ways in *High Sierra* and The *Desperate Hours* (1955), where he played characters at cross purposes with the law. In films such as *The Barefoot Contessa* (1954), *Sabrina* (1954), and *The Harder They Fall* (1956), he came across as a world-weary oracle. His brilliant Academy Award-winning effort opposite Katharine Hepburn in *The African Queen* (1951) displayed an anarchistic rebel willing to drink his whisky, drop out of the rat race, and laugh at what he sees as an absurd world, that is until Hepburn fills him with some idealism. While other characters played by Bogart in films such as the aforementioned put his quick wit and no-nonsense rebelliousness on display, never were the deep internal frustrations of the actor and the man captured on celluloid in the manner depicted in the Dix Steele character from *In a Lonely Place*. Evidence exists that the self-doubt and sober, often bitter internalizing of Dix Steele was a reflection of what Bogart was experiencing at the time. Richard Brooks, whose novel, *The Brick Foxhole*, was later made into *Crossfire* (1947), was told by producer Mark Hellinger to go see Bogart about making a film of his book. A meeting was arranged at The Players, the Sunset Boulevard restaurant owned by director Preston Sturges. When Bogart expressed praise for Brooks's novel, the then-writer and future directing great sought to compliment the actor. A snort cut off the compliment with the wry observation, "Hell, I've been playing George Raft's brother-in-law for years!" Bogart then launched into a diatribe about his early days at Warner Bros., prompting Brooks to conclude that he was uncomfortable with praise, and that past rejections stood out more than current triumphs. Brooks, who would soon become a close friend of Bogart's, focused on the actor's underlying pessimism: "From his own experience he knew that the people with the power loved you as long as you could make a dollar for them. That was the bottom line. Were you successful? And were your movies successful? Without that, you were gone, they wiped you off the slate. You never existed."

Bogart not only brooded over what he viewed as an absence of permanence in his unique world as a superstar, he also internalized about the value of how he made his living. Lizabeth Scott, Bogart's co-star in *Dead Reckoning* (1947), watched Bogart pause periodically, look into the distance, and say to no one in particular, "Isn't this a stupid way to make a living?" Scott and Bogart's other on-set colleagues remained aware of his discontent. "Not that he didn't want to be an actor," Scott explained, "that he didn't enjoy the fame, the success, the material aspects; but that somewhere within himself, he thought he should be doing greater things."

There was no doubt among those who knew the brooding intellectual side of Bogart that the actor was an ideal choice to play Dix Steele. An on-screen bonus was that, whereas Bogart's pithy one-liners and brooding quietude in real life embodied self-control against an inner turmoil, playing the troubled scenarist enabled him to cut loose and externalize for audience purposes any troubling demons of his internal nature. As a man of intelligence and sensitivity, Bogart could empathize with the Steele character, understanding both his charmingly gregarious side as well as the dark, brooding beast also desiring expression.

A PERFECT COUNTERPART

If Bogart's true-life persona was geared to empathize with Dix Steele, the same would have to be said for Gloria Grahame embodying the characteristics to artistically relate to the troubled actress and love interest of Steele in *In a Lonely Place*, Laurel Gray. The vulnerability of Gloria Grahame extended to her troubled marriage to the film's director, which ended not long after *In a Lonely Place* was completed. It was a case of art imitating life in that Ray rewrote portions of the script to coincide with the turmoil he was then experiencing with his wife and leading lady.

Grahame became friends with RKO's film noir leading lady, Jane Greer, after they were flown to Las Vegas to pose for a series of publicity photos. "Gloria was a fine actress and I liked all of her films," Greer said. "If there is one word I would use to describe Gloria it is vulnerable. She was very child-like and did not like her appearance. I would tell her that she looked fine, but so many times she would come to see me and would be holding her hand over her mouth or over her face after she'd had an operation. Once, while she was making a film in Germany, Gloria had an operation on her mouth and the doctor hit a nerve by mistake. Her whole lip was paralyzed as a result."

Born Gloria Grahame Hallward, the future actress was a Los Angeles-born product of the industry who attended Hollywood High, the world's leading spawner of film talent. Grahame is included in legendary ranks consisting of Lana Turner, Mickey Rooney, Jackie Cooper, Nanette Fabray, Lionel Stander, David and Ricky Nelson, Tuesday Weld, Yvette Mimieux, Stephanie Powers and Linda Evans. When Gloria Hallward appeared in dramas at the famous Highland and Sunset high school, she appeared with a future star, but from the world of international diplomacy rather than films, Warren Christopher, who would ultimately become a U.S. Secretary of State after a stellar legal career in Los Angeles.

The camera's all-perusing eye detected a sensitivity and aloofness in Grahame that was a mask for vulnerability that existed off screen as well. She received a Best Supporting Actress Oscar nomination for her fascinating portrayal of Ginny the B girl in *Crossfire*. Some two years after *In a Lonely Place*, she secured an Academy Award in the supporting category for playing the mischievous southern belle wife of writer Dick Powell in *The Bad and the Beautiful*, who is lured on a weekend dalliance with playboy actor Gilbert Roland by film producer Kirk Douglas so Powell can finish his screenplay away from his distracting wife. A fatal plane crash kills both Grahame and Roland. Grahame's presence was so explosive that she garnered an Oscar for the shortest time on screen of any supporting category recipient until Dame Judi Dench won recently for her role as Queen Elizabeth in the 1999 release, *Shakespeare in Love*. Another attention-grabbing Grahame vehicle was in C.B. DeMille's *The Greatest Show on Earth* (1952), where she received lavish praise playing the elephant girl. Jane Greer remembered an incident from that period.

"I remember that after *The Greatest Show on Earth* was finished the circus was coming to town and Gloria got tickets for ourselves and our children," Greer recalled. "Gloria had done all of her own stunts and had become well acquainted with Elizabeth, the elephant she worked with in the film. When the show started and Elizabeth, the same elephant, paraded out she told me, 'Jane, she recognizes me. I've got to see her. I'll be back later.' When she walked over to where the elephant was Elizabeth caused a great commotion by beginning to walk up the steps toward where Gloria was standing, which could have caused great damage. Finally Gloria walked down to the ground area and was reunited with Elizabeth."

Laurel Gray is wary in her approach to life. Even though immediately attracted to Steele, as someone who has struggled as an actress as well as in life generally, Laurel exercises a shrewd wariness. Her diffidence concerning Steele is heightened by her awareness of his volcanic mood swings from thoughtful and intelligent sensitivity to dangerous temper tantrums in which rage dominates and all restraint vanishes.

A GREAT HOLLYWOOD FILM

In addition to being one of the memorable noir classics, *In a Lonely Place* is one of the rare great films about the movie industry, along with another significant Grahame vehicle, the aforementioned 1952 classic, *The Bad and the Beautiful*. In the finished shooting script of Andrew Solt, the restaurant that Dix Steele frequents is no longer Romanoff's. It resembles instead Chasen's, which was a Bogart favorite. Restauranteur Mike Romanoff appears in the film, however, playing himself.

The Steele residence is an apartment overlooking a courtyard, from which Laurel Gray can look out the window and observe him. It was said to be the actual residence of Ray earlier in his career. Its courtyard ambience resembles the Garden of Allah on Sunset Boulevard, which was used in *D.O.A.*, the history of which was discussed earlier. Bogart's faithful agent, played by Art Smith, resembles the star's actual longtime representative, Sam Jaffe.

The original Edmund North screenplay initially brought out Dix Steele's penchant for violence shortly after he arrives at the Chasen's-like restaurant he frequents. The completed Solt script reveals his violent side in the movie's first scene. When Steele, en route to the restaurant, stops at a signal, an actress calls out a greeting to him. When he admits he does not remember her, she tells him she appeared in a film he had written. Her husband, becoming immediately jealous, testily orders the writer to "stop bothering my wife." The quick-witted Steele, brooking no nonsense, tells the attractive actress that it was too bad she had "married a pig." When the stockily built husband asks Steele how he would like to pull over at the curb, the explosive writer exclaims, "What about here?," promptly jumping out of his car in the middle of the street and raising his clenched fists. The light then changes and the man drives away.

The recurring violent theme surfaces anew when Bogart arrives at the restaurant. His agent is elated to tell him that he has a job for him, adapting a blockbuster soap opera novel to the screen. Bogart's brutal outspokenness is evidenced when he tells the director of the project that he has spent his entire career doing the same film. "You're a popcorn salesman," Bogart tartly declares.

An explosion promptly occurs when a young producer played by Lewis Howard, said to resemble Carl Laemmle Jr., arrives heady with delight after attending a studio preview of his latest film. When the writer's old actor friend, who has appeared in many films produced by the obnoxious producer's father, is insulted and spurned after seeking to shake his hand, Bogart goes ballistic and shoves him around, finally being restrained.

The inebriated actor, who delights in reciting Shakespeare, resembles Broadway legend John Barrymore. Playing him is Robert Warwick, a Broadway veteran who, in the early struggling stages of Bogart's career, found him work and provided him with encouragement, which Bogart never forgot. Warwick appeared with Bogart in the younger actor's Broadway debut in *Drifting* in 1922.

When he is cautioned by tolerant establishment host Romanoff to settle disagreements outside rather than within the restaurant, the comment is reminiscent of one said to have been uttered by the restaurateur to Errol Flynn. The warning occurred after the fiery actor had been involved in a confrontation with noted Hollywood columnist and commentator Jimmy Fidler and his wife.

Despite the enthusiasm of his agent for landing a job for Bogart, who has been experiencing hard times, the writer's stubborn reluctance is revealed as he loathes the idea of reading what he considers to be a potboiler novel unworthy of his time. He finally decides to recruit hatcheck girl Martha Stewart, who has read the novel and adores it, to accompany him to his apartment and provide him with the skeletal plot outline, saving him the bother of an unpleasant task. She breaks a date with her boyfriend to do so.

When they arrive back at his apartment and Bogart has put on his robe and mixed himself a drink, Stewart becomes so loudly animated in describing the story that the writer calms her down, explaining that the hour is late and neighbors are trying to sleep. At one point, a celebrity-struck Stewart comments that she used to believe that actors made up their own dialogue. "When they get to be big stars they usually do," Bogart responds.

The Bogart comment about dialogue from scriptwriters is reminiscent of another great film which debuted in 1950 and dealt in a hard-hitting way with the film industry, Billy Wilder's bombshell, *Sunset Boulevard*, starring Gloria Swanson, William Holden and Nancy Olson. At one point, Holden, like Bogart cast as a screenwriter, exclaims morosely, "Most people think that the actors make up the words as they go along."

The noir emphasis of evening is evident in Bogart's comments and manner. He lets it be known that he is an evening person and does not like to see people before noon, but in the case of Stewart, having heard her verbal summary of the book he intends to adapt to the screen, he laments that he is very tired and has to get up early the next day. The writer begs off driving the young woman home, providing her with cab fare as well as something extra for her time and effort in helping him. He tells Stewart that there is a cabstand one block away. Stewart has told him earlier that she lives with her aunt in Inglewood and that her regular transportation is the Beverly Hills bus. Bogart notes that there is a taxicab stand just around the corner on Sunset Boulevard, establishing the location of the apartment building.

The association between beautiful young hatcheck girl Stewart and Bogart will provide beneficial clues to analyzing the tragic event which will occur shortly, dramatically complicating the writer's life. The celebrity-conscious Stewart, who works at a restaurant frequented by the Hollywood famous, is ecstatic that an important writer like Bogart is interested in her opinion. While she is plainly impressed by him, she demonstrates an absence of enthusiasm about her fiancé, from whom she broke off a date to assist Bogart. She explains that he lives with his folks and is "substantial." The word *substantial* is a case of damning with the faintest praise. It is clearly meant to reflect that he is boring.

MAN IN THE MIDDLE

Bogart is awakened early in the morning by a soldier formerly under his command in WWII who now works as a Beverly Hills police detective. Frank Lovejoy as Detective Brub Nicolai informs Bogart that Martha Stewart's mangled body was found off Benedict Canyon. He takes Bogart in for questioning, as he was the last person known to have seen the dead woman alive. Lovejoy, while believing that his old commanding officer did not kill the young woman, is soon caught in the middle. His boss, Captain Lochner, played by Carl Benton Reid, gives Bogart a solid initial grilling, then has increasing suspicions after perusing the volatile writer's police record. Bogart had broken a film producer's jaw, had been arrested after a bar-room brawl, and was involved in a disturbing the peace charge, after which his girl-friend, who had a broken nose, refused to press charges and asserted that her injury resulted from an accident.

Bogart's initial police interrogation results in a dramatic first formal meeting with new neighbor Grahame. While a highly interested Bogart listens, she reveals that she had actually seen the hatcheck girl leave his apartment alone, providing the writer with an alibi. At one point, she says concerning Bogart, "I like his face."

While Lovejoy's boss remains unconvinced of Bogart's innocence, pointing to his record of violence and confrontational manner when being interrogated, his wife develops suspicions of her own about the screenwriter. After dinner at the Nicolai home, the eager detective invites Bogart to present his own slant on Stewart's mur-der. He demonstrates with an all-too-apparent relish, especially from the stand-point of Lovejoy's wife, Jeff Donnell, how the homicide might have occurred.

Bogart's shrewd analytical instincts impress Lovejoy. In Bogart's view, the mur-der could have been committed by "an ex-GI who can kill without using his hands." He has Lovejoy and Donnell act out a would-be killing under his instructions. Love-joy grips his wife's throat with his forearm. Bogart with cold lucidity then explains the motivation behind the killing, concluding that the killer felt a resentment over not being considered important enough by a young woman working in a famous restaurant where she met many of the greats of the film industry, recalling the words Martha Stewart expressed in his apartment.

WOMANLY INTUITION

After Bogart leaves, a conflict is revealed in the Nicolai home. The detective's professional side prompts feelings of satisfaction and gratitude from Lovejoy for the writer's shrewdly analytical insights. Donnell sees a coldness she does not like, the manner in which Bogart was able to describe such a brutal strangling unfeelingly, using her as a guinea pig to make his point. Lovejoy protests that Bogart has sup-plied him with insights on the case that he had never thought of, asking her to let go of her abnormal psychology college training. Donnell concedes genius on Bog-art's part, but is happy that she married an average guy like Lovejoy.

The apprehension displayed by Donnell provides a building block in under-standing the responses of Gloria Grahame as her relationship with Bogart evolves. Womanly intuition is frequently used as a safeguard. The radar warning significantly rises in cases involving potential violence. A shrewd woman who has studied psy-chology in college, Donnell is frightened by the enthusiasm displayed by Bogart in describing a murder. She sees in the writer what so many others have indicated, that here is an intelligent and interesting man capable of sensitivity, but who also is a ticking time bomb with a penchant for periodic eruptions.

A ROMANCE BLOSSOMS

Bogart is immediately drawn to his new neighbor. He hopes that their dramatic meeting at the police station will lead to much more. Grahame is a more cautious sort, and after he reminds her about a comment at the police station in which she stated that she liked his face, she coolly responds, "I said I liked it. I didn't say I wanted to kiss it."

Grahame has good reason to be diffident about a romantic liaison with Bogart. She becomes aware of his violent past. Her tough-minded friend and masseuse Martha, played by Ruth Gillette, reveals a strong liking for the sultry actress, telling her about the actress before her who had her nose broken. She criticizes Grahame for foolishly turning aside her last pursuer, a successful real estate operator with a lovely home and a freshly constructed swimming pool. Her comments trouble Grahame enough that she asks Martha to leave.

The romance instills both Bogart and Grahame with a zest for living, which the two world-weary rebels had not previously known. The writer reacquires his old discipline, working nonstop and swiftly penning words in longhand all through the night on his new assignment, while Grahame serves as his dutiful typist.

A RAPID TRANSITION

After Bogart and Grahame begin dating, he takes her with him to a beach party given by Lovejoy and Donnell. Things go well until Donnell lets it slip that Grahame has met with police for a second time, something she has not revealed to Bogart. While Grahame's reason was not to unduly worry him, the chips on his shoulders, which loom as ponderous blocks of granite, precipitate a quick and decisive response. He cuts the party short, angrily lamenting that he is being victimized by those around him.

Bogart darts to his car with Grahame in pursuit. She gets in and he manifests his frustration by driving at dangerous breakneck speed amid the twists and turns of a canyon in darkness. Bogart's car meets another vehicle at a fork in the road driven by a college-age man. After Bogart sideswipes the young man's car, he gets out and moves angrily toward Bogart, who remains seated in the front seat of his vehicle. The young man shouts that his car had just been recently painted, calling Bogart "a blind, knuckle-headed squirrel."

The ugly side of the writer's nature surfaces. An enraged Bogart charges from his car and begins pummeling the young man until he knocks him down. As he lies on the ground unconscious, a still-furious Bogart picks up a large rock, holding it aloft in apparent preparation to strike his victim. Grahame shrieks, "You'll kill him!" The warning snaps Bogart back to his senses.

When they drive away, the victim still lying on the ground and eventually awakening, Grahame emphasizes the importance of controlling himself. Bogart argues that after being called the names that the young man shouted, his victim deserved his fate. He explains that a matter of principle is involved, and that he has had "a hundred fights" for similar reasons. Grahame replies that calling someone "a blind, knuckle-headed squirrel" hardly rates with the most scurrilous insults.

The rapid-fire mood swing of the volatile Dix Steele is then revealed when the writer, now driving at a moderate speed, waxes romantic. His sensitive side emerges as he tells Grahame about some lines he seeks to work into his screenplay, which obviously parallel his feelings for her: "I was born when you kissed me. I died when you left me. I lived a few weeks while you loved me."

The next day, when an article about the beating appears in the local paper, Bogart, after reading the name and address of the victim, sends him a check and provides the postal clerk with the name "Mr. Squirrel," a reference to what he had been called after the collision. Once more, a shift has occurred. The furious writer, convinced he has been tragically wronged, on the verge of killing his unconscious victim, undergoes an about-face and feels for the young man he ferociously assaulted.

A Proposal and Misgivings

While Steele, spurred on by his new-found love, reaches a level of creative activity he has not scaled in years, with Laurel ably assisting him as a one-woman cheering section and by typing the pages he provides, the breakneck pace of the relationship along with concerns about the volatile scenarist's violent side cause misgivings at a pivotal moment in their relationship. A headily romantic Dix has proposed to Laurel, and she has accepted. Steele's agent is ecstatic, gleefully volunteering himself for duties watching the Steele children, telling her that he could not remember seeing his client and friend on such an emotional high. When Laurel expresses misgivings about Dix's dark side, the candid and folksy agent is brutally frank. He explains that he has represented Dixon Steele for twenty years. While it has been an exciting experience representing such a colorful, intelligent, and fascinating personality, agent Mel Lippman concedes that, with Dix Steele, one has to accept the bitter with the sweet. Pulling no punches, he holds out no hope for the violent trigger mechanism within Steele to go away. In his terminology, with Dix Steele, you have to "accept the total package." This underscores her doubts and fears concerning Steele and a longstanding relationship with him.

Eventually Grahame and Smith reach an understanding. The actress is fearful about a potential marriage to a brilliant but complexly violent man who is eager to whisk her off to Las Vegas, then go house hunting. Successful agents need to be good listeners, and here the avuncular Smith excels. She expresses a need to leave for New York and get away from the volatile writer, whom she justifiably fears, while Smith agrees to keep her decision a secret.

Like Jeff Donnell, Art Smith has more than a little of the psychologist in him. Could this not be linked to his agent's career? Smith, who knows Bogart better than anyone, explains that his friend and client has a deeply rooted pride. If Grahame promptly breaks off the engagement, he will feel defeated and erupt in a fury. He poses a theory. If Bogart had a major triumph, such as acceptance from the producer of the film on which he has labored so mightily on the script, then in Smith's view, this would enable him to endure what would otherwise be a catastrophic shock from Grahame's rejection of marriage.

Grahame warms up to the opportunity to provide Bogart with a triumph. She tells him that the script is completed and that she is more than happy to give it to him. She does and Smith gleefully promises to deliver it into the producer's hands. Meanwhile she checks on plane reservations that evening for New York.

RATTLED BY MISGIVINGS

When the writer takes Grahame to his old Chasen's-like haunt, Bogart's trigger mechanism enters the danger zone. Prodigious chips overload his shoulders. His instincts tell him something is not right, but he cannot ascertain just what it is. A frightened Bogart is painfully aware of Grahame's recent rejection of a marriage proposal from a successful realtor. He is mortally afraid that she will walk out on him.

When agent Smith expresses concern that Bogart has altered his screenplay too far from the potboiler he is expected to adapt to the screen, the writer throws a temper tantrum and roughs up his agent, accusing him of holding back on him, certain that the producer hates his script. Bogart's fear is disproved when the ebullient director surfaces and delightedly tells the writer how much the producer likes his screenplay. Bogart asks Smith if he should get a new agent. Lippman shrugs it off, remarking, "Business isn't so good."

Bogart also erupts about his script being submitted without his approval. His paranoia heightens, aware that something is wrong in his relationship with Grahame. When her longtime friend Martha attempts to reach her, a suspicious Bogart grabs the phone. His suspicions increase through his recognition that Martha holds only negative feelings toward him.

A VINDICATION MADE HOLLOW

The tempo of the film builds to a fever emotional pitch with one of the most unique endings in the annals of noir. Bogart, who remained a police suspect for a brutal murder during almost the entire picture, is vindicated after the hatcheck girl's boyfriend attempts to take his own life, then confesses with overwrought guilt from his emergency room hospital bed. Bogart's analysis revealed to Lovejoy proves accurate. The boyfriend was apparently driven homicidal over Martha's Stewart scant regard for him, which she expressed in front of Bogart. He looked smaller and more boring to her due to her contact with exciting movie people such as Bogart.

Humphrey Bogart and Gloria Grahame stand in the courtyard of the Beverly Hills apartment complex where they are neighbors and ultimately become lovers in *In a Lonely Place*.
When Warners boss Jack L. Warner refused to provide permission for Lauren Bacall to
star with her husband in the film, which was produced by Bogart's company, Santana Productions, director Nicholas Ray obtained the services of his wife, Gloria Grahame, to
appear opposite Bogart. The casting worked superbly and the duo sizzled as a love team.

As for his relationship with Grahame, after the stormy restaurant meeting, an
increasingly suspicious Bogart turns up the pressure on her to marry him immediately. The telephone rings and he picks it up, suspicious about the nature of the call.
A ticket agent tells Bogart that there is a ticket available for Grahame on a plane
to New York that evening. Once more the angry beast of the writer's nature surfaces as he grabs Grahame by the throat and begins choking her. He lets go, not
following through to the fatal point, but a fatality he immediately becomes in his
relationship with Grahame. His sad look of defeat reveals acceptance of his fate. As
he is preparing to leave her apartment the telephone rings, and he is told that he
has been cleared of any suspicion of murder with the confession of Martha Stewart's boyfriend. Captain Lochner then apologizes to Grahame for putting her through
such a terrible ordeal. She replies in a sad tone that such a disclosure would have

meant everything yesterday, but means nothing now. A crestfallen Bogart hears her lachrymose words as he departs. The film ends with Grahame, after hanging up the phone, walking toward the doorway and watching a thoroughly crushed Bogart walking slowly in the courtyard toward his apartment.

Tears stream down Grahame's face as she watches Bogart departing for good from her life. She repeats a fitting line from his screenplay, then bids him a sad farewell: "I lived a few weeks while you loved me. Goodbye, Dix." The tears in Grahame's eyes and pathos in her voice could well have stemmed from the "art imitating life" element of the story's conclusion, the blunt realization that her marriage to the film's director was reaching a sad and rapid conclusion.

In order for a film, stage play, or work of literature to attain the status of a classic, it must vitally tap into life's essential verities. The ring of truth must dominate, and such is the case with *In a Lonely Place*. The film contains the following major dramatic elements:

1) A Ticking Time Bomb Figure—A basic truth was revealed by Art Smith as Mel Lippman, the person who knew Bogart the longest in the film, having been his agent for twenty years. Seeking to hide nothing, he tells Grahame that Bogart, while a man of excitement, remains violent, and that one has to accept the bad to experience the good. Bogart looms as a perpetual ticking time bomb ready to explode any second. Nicholas Ray doubtlessly saw and helped shape the film as a fifties, postwar allegory, in that the period in which the film was made and released to theaters was one of perilous uncertainty in which both the United States and the Soviet Union possessed and were testing atomic bombs en route to the next breakthrough of the hydrogen bomb. Ours was a ticking time bomb world of uncertainty, much like the unforgettable Dixon Steele character blossomed to perfection by the moody Bogart.

2) Hollywood's Uncertainties—The film reveals the pervasive uncertainties of the film industry and the fears of the creative people comprising it in a brutally realistic fashion. Bogart, who in real life registered constant fears about a downfall should he experience a flop or two at the box office, remains sensitively attuned to the status of Robert Warrick as the once-successful actor who is now no more than an object of ridicule to the spoiled producer son of the man who had earlier made a fortune for his father. When Bogart reveals this early in the film and the spoiled young producer continues to ridicule Bogart's friend, who had in real life provided him with aid and encouragement during his struggling days as a young actor, the writer erupts and roughs up a man who represents the industry mind-set Dixon Steele loathes, the "What have you done for me today?" mentality. The image of Warrick is a haunting figure, a ghost from the past, a Tinsel Town Jacob Marley reminding Bogart of what his own future might hold.

3) Similarities Attracting and Repelling—As shrewd and independent loners with rebellious streaks, Bogart and Grahame are able to relate to each other at the outset because they understand one another while confounding others they encounter. The acute sensitivity and strong emotions in Bogart that immediately

draw Grahame emotionally toward him are part of a double-edged sword, however, as the strong positive emotional reactions are part of a syndrome wherein he feels every bit as strongly in a negative direction, with violence the result. As Mel Lippman has correctly analyzed, with Dix Steele, one has to accept the entire package or not deal with him at all. The very standoffishness and sensitivity that help make Grahame initially fascinating to Bogart prompt her to reevaluate her relationship with him. The cautious individualist pulls back from fully committing herself to a man split dangerously down the middle.

Despite high critical notices for *In a Lonely Place*, Bogart, an actor seeking to rise above run-of-the-mill films, who had seen his own Santana Productions craft a winner, was unhappy with the picture. Bogart biographers Sperber and Lax offered a reason: "Perhaps the characterization was too close to the part of himself that he protected with barbs and wisecracks."

STAR SIMILARITIES

While the roles of the two lead performers in *In a Lonely Place* revealed similarities between their off-screen lives and dramatic personas, Humphrey Bogart and Gloria Grahame appeared to possess significant real-life similarities. While both were highly suspicious of praise and approached their careers in the manner of ship captains confronting a lull with trepidations of an oncoming storm, as mentioned earlier, each would receive an Oscar not long after working together in *In a Lonely Place*. The following year, Bogart's work opposite Katharine Hepburn resulted in a Best Actor statuette for *The African Queen*. Grahame would receive a Best Supporting Actress Oscar for the 1952 release which, like *In a Lonely Place*, was a film about Hollywood, *The Bad and the Beautiful*.

Both Bogart and Grahame also had complicated and well-publicized love lives. Bogart had three marriages, the last of which to Lauren Bacall was successful, but his second to stormy, heavy-drinking actress Mayo Methot produced a turbulent triangle in which, after falling in love with Bacall, he feared that violence would result when his temperamental second wife was intransigent about giving him his freedom. Nicholas Ray was Gloria Grahame's second husband, preceded by an earlier marriage to actor Stanley Clements from 1945 to 1948. She married Ray in 1948, a union dissolved in 1952. Her third marriage was to writer-director Cy Howard and spanned a period from 1954 to 1957. In 1961 the actress married Tony Ray, her earlier husband Nick's son by an earlier marriage.

Bogart and Ray both died of cancer in their fifties. Chain smoker Bogart died a slow and painful death in 1957, becoming increasingly weaker until his hands shook as he sipped grape juice through a flexible straw. "Goodbye, kid," he told the love of his life, Bacall, before she went out to run an errand. "Hurry back" were his final words to her as he slipped into a coma and never recovered. Toward the end of her life, Gloria Grahame moved east to New York. She received an opportunity to act in London in a play, *The Legend of Lilly Lamont*. Following the drama and an intermission, clips would be shown of some of her selected films, upon which she would comment, a practice employed later by Cary Grant and Gregory Peck.

After Gloria Grahame's 1981 death in New York, an actor who appeared in the London play with her wrote a book about their romantic relationship. In the early nineties, a film based on the book was considered. Kim Novak and Ellen Barkin were discussed as possibilities for the Grahame role.

THE STRANGER IN TOWN

When the title character in Ray's 1954 unconventional western, *Johnny Guitar*, played by Sterling Hayden, voiced the epigram, "I'm a stranger here myself," it was thought by many to embody Ray. His characters loomed from the shadows, frequently alone, disaffected, trying to make sense out of a world riddled with anarchy and heartbreak. They appear to follow the credo voiced by Robert Mitchum to Jane Greer in Jacques Tourneur's *Out of the Past*, "If I've gotta die I'm gonna die last."

Before leaving RKO, Ray crafted two memorable films dealing with tough, often disillusioned loners. It was said that the director, a man with notably left-of-center political views, had been aided during the dangerous Hollywood Ten period by his friendship with RKO boss Howard Hughes. The 1951 release, *On Dangerous Ground*, depicted Robert Ryan as a disillusioned big city cop affected by the unbending pattern of violence surrounding him. He receives badly needed comfort from good listener Ida Lupino, who plays a blind woman living in the country, away from the violent world which has hardened Ryan. Bernard Herrmann's musical score was the Oscar-winning composer's personal favorite. In 1952, RKO released *The Lusty Men*, in which Robert Mitchum starred opposite Susan Hayward and Arthur Kennedy as a washed-up rodeo king forced to the sideline after being gored by a Brahma bull. The film concludes on a note as uniquely ironic as the finale of *In a Lonely Place*. After accepting the challenge of protégé Arthur Kennedy, who has grown cocky and calls him a coward and a has-been, besting him in rodeo competition, Mitchum catches his foot in a stirrup. He is trapped beneath the hoofs of a bronco and trampled to death. His parting words as he is carried out of the arena and dies in the arms of Hayward and Kennedy are to caution against any mourning, revealing that he "made a thousand bartenders rich."

During the height of the McCarthy era, Ray directed *Johnny Guitar*, which symbolically attacked the witch hunt concept in the same manner of Arthur Miller's gripping play produced during the same period, *The Crucible*, which focused on seventeenth-century America and the Salem witch trials. *Johnny Guitar* was a highly unconventional western, pitting two strong-willed women against each other, saloon owner Joan Crawford and embittered landowner Mercedes McCambridge. Despite the fact that it was a color film, black and white master Ray found a way to make his point and incorporate a flavor of his moody earlier style by depicting Crawford and her contingent, representing the forces of good, in white, while McCambridge and company were attired in black.

Not only did *Johnny Guitar* become a cult favorite in America with its stamp of daring originality, but also that same ingenuity prompted Nicholas Ray to be recognized in France, the land of Sartre and Camus. England had provided a major boost to Ray early in his career with the enthusiastic success accorded *They Live by Night*, prompting RKO to put the film in general U.S. release. Now France's prestigious film journal *Cahiers du Cinema* trumpeted the director as a genuine author and a great visionary of film.

CASTING THE IDEAL REBEL

The reason given, along with the preachiness of the script, as to why *Knock on Any Door* failed to ignite the kind of sparks that Ray at his best generated dealt with the fact that young rebel type Marlon Brando was unavailable and handsome John Derek failed to project the level of rebellion needed to put his role of Nick Romano across. After leaving RKO, the director received the opportunity he was looking for when he did another film about disaffected youth, *Rebel Without a Cause*, which soared at the box office, was identified with closely by waves of youngsters, and received high critical praise. Before he got his way and cast the ideal star, however, Nick Ray had to argue with the top brass of Warner Bros. While the director proposed casting James Dean and Natalie Wood in the lead roles, Warners countered with what it deemed a safer and more commercial pairing of Tab Hunter and Jayne Mansfield. Ray proposed pulling out of the film, which the studio believed had strong merit, unless his casting choices were accepted. They were, and the rest is film history.

The brooding defiance and restless rebelliousness of James Dean registered strongly on audience members of all ages. The nation's youth felt a particular empathy, as the pressures of Cold War angst among those growing up were defiantly expressed by a new poster boy who had died in a tragic automobile accident just ten days before *Rebel's* release. Natalie Wood, saluted in print as "America's most beautiful teenager," used the vehicle to launch a brilliant career as a leading lady. Her career was cut short by her tragic drowning death in 1982. While the film was a huge success, much would later be written about a possible curse attached to it, made all the more ironic by its often disquieting subject matter. Sal Mineo, who, along with Wood was nominated for an Oscar in the Best Supporting Actor category, was stabbed to death by a petty robber while arriving at his Sunset Strip apartment at 8563 Holloway Drive following a rehearsal of the play *P.S. Your Cat Is Dead*, in which he was slated to star. Nick Adams, a feature player in *Rebel*, was a suicide victim. Adams, ironically, had sprung to fame in the early sixties by starring in the television western series, *The Rebel*.

Perfectionist Ray busily culled Los Angeles Police files researching cases involving wayward teens in preparation for *Rebel Without a Cause*. He shot the Cinema-Scope movie in black and white for a few weeks during pre-production to get the mood and feel for the muted color patterns he would later use in the final color print. *Rebel* combined Ray's strong concern for disaffected youth with his flair for the poetry of night, evidenced through his photographic mood pieces. He was truly the Edward Hopper of the cinema world. The moody aura of *Nighthawks* surrounded so much of his most compelling cinema. The car race which resulted in Corey Allen's death when he was unable to extricate himself from his speeding vehicle occurred in the evening's bewitching period. Rebel group Dean, Wood and Mineo escape from troubled family existences by meeting in a deserted mansion. Mineo, after shooting a policeman investigating a possible break-in at the deserted mansion, takes refuge in Griffith Park Planetarium. These events are made all the more powerful because they occur in the darkness of evening amid the moody cinema poetry of Nicholas Ray.

Ray was named Best Director for 1955 by the New York Film Critics for *Rebel Without a Cause*. In 1956, having tackled tense vulnerabilities of disaffected youth in Cold War America with *Rebel*, he set his sights on the adult world with *Bigger Than Life*. Rather than make his case by using a brooding rebellious type such as Bogart as Dix Steele in *In a Lonely Place*, Ray ingeniously presented a sophisticated and successful James Mason as a man cracking up from the effects of cortisone and the imploding pressures of current society.

Ray's career ended with two international high-budget features for producer Samuel Bronston, *King of Kings* (1961) and *55 Days at Peking* (1963). He spent most of the remainder of the decade in Europe, suffering from a myriad of illnesses. When he returned to America in 1969, the spokesman for disaffected youth found himself a cult hero and popular figure on the college lecture circuit. It was only natural for Ray, director of *They Live by Night*, *Knock on Any Door* and *Rebel Without a Cause*, to take a college teaching position, where he could interact with bright young minds. He began teaching film at the State University of New York at Binghamton and, in collaboration with students, made a film, *You Can't Go Home Again* (1973). Increasingly poor health limited him to appearances in cameos of films by other directors. Finally, battling cancer, he collaborated with Wim Wenders in a moving film, *Lightning Over Water*, which was released in 1980. Ray did not live to see the film, having succumbed to the ravages of the same disease that earlier took the life of his *In a Lonely Place* male star Bogart and one year later would claim the female star of that same film, his onetime wife Grahame. The director died in New York City on June 16, 1979.

According to his friend and colleague Elia Kazan, who had given Ray his initial New York stage break and Hollywood film job, this complex one-time student of Frank Lloyd Wright "had never been just one man, but had been many different men at different times, matching where he was and whom he was with and what the scene needed. His way of being was characteristic of a certain kind of actor and director—to be a tough guy when you're with tough guys, a poet when you're with poets, a bar fighter when you're with bar fighters, a lover who believes a life well lost for love when you're with a woman. It was an aspect of the Stanislavsky system, in which Nick, long ago, had been trained."

Ray's emphasis of camera and mood was reflected in a remark attributed to him, "If it were all in the script, why make the film?" In exploring the man and his vividly enriching cinema, David Thomson revealed, "He remains a test case of the way such gathered moments exceed the hackneyed idioms of commercial cinema; with the piercing enactment of human solitariness through gesture, color and space, and because—with any great director—one comes away from his work moved by the spectacle of nature that he has revealed."

While he presented a dark world in which characters grappled against a merciless fate and explored the great unknown, when it came to presenting this view, Nicholas Ray came, saw, and conquered. He was and will remain a richly evocative poet of night.

FIVE

McCarthyism and
Cold War Paranoia

It was the first picture after the McCarthy business. Maybe that's what made me so venomous.
The Blue Gardenia (1953)

Fritz Lang was a director noted for films exploring the nuances of moral ambiguity. Film noir would seem to be a perfect vehicle of expression for the Austrian-born director who made his mark in Germany before migrating to America. *The Blue Gardenia* embodies film noir and much more, a foray into the paranoiac world of the early fifties when people in the United States were experiencing McCarthyism and its accompanying fears of nuclear warfare with developing superpower and U.S. archenemy Russia.

"It was the first picture after the McCarthy business," Lang would remark later concerning *The Blue Gardenia*. "Maybe that's what made me so venomous." The scourge of McCarthy and the committee which bore his name sent waves of fear reverberating through the film community. The McCarthy Committee, whose hearings drew large television audiences, operating within the U.S. Senate, was one of the twin pillars of exposure existing during the period, the other being the House Un-American Activities Committee (HUAC). The HUAC held highly publicized and sometimes televised hearings in Washington and Los Angeles, interviewing large numbers of witnesses, some of whom were deemed friendly and came from the rightward spectrum of the industry, with others noted as unfriendly, meaning a refusal to cooperate. The most notable of those examples comprised the Hollywood Ten, who did time in federal prison for refusing to cooperate. These individuals steadfastly refused to name names and implicate others. The message they sent to the investigators of HUAC was clear: If you have any evidence I violated a law then prosecute me, otherwise leave me alone. My ideas belong to myself and are nobody else's business.

Lang's European background gave him reason to be dubious about any committee which seeks to pry into the realm of personal beliefs. Born in Vienna in 1890, Lang's mother came from a Jewish background but converted to Catholicism, which her son also embraced. Lang studied architecture as a young man, as had another laureate of the world of darkness, Nicholas Ray. As noted in Chapter 4, an architectural background gave a director a working familiarity with spatial considerations. This consciousness could also extend to the realm of psychological confinement, a perfect element for exploration in film noir. Lang longed for a creative life and threw himself headlong into painting, at which point he was conscripted for WWI.

A bout with tragedy ultimately resulted in a substantial career break for Lang. After losing an eye in the conflict, he was given a part in a drama put on at the camp where he was then assigned. He was discovered by a talent scout for a Berlin studio, who ultimately provided him with the opportunity to begin his directing career.

Lang surged to the top ranks of directing in Berlin. While he directed many films, the two which stood out in America and internationally were *Metropolis* (1927) and *M* (1931). The films brought out different creative facets of Lang. *Metropolis*, made following the director's first visit to New York, presented Lang's vision of Manhattan in 2000. While presenting a bleak portrait of a future world where the citizenry is divided between the rich and slothful and their slaves, who provide all the manual work, what impressed audiences in this engrossing silent was the brilliant depiction of skyscrapers and trains in an imaginative future world. The grasp of technology and space, in which tall skyscrapers were captivatingly presented, represented the architectural side of Lang's creative nature. *M*, an early talkie which propelled its young leading man Peter Lorre to international stardom, depicted him as a serial killer operating within a terrified Berlin. "It was my picture against capital punishment," Lang explained afterwards. "I have always opposed capital punishment for the basic reason that in killing a murderer society has created another killer to carry out the job." Rather than showing Lorre's gruesome handiwork, the visual Lang would display killings in other ways, using symbolic illustrations to make his point.

A MEETING WITH GOEBBELS
AND A NIGHT JOURNEY TO PARIS

With Hitler's Third Reich ensconced in power, Propaganda Minister Joseph Goebbels summoned Germany's most notable director for a meeting in his office. Goebbels offered Lang the reins of the Film Division of the Ministry. Lang immediately suspected a trap and, following the meeting, moved swiftly.

Concluding that he did not have long before Hitler's forces would come calling, Lang left behind his residence, his valuable collection of paintings, as well as his wife, catching a train that evening for Paris. His wife would stay behind and utilize her directorial talent on films approved by the Third Reich.

Lang's sense of humor is brought into play in describing what happened next in his career. While residing in Paris, a talent scout from MGM visited the city. "When the big cities sent talent scouts to Europe they were expected to come back with a trophy," Lang recalled. "I became a trophy."

Once Lang arrived at MGM's Culver City studio, he found reason to believe he was a trophy. Trophies are objects to collect and often sit on shelves. Lang sat on the shelf for better than a year at MGM and ultimately complained to Louis B. Mayer's right-hand man, Eddie Mannix. When he finally was permitted to spring into action, it was with a sonic blast, a film based on a theme dear to Lang's heart. *Fury*, a 1935 release, starred one of the studio's leading lights and box office magnates, Spencer Tracy, who was cast as a victim of mob rule when he is arrested for a murder he did not commit. Sylvia Sidney provided meaningful support as the steady, always-supportive woman in his life. Lang copped a New York Critics Circle award for his direction in his first American effort. The lynch mob mentality theme proved bountiful for MGM. Just two years later, the same theme proved a winner for Mervyn LeRoy in *They Won't Forget*, based on an actual lynching case in Georgia. It had been preceded by another LeRoy hit based on the memoirs of a victim of justice, *I Am a Fugitive from a Chain Gang* (1932) with Paul Muni.

The man who barely escaped Hitler's Germany was a director whose entire career would deal with the anarchistic, the ambiguities of a society wherein people perpetually went over the edge. In such an atmosphere, injustice often resulted. *Fury* was a timely choice at a point where the twin-edged swords of the Great Depression existed alongside the discomforting international specter of Hitler and his legions on the rise. An important element of Lang's message in *Fury* and other works was the danger of the common folk displaying their worst side, falling victim to prejudice and injustice. In this case, one of filmdom's good guys, Spencer Tracy, a quintessential American every man, was victimized. While Frank Capra would provide scenarios in which Jimmy Stewart would prevail with the aid of the common folk, Fritz Lang would depict the flip-side of human existence, the degradation, often through mob rule, of the masses into a force of ugliness bent upon wreaking injustice on innocent victims.

ENTER NOIR PHASE

With America at war and audiences willing to accept an increasing amount of searing realism, it was predictable that Fritz Lang would enter the film noir sweepstakes. He landed there with the 1944 release, *The Woman in the Window*. Edward G. Robinson, a college psychology professor, plays a victim of circumstances, with the script of veteran Twentieth Century Fox mainstay Nunnally Johnson, who also produced, taking significant twists and turns, keeping the audience fully absorbed. Robinson sees a portrait of Joan Bennett in a window, then meets her and is swept off his feet, engaging in an extramarital affair. After he kills a powerful Wall Street magnate in self-defense, he is blackmailed by Dan Duryea, a tarnished ex-cop, once more at his ruthlessly entertaining optimum. Lang had used the talented character actor in a film he did at Paramount, *Ministry of Fear* starring Ray Milland and Marjorie Reynolds, also released in 1944. Duryea's propensity for smarmy rebelliousness made him a natural for film noir heavies. As earlier noted, he was at his best as gangster Slim Dundee, the rival to Burt Lancaster in their pursuit of Yvonne De Carlo in *Criss Cross*.

Just when the situation appears particularly bleak for Robinson, a story ploy is invoked. The professor awakens at his private club. He observes that the characters in the drama he dreamt work in the establishment, explaining everything and leaving him in a state of contentment.

Some critics explained the ending as necessary to please the powerful Breen Office and its perpetual concerns about censorship. Lang denies this, explaining that this was a ploy on his part to give the film a surprise twist as well as an upbeat ending. Some dubious critics contended that Lang had painted himself into a corner, and the dream ending enabled him to salvage a story going awry and needing a solution. He denied the charge, and once more there was controversy surrounding Lang. The veteran director was always up to the task of confronting controversy with crisply detailed responses.

PARTNERSHIP WITH BENNETT

Following the success of *The Woman in the Window*, Lang brought back the major principals, Robinson, Bennett and Duryea for a film released the following year, *Scarlet Street*. This time the beautiful brunette actress Bennett was back not only as a performer, but as a partner with her husband, producer Walter Wanger, and Lang.

Scarlet Street offered no upbeat surprise twist ending, such as *The Woman in the Window* supplied. This film, an adaptation of Jean Renoir's *La Chienne*, provided definitive Lang moral ambiguity and victimization. Dudley Nichols, who won an Oscar penning the 1935 John Ford hit, *The Informer*, handled the writing assignment with purposeful gusto, giving the story a strong noir bite, with Bennett as an opportunistic *femme fatale* and the always effectively surly Duryea as her rapacious so-called "bodyguard" feeding her greed.

Set in New York, the film begins with Robinson, a timid, henpecked, obscure cashier leaving a stag dinner where he has been honored by his boss for 25 solid years of service. En route to the subway to catch a ride back to his Brooklyn apartment, he observes Bennett being kicked by Dan Duryea as she lies on the ground. He comes to her rescue, knocking Duryea unconscious with a swipe of his umbrella.

Robinson rapidly falls in love with Bennett, who appears to take an interest in him in a way that his shrewish wife, who constantly berates him, does not. In actuality Bennett loathes his gentlemanly ways, as she is a masochistic prostitute who enjoys being beaten and dominated by her unscrupulous pimp, Duryea. Bennett, who masquerades as an actress, seeks money from Robinson, who begins embezzling funds from his employer. He sets her up in a spacious Greenwich Village apartment, where he stores his paintings and visits her. Very much in love, he begins painting more frequently away from his perpetually lamenting wife, who scorns his efforts and tells him he is only a shell of a man compared to her earlier husband, a New York police detective. Robinson provides some deception of his own, never telling Bennett that he is a cashier, preferring to have her believe he is a successful painter. When the world-wise Duryea becomes suspicious of Robinson, Bennett quips sarcastically, "He's too dumb to be a phony!"

Robinson, who is actually a skilled painter, but who has pursued the activity as a hobby, becomes a Lang tortured victim in the worst possible sense with failure ultimately looming in every direction, prompting him to finally erupt into an unanticipated homicidal state. His embezzlement is uncovered and he loses his job. Duryea takes his paintings and sells them. When a prominent New York art critic seeks to meet the city's new modern art painting sensation, the always-conniving Duryea, his sneering grin intact, points in the direction of an astounded Bennett. Robinson would otherwise be acclaimed as an artistic genius very much in demand were it not for the bitter noir twist brilliantly exploited in the Nichols script.

With Bennett posing as the creator of the paintings, Robinson is checkmated from capitalizing on his own genuine talent while an opportunistic prostitute is acknowledged as New York's newest artistic genius and pursued romantically by the critic who discovered her.

BENNETT'S FATAL ERROR

Robinson's world caves in on him at a time when he believes he has reached a brilliant new beginning in his relationship with Bennett. As a means of putting him off, Bennett constantly refers to his married status. When his wife's first husband returns after being presumed a suicide drowning victim and seeks to blackmail him, he instead shrewdly turns them back toward each other as he makes a surprise visit to the apartment on the assumption of receiving blackmail money from Robinson.

Gentle almost to the end, Robinson's pride will not allow him to be ridiculed by a woman he has deeply loved and broken the law to assist. As he rushes toward her apartment to tell her what he believes will be wonderful news regarding his own marital status, he sees her delivering a solid goodbye kiss to Duryea. Bennett later reacts by throwing her head on the pillow. A misunderstanding arises when Robinson believes she is crying, but learns to his shock that she is laughing at him. With tempers rising, she makes the cardinal mistake. When a man is emotionally distraught, his temper will likely rise, perhaps dangerously, if his masculinity is questioned. Bennett drops the saccharine mask she has worn for so long to manipulate the trusting cashier, angrily telling him that he is "old and ugly," then contrasting

him with lover-business confidante Duryea with the cutting words, "He's a man!"
Robinson attacks her with an ice pick, killing Bennett instantly.

Duryea is then buried in a shocking story twist. Aware of the type of relationship he had with Bennett, and that he, in a drunken state, threatened to go back to
the apartment and beat her up, authorities succeed in convicting him of the murder committed by Robinson. He desperately protests his innocence to the bitter end,
a date with the electric chair at Sing Sing Penitentiary. The story ends with bitter
irony as Robinson, in a deeply forlorn state, observes his painting of Bennett being
taken out of the window of a Manhattan art gallery, where it has been sold to a
wealthy art patron for $10,000. Meanwhile the great painter is reduced to sleeping
on park benches, from which he is evicted regularly by the police. They fail to listen to his frequently repeated confession to killing two people, believing it to be no
more than the ranting of a deranged street derelict.

A Bout with the Breen Office

It was erroneously believed that Lang's concern about the Breen Office resulted
in the ending that was used in *The Woman in the Window*. An actual confrontation
did occur one year later when Joseph Breen expressed misgiving about *Scarlet Street's*
ending. Unlike the prevailing wisdom during a period of concern about arousing
the wrath of the powerful Breen Office, this was a film that did not follow the regular formula of a crime's perpetrator paying for his misdeed. In this case, the devi-
ation from this principle was accentuated by having an innocent man, at least
regarding the specified crime in question, executed for the death of Joan Bennett.

Fritz Lang, inventive in every way, had an answer for Joseph Breen when his
misgivings about the film's ending were stated. "We're both Catholics," Lang
explained. "Here is a man undergoing torture who will go to hell for his crime. That
is the ultimate penalty."

Breen dropped his objection and the ending remained. It was a film that captured the brooding nature of the tortured Robinson and the dark hues of the noir
world. Lang made his point, with cinematographer Milton Krasner, who won an
Oscar for *Three Coins in the Fountain* (1954) and was nominated for coveted statuettes on six other occasions, providing the proper shadowy hues to underscore the
film's somber nature. *Scarlet Street* is an instructive guide to future Lang noir for-
ays, including his prolific bag of tricks, always structured around the shadowy twists
and turns from an ideal world of morality, in which vulnerable characters plummet,
sometimes to destruction.

A Highly Unique Western

After Lang's death, a number of paperback western novels were reportedly
found among his possessions. During the period of inactivity forced by MGM after

his arrival in America in the thirties, Lang lived among the Navajo Indians for six months, recounting the enjoyable sociological experiment for the remainder of his life. He revered the western as a fascinating part of Americana, and he began the fifties by directing one of the most unique films ever achieved in that specialized genre.

Rancho Notorious debuted in 1952 and was filmed at RKO during a period of upheaval in which the studio was sold and Howard Hughes returned to assume control. A major reason for Lang undertaking the assignment was the opportunity to work with the film's star, Marlene Dietrich. "By the end of the picture we were no longer speaking to each other," Lang observed. Dietrich, by all reported accounts, was a wily expert in the field of lighting and other technical phases of filming. She drew upon her experiences from her link to the famous director who discovered her in Berlin and brought her to Hollywood, Joseph von Sternberg, citing knowledge gleaned from the association to Lang, who noted that "Sternberg's ways were not necessarily my ways."

Despite emerging difficulties with Dietrich, the film became a cult classic. It broke new ground in the western genre by showcasing a theme tune which was repeated in various settings throughout the film, known as "Chuck-a-Luck." Written by Ken Darby, it unifies the film's plot in a similar manner to Dimitri Tiomkin's memorable "Do Not Forsake Me, Oh My Darling" from *High Noon*, released the same year, 1952. Ballads written by Darby are also used as devices to move the story along.

The film has been called a noir western by some film historians. It had the twin themes of hate and obsession inter-linked like Siamese twins in the script by Daniel Taradash, who the following year would win an Academy Award for his adaptation of James Jones's novel, *From Here to Eternity*. Arthur Kennedy's life is dominated by his compulsion to avenge the brutal robbery and murder of his fiancée. His excursion from Wyoming to the Southwest ultimately leads him to a ranch known as Chuck-a-luck run by saloon chanteuse Dietrich, which serves as a hideout for desperados. He finds the killer there, becoming involved in a romantic triangle involving gunslinger Mel Ferrer and Dietrich, who, while better than a decade older than either actor, possessed at 50 the requisite physical assets to render the story plot credible.

The Dietrich character was modeled after Belle Starr, who operated a ranch comparable to that depicted in *Rancho Notorious*. Starr was played by Gene Tierney in a 1941 release based on her life, *Belle Starr*.

Lang was able to tiptoe through the RKO experience without locking horns with the reclusive and erratic Hughes, but was disgusted when the mogul insisted on changing the proposed title of *Chuck-a-Luck*, which resonated with the film's theme. One casting move Hughes made certainly rankled Lang, given his anti-authoritarian disposition. Exercising a paranoiac Cold War McCarthyite propensity, Hughes, following Lloyd Gough's refusal to testify before the HUAC, took a unique step. In the only known case in film annals, the studio boss, given the fact that Gough was a central figure in the film, and recognizing the tremendous cost of re-shooting all the scenes in which he participated, opted to take his name out of the credits, despite his consequential involvement in the film.

FROM MCCARTHY TO COHN TO *THE BLUE GARDENIA*

Despite never having been a member of the American Communist Party or notably active in political activity, Fritz Lang was victimized by McCarthy period hysteria. He noted that the stigma must have stemmed from giving some money to a committee he was asked to support. He never appears in Robert Vaughn's thoroughly documented history of the period, *Only Victims*, but a frightening aspect of the McCarthy era was that many individuals were punished through a silent whisper campaign that never matured to the point of being called to testify. The stigma attached all the same.

During this forced career interregnum, Lang received an opportunity to return to work by controversial Columbia studio boss Harry Cohn. The result was a film which director-film historian Peter Bogdanovich termed "a particularly venomous portrait of American life." It was released in 1953, and its inventive director and veteran scenarist Charles Hoffman propelled the story line above a mystery drama to a full-fledged noir classic displaying the paranoiac fears of a decade in which an American society riddled with fearful uncertainty in a burgeoning Cold War sought victims as an easy solution alternative to complex answers. As an acutely sensitive Lang was well aware, cinema capital fears extended beyond HUAC hearings. This was a period in which the industry felt increasingly challenged by television as a competitive force. It will be noted how many principals involved in the film ultimately attained significant employment in the feared new competitor of films. Adapted from a novel by Vera Caspery, author of *Laura*, the film explores mob psychology and manipulation of the masses through a vigilant press zealously committed to profits through market control.

The film begins with a view of the Los Angeles Freeway, focusing on the activity of a busy city. The camera then concentrates on the then-focus of political and police control of Los Angeles, City Hall. The action commences outside the large downtown switchboard room, where artist Harry Prebble, played by Raymond Burr, wearing a broad Cheshire-like grin, draws a portrait of world-wise switchboard operator Crystal Carpenter, played by Ann Sothern. Her shrewd expression indicates an awareness of distancing herself from the artist's wolfish advances. Newspaper columnist Casey Mayo, played by Richard Conte, joins the group, at which point Sothern gives him her phone number, which a grinning Burr then jots down above the portrait he is painting. Burr notes that he had tried unsuccessfully to obtain Sothern's number. He has an office in the building and concentrates significant time doing sketches of the telephone operators as well as getting to know them. It is evident that Sothern trusts Conte and is self-protectively standoffish toward Burr. Burr's cold nature is revealed in a brief telephone conversation in his office, when a former lover desperately tells him it is urgent that he see her. "I told you not to call me here," Burr cavalierly scolds, hanging up.

The action shifts to the apartment Sothern shares with fellow telephone operators Anne Baxter and Jeff Donnell. Sothern, with a marriage and divorce behind her and older than her two roommates, is den mother of the group, a font of wisdom whose counsel is sought and appreciated. Her shrewd wisecracking ways serve as an intelligent contrast and relief to a story line that otherwise would be in danger of becoming morose. She goes out on a date with her equivalently wisecracking former husband, played by Ray Walker, with whom she proclaims she gets along with much better now that they are no longer married. Donnell, cast as Sally Ellis, receives a call from a local store indicating that the latest murder mystery has arrived. By no coincidence the author's first name is Mickey, reminding viewers of the then-highly popular mass market paperback mystery king Mickey Spillane, who wrote voluminously with staggering sales results about the exploits of his detective creation, Mike Hammer, a topic to be explored in the following chapter.

Before Sothern also leaves the apartment with steady boyfriend Walker, the sensitive introspection of Anne Baxter, cast as Bakersfield girl and recent migrant to Los Angeles, Norah Larkin, is displayed. Walker, cast as the good-natured, happy-go-lucky Homer, becomes concerned when Baxter, on her birthday night, expresses her preference for staying in and enjoying a candlelight dinner, complete with champagne, with the man in her life. What causes concern on Homer's part is that it is an imaginary date with her fiancé, who is serving as an army lieutenant in Korea. His presence is revealed by his photograph on the table. Also perched on the table is his most recent letter to her, which has been saved for the auspicious occasion.

The solitariness of the lovely and sensitive Baxter concerns Homer, whose extroverted nature complements that of love interest Sothern. He tells Baxter from a perspective of wisdom that she should not stay in every night dreaming about the man of her dreams in faraway Korea. She ought to go out. "Lots of guys would like to take you out and without any fooling around," the sympathetic Homer exclaims. "I'd like to myself if it weren't for Crystal." His remark draws a glance from the wily Crystal.

After Sothern and Walker leave, Baxter pours herself champagne and opens the letter. The message is rendered through a voice-over. The insertion of a distant romance between Baxter and her early youth sweetheart from Bakersfield who is in Korea fighting against Communist forces with the U.S. Army is yet another reminder of the continuing Cold War conflict and the pains it renders on Americans.

The letter begins routinely with the soldier apologizing for not writing more frequently. It shifts abruptly to Baxter's Bakersfield sweetheart explaining that he was injured in battle and flown to a Tokyo hospital for treatment. There he met a nurse who assisted him back to health, and with whom he fell in love. The letter ends with the line, "Best wishes for your future."

CROSSING CURRENTS

As a crestfallen Baxter reels under the shocking disappointment over a "Dear Jane" letter from the man toward whom she maintained total fidelity during his service in Korea, the story takes a shrewd twist with the audience being exposed to a surprising shock current. The turn of events renders Baxter, already a victim, increasingly vulnerable.

The telephone rings and Baxter, the only person in the apartment, answers. A grinning Raymond Burr is on the other end of the line. Events develop through a misunderstanding when she tries to explain that he is talking to the wrong person, aware that the wolfish artist is pursuing the wisecracking woman of experience of the household, Ann Sothern. When an invitation is extended to meet him for dinner at The Blue Gardenia, she succumbs. Under other circumstances she assuredly would have spurned Burr's invitation and finished the explanation she had earlier begun—that he had reached the wrong person and wanted to talk to Sothern, who was out on a date with her former husband and current boyfriend.

The story ploy involves a surprise along with a quick story contrast. As a depressed Baxter prepares to sulk alone, an invitation is extended for dinner on what would otherwise be a dreary birthday evening for her. The crossing current of Burr's desire for a good time coincides with her loathing of her self-imposed alienation in deference to a man in faraway Korea who has suddenly dropped her.

When the emotionally vulnerable Baxter accepts the artist's invitation, the audience knows that she is headed for trouble, a lamb heading into the wolf's den. Where was den mother Sothern when she needed her? The wily Sothern would have warned her away from Burr and recognized her dangerous state of emotional vulnerability.

Burr has explained that The Blue Gardenia, a popular local restaurant and nightclub, is located on "Hollywood Boulevard just off Vine." The reference to the familiar corner that evoked recognition magic throughout the world of Hollywood and Vine was mentioned, indicating that the restaurant was in the heart of the city known as the movie capital. The restaurant with its Polynesian accent bears a familiar resemblance to Don the Beachcomber, long a popular favorite for movie celebrities and currently a parking lot. Don the Beachcomber was located at 1727 McCadden Place, just off Hollywood Boulevard and the corner occupied for years by the popular Pickwick Bookstore. The restaurant was one block east of Highland Avenue, where the famous Hollywood Hotel and Lee's Drugstore, used in a climactic scene of *D.O.A.*, were situated. It was understandable, even in the event that Don the Beachcomber was the model for The Blue Gardenia, to mention Hollywood and Vine rather than Highland, considering the notable name recognition of what was then the most famous corner in the world.

PLENTY OF RUM AND A RIDE HOME

As a skilled predator, Burr knew the approach he wanted to take as Baxter agreed to meet him at the restaurant. He instructs the waiter before her arrival to put "plenty of rum" in the drinks. The game plan is clear, 1) render your intended future conquest vulnerable through excessive alcohol, and 2) in an intoxicated state, with inhibitions presumably lowered, take her back to your place.

Lang cynicism plays out in the cat and mouse game which develops when Baxter arrives. Burr is surprised, expecting Sothern, but the gleam in his eye indicates what he is thinking. The younger Baxter is seen as a more vulnerable target than Sothern, who has more experience at working her way out of clinches with the likes of Burr. He recommends the specialty of the house, the Polynesian Pearldivers, explaining that they do not contain much alcohol, knowing that the opposite is true.

While Baxter busily engages herself in seeking to throw off the painful memory of the man who has spurned her, drowning herself in potent Polynesian Pearl-divers, which, Burr reveals, hearken thoughts of "trade winds over lagoons," the brilliant song stylist Nat "King" Cole, at the peak of his popularity in the fifties when the film was made, sits at the piano and accompanies his own haunting rendition of the movie's theme tune, "Blue Gardenia." The tune will be played periodically through the remainder of the film. Its slow, rhapsodic beat adds a note of melancholy or romanticism, depending upon the situation.

A somewhat stumbling, slightly incoherent Baxter is next whisked off in Burr's convertible to his apartment. When it begins raining, he puts up the top, referring to the rain as "California dew." The arrival at his apartment helps Baxter shake off some of the cobwebs. Even with the abrupt intrusion of the Polynesian Pearldrivers, and without a warning from Sothern, she begins feeling tentative around Burr. She immediately asks for a cup of coffee. After the coffee, she enters a daze in which she mumbles words concerning her former boyfriend. Burr puts on a record of Cole singing "Blue Gardenia" and springs into action, attempting to kiss Baxter.

Burr receives a rude awakening when Baxter, reacting to the urgency of the moment, quickly comes out of her fog enough to resist. In the ensuing wrestling match, as she seeks to free herself from Burr's determined tentacles, she jolts him by smashing a window. After that, she blacks out again.

WHAT HAPPENED?

The action proceeds from Baxter's viewpoint. When Baxter awakens, a record is playing. She does not see Burr and apprehensively steals off into the rainy night without her shoes, roaming in the darkness back to her apartment.

The story then spins into a fresh direction. Lang has an opportunity to display his venom against the forces of incrimination, his artistic response to McCarthyism. A leading figure in the film used to make some of Lang's bluntest points is

Richard Conte, the suave, shrewd columnist from *The Globe* known as Casey Mayo. Conte, battling for headlines and circulation in Los Angeles journalistic competition, pounces on the story like a cat descending on the proverbial mouse. He explains to his sidekick, young photographer Richard Erdman, and a copy boy that what makes the story a great potential seller is the sex angle combined with murder. Conte jumps on a comment the copy boy makes to determine the name designed to sell headlines. "The Blue Gardenia!" Conte exults. "Not bad!"

Young, naive, recently spurned, vulnerably beautiful Norah Larkin, transplanted from the desert city of Bakersfield north of Los Angeles to her current status as frightened switchboard operator, becomes the most hunted person in the sprawling metropolis. She learns about the murder investigation into playboy Harry Prebble's death from the operator next to her, who is called away by her supervisor to talk to police. When she returns, she explains, "I posed for Prebble and I have a cold." Police wonder if she could have been the person wandering through the streets of Los Angeles barefooted in the wake of a murder. The camera closes in on a petrified Norah.

At one point, intended humor is used to achieve frightening dramatic results. A rattled Baxter, feeling a helpless confinement as Conte garners headlines with his column, in which he seeks to correspond directly with "The Blue Gardenia," jumps every time the telephone rings. On one occasion, when she picks it up after a long, nervous pause, the caller asks, "Is this The Blue Gardenia?" Baxter slams the phone down in an agitated state. Moments later the phone rings again and Sothern answers it. A perplexed Walker, always the humorist, asks why his call was terminated, assuming that the person answering the phone would know that it was just another case of him cracking a joke, this time about a subject that was paramount in the minds of Los Angeles residents.

Lang and cameraman Nicholas Musuraca, an RKO veteran who was cinematographer for *Out of the Past*, utilize a series of quick cuts to demonstrate the dominance of The Blue Gardenia case as trumpeted by Conte. Papers are rushed out onto the streets by eager vendors, while people from all walks of life are observed reading the details of Conte's columns with rapt attention. Meanwhile Baxter feels more helpless, trapped in confinement within a cold, large city whose citizens, targets of a media feeding frenzy, are curious to know her identity.

The tortured Baxter sees black uniformed police officers everywhere. With a description of the black dress she wore when seen the night of the murder with Burr at The Blue Gardenia being bandied about by Conte and others in print, she steals into the backyard late one evening to burn the evidence. As the fire burns, destroying the potentially incriminating evidence, an officer stops and reprimands her for violating the city ordinance to use incinerators after dark. He tells her, "It's too late this time, but don't do it again." On another occasion she opens her apartment door and finds a uniformed officer standing there. She stands frozen with fear. He routinely asks for the number of the manager's apartment.

A BLACK DAHLIA LINK

On the morning of January 15, 1947, the body of a 22-year-old woman, Elizabeth Short, was found neatly cut in half at the waist in a vacant lot at 3925 S. Norton Avenue in Los Angeles near the University of Southern California campus and the Coliseum. The would-be actress who had come from Massachusetts was known to prowl Hollywood Boulevard by night and was called "The Black Dahlia." The name was almost certainly inspired by the Paramount film noir hit of 1946 starring Alan Ladd, *The Blue Dahlia*, the screenplay of which was written by none other than celebrated mystery writer Raymond Chandler.

The ingredients that fit into the mix for the Charles Hoffman screenplay for *The Blue Gardenia*, a similar name to Black Dahlia, can be found in the fascinating murder case which is still prompting media attention. As Conte noted, the sex ingredient was a major mass-market seller, along with the mystery element of who perpetrated the crime in question. In the case of the film, the mysterious Blue Gardenia was thought to be the crime's perpetrator. In the real-life instance, a case which rocked Los Angeles, dominating newspaper headlines at the time, as in the Lang movie, scores of individuals confessed to the murder. The pattern continued after the frenzy diminished and no suspect had been apprehended. Some 40 people have confessed to killing The Black Dahlia.

The biting cynicism of director Lang was at work in one scene, where venom-etched humor produces hilarious results. In The Black Dahlia case, L.A. police detectives withheld certain key evidence about the killing from the press. Questions were asked which eliminated mentally disturbed confessors from consideration. In the film, columnist Conte uses the pair of black shoes found in Burr's apartment, which had been abandoned by Baxter in her frightened haste, as a means of eliminating confessors. A chain-smoking woman calls who displays her huge feet. The contrast between them and those of the petite Baxter is vast enough to produce a humorous result.

Reading the open letters to The Blue Gardenia from Conte, which increasingly urge the importance of contacting him, along with an offer to assist her, prompt a petrified Baxter to respond. By then Baxter is immersed in total doubt as to whether she is Burr's murderer. She makes initial contact on an appropriately foggy night in the beach community of Santa Monica. To disguise her voice, she holds a handkerchief over the pay phone she uses. Baxter will only go so far, telling Conte that she is not The Blue Gardenia, but a friend of the woman. His interest is sparked when she correctly tells him the 5½ B shoe size. The story then hits another bump in the road, the pattern of imposed obstacles of mystery writing again surfacing. A policeman arrives on the scene, in no way connected to her, but troublesome all the same, particularly in view of the conversation in which she is engaged. She immediately vanishes, and the officer steps into the phone booth, picking up the dangling phone. Conte then explains what has been happening.

Baxter contacts Conte again and agrees to meet him in his office. He tells her to enter through the Olive entrance, the heart of the downtown location of the *Los Angeles Times*. An immediate mutual attraction occurs, and the columnist takes her next door to Bill's Beanery, the small restaurant which serves as a hangout for reporters. Over hamburgers, she makes arrangements to have her "friend" turn herself in. Conte reveals his background in one succinct sentence: "I was born in a bus between L.A. and Tucson and I've been here ever since." His one sentence summary is reflective of the rootlessness associated with Los Angeles in the works of Chandler and other writers. In Conte's case, he became columnist Casey Mayo, where his reputation and future hinge on stirring up interest in the restless masses of the sprawling city.

Before Baxter follows through on her next move, the always-shrewd Ann Sothern asks her friend to come clean and tell her about what she has figured out on her own by piecing together clues: the constant panic, the unexplained anger at Sothern for asking where she is going before she leaves to telephone Conte, the mystery date she will not discuss and Baxter's hangover status the next morning. Sothern's detective instincts are unerring and Baxter levels with her, after which Sothern accompanies her to Baxter's next meeting with Conte at Bill's Beanery.

ANOTHER CYNICAL TWIST

After intermediary Sothern opens the discussion, she points toward the next booth, where Baxter sits. When Sothern leads and the discussion begins in earnest, Conte expresses shock. "Why did it have to be you?" he asks. The formerly naive girl from Bakersfield has been learning fast in the ways of men, realizing the implication. "What difference should that make?" she asks, as his question draws a probing question from her. Baxter had been earlier told that if The Blue Gardenia turned herself in to police, *The Globe* would extend every effort to assist her, including providing the best criminal defense attorney in the city. His awkwardness in the wake of his attraction toward her reveals a lack of candor earlier. When she asks if he meant what he said earlier, Conte says with a truthful awkwardness, "Frankly no."

Conte's candid response reveals him as an opportunistic journalist, interested in garnering continuing headlines and an attentive readership whatever the cost involved. He is not, however, responsible for the next event, for which Baxter blames him. Police Captain George Reeves descends with a contingent of uniformed officers, immediately arresting Baxter. She believes that Conte has set her up. As Reeves leaves, he looks over at the tall, silent proprietor of the eatery. "Thanks for keeping your ears open, Bill," he acknowledges.

Hoffman's script contains twists and turns, but all within the scope of a tightly structured story line, which includes the following:

1) An appropriately naive and attractive young woman whose vulnerability is enhanced in the wake of the tragedy of being bumped by her one and only love, the boyfriend from her early years in Bakersfield.

2) A big bad wolf, the womanizing photographer she would be better off avoiding, and would have if the apartment den mother had not been out on a date.

3) The clash seemingly ordained by the fates, the shark moving in on the barracuda. In a drunken haze from too many Polynesian Pearldivers, Baxter visits the lair of the predatory beast. When she comes to and resists, a window is smashed and a whirlpool of uncertainty intervenes as she passes out. Did she or did she not? She wonders after learning the next day of Burr's demise.

4) A media feeding frenzy sparked by an opportunistic columnist with a talent for grabbing headlines. The more intense the frenzy, reminiscent of the Black Dahlia case which gripped Los Angeles several years earlier, the more solitary the victim becomes.

5) The columnist and murder suspect ultimately meeting, with the added twist of a mutual attraction that immediately surfaces between them.

6) The moral ambiguity of the columnist revealed when he expresses disappointment over the woman toward whom he is attracted being the suspect. This drama-filled meeting contains yet another story twist, that of an alert police captain making an arrest with the victim understandably believing that she was set up by the columnist when the tipster was the lean, silent restaurant proprietor.

THE WRAP-UP

Police Captain Reeves seeks to keep aggressive newspaper columnist Conte in his newspaper domain, but he feels an added obligation to solve the crime when Baxter, someone he cares for, has been arrested. Symptomatic of the fifties, Conte has been handed the assignment by his editor of covering a hydrogen bomb test in Nevada. Nuclear war concerns rivaled murders with sexual overtones in the rush for headlines in the fifties. As Conte sits with his young photographer, played by Richard Erdman, waiting to board the plane to take them to their Nevada destination, his attention is riveted by a recording he hears over the airport loudspeaker system. He recognizes it as the same recording he heard playing on Burr's phonograph when he arrived to investigate the murder when the apartment was swarming with policemen. Conte recalls that when Baxter awakened following her involuntary sleep, "Blue Gardenia" was playing on Burr's record player. Listening to the sound of Richard Wagner's *Tristan and Isolde* alerts him that he might hold a valuable musical clue.

Convinced that the recording could hold a link to solving the murder, Conte is next seen with Reeves at the Melrose Music Shop, the label having been obtained by checking Burr's collection. Melrose Avenue was where RKO Studios were located, as well as being just one block south of Paramount. The proprietor recalls that the record album had been sold to Burr by Miss Miller. She had appeared briefly at the start of the film being brushed off on the telephone by the constantly stalking womanizer Burr. When Rose Miller, played by Ruth Storey, is summoned, Reeves becomes impatient over the delay. He snaps impatiently at Conte, convinced that he is wasting his time and already has the killer, Baxter, now in custody at Los Angeles County Jail. No sooner does Reeves express his disgust than an anguished cry from a woman in the distance pierces the air, propelling the detective into immediate action.

The action then shifts to a hospital bed with Storey explaining why she attempted to commit suicide by slitting her wrists. The selection on the record player held special meaning for her since it marked her first meeting with Burr, who became a regular customer at the music shop, romancing her in the process. On that rainy night, with Baxter fast asleep, the jilted woman who was desperate and carrying what would be Burr's child, arrived for what she hoped would be a reconciliation meeting. Instead Burr attempted to brush her off. When the selection she associated so closely with their relationship played, she became desperate and enraged, picking up the poker and striking the fatal blows. Baxter, in jail attire, is brought in to listen to the confession of the woman, who has been spared death through her unsuccessful suicide attempt, but stands to do a stretch in prison for murder or manslaughter. The gas chamber and a first-degree murder conviction would be unlikely due to the heat of passion element of the crime and possible absence of premeditation. Storey's spontaneous fury over being rejected by a man she loved is cited by her as the murder catalyst and appears highly plausible under the facts.

By the film's end, Baxter appears ready to resume her romance with Conte, but as a much wiser woman. Listening to psychological guru Sothern, she plays a temporary game of hard to get when she is released from jail and a battery of reporters and photographers, including Conte, are there to greet her. Baxter walks away without recognizing Conte, but Sothern cautions her not to carry the game too far. Sothern then approaches Conte and says with a grin, "The number is Granite 1466." This concluding dialogue lends thematic unity to a well-structured movie, since the trouble began with Burr jotting down the number in pursuit of Sothern.

AN EERIE REAL-LIFE ELEMENT

A graphic incident of life seemingly imitating art occurred in the case of husky, broad-shouldered George Reeves, who played Police Captain Haynes in *The Blue Gardenia*. At the time he appeared in the film, Reeves enjoyed high popularity as the legendary man of steel in the television series *Superman*, beginning in 1951, when the new medium was beginning to hit full popularity stride.

In 1959, after the cancellation of the once-successful *Superman* series, Reeves, 45, was found dead on the bedroom floor of his home at 1579 Benedict Canyon. He had been shot in the head and a gun lay on the floor between his legs. The coroner ruled Reeves's tragic death a suicide, the result of despondency relating to his career slump.

Reeves's mother shipped his body back east, insisting that he had been murdered. Rumors circulated that she had put his body on "ice" until she could prove that he was a victim of foul play rather than a suicide victim. Many persons in Hollywood today believe that his body is still on ice. He lay unburied in the East for eight months until he was cremated and his ashes returned to Los Angeles and placed secretly in an unmarked urn in a local cemetery. His mother died in 1964 still attempting to prove her son had been murdered.

The tragedy of Reeves's death, which was explored on the popular *Unsolved Mysteries* television show narrated by Robert Stack, had startling future repercussions. Occupants of the home where he died reported ghostly incidents, prompting them to move.

Abrupt Burr Career Departure

Raymond Burr, who played the role of the scheming womanizer artist with the proper measure of oiliness, began his lengthy acting career playing unpleasant figures. The Canadian-born actor, who was compelled to drop his weight from 340 pounds to a fighting trim 210 to get a shot at movies, was a dark, convincing villain on the screen. He played the ferocious district attorney determined to send murder suspect Montgomery Clift to death by execution in George Stevens's 1951 classic, *A Place in the Sun*. Another memorable villain's role came one year after *The Blue Gardenia* in the 1954 Alfred Hitchcock masterpiece, *Rear Window*, delivering a chilling portrayal of a killer determined to bury his wife and evade responsibility, but under the shrewd and watchful eyes of James Stewart and Grace Kelly in the adjacent apartment building.

Characteristic of the fifties, many film performers made their mark on television. Burr's image changed, and he became a force for good as he garnered the lead of the popular *Perry Mason* television series, based on the novels of Erle Stanley Gardner, who reportedly jumped to his feet and shouted, "That's him!" after spotting Burr in what was to have been a test for the role of the district attorney. The series began in 1957 and lasted for almost a decade. After a hiatus of less than a year, Burr was back at work as the wheelchair-bound San Francisco Police Commissioner *Ironside*. That series also had enormous staying power, running from 1967 to 1975.

Ann Sothern, who played the wisecracking beacon of experience in the film, also had a successful career in television during the fifties after having ridden to fame playing a lovable scatterbrain in the *Maisie* series. She starred on the small screen in *Private Secretary* and the *Ann Sothern Show*.

Jeff Donnell, the addictive murder mystery reader and roommate of Baxter and Sothern, played the wife of George Gobel in the show of the same name, which was a big hit in the mid-fifties, while Richard Conte's sidekick, photographer Richard Erdman, supplied the laughs as pinup photographer Tab Hunter's sidekick in the early sixties' *Tab Hunter Show*. Alex Gottlieb, the film's producer, began writing for radio, working for such stars as Al Jolson and Eddie Cantor, moved into scriptwriting in films, wrote a play, *Susan Slept Here*, which became a 1954 film starring Dick Powell and Debbie Reynolds, and finally moved into successful television producing with such shows as *The Bob Hope Chrysler Theater*, *The Donna Reed Show*, and *The Smothers Brothers Show*.

While the Anne Baxter-Richard Conte duo displayed on-screen chemistry, the pairing emerged as a result of Lang favorite, Dana Andrews, the prince of moral ambiguity, having another commitment. This brought Conte onto the scene, a natural in that one of his finest roles was as the sensitive and committed young prizefighter who donated his earnings to a revolutionary cause in the 1952 release, *The Fighter*, produced by Gottlieb and directed by Herbert Kline. An actor with a dark and brooding charisma, Conte failed to receive breaks commensurate with his talent. He made a brilliant nemesis for idealistic detective Cornell Wilde as a mob boss seeking total domination in the Joseph Lewis 1955 low budget noir success, *The Big Combo*. Conte also won solid notices in the 1949 Jules Dassin film, *Thieves' Highway*.

Fritz Lang shot *The Blue Gardenia* in a compact 10 days. He had little regard for the film, perhaps due to the brevity of the assignment. He was impressed with the acting performance of his leading lady, the elegant Anne Baxter. The granddaughter of famed architect Frank Lloyd Wright, she began her acting training at 11 under the famous Maria Ouspenskaya. Baxter won an Oscar for Best Supporting Actress as the alcoholically troubled wife of Tyrone Power in the 1946 Fox hit, *The Razor's Edge*. Four years later, she was nominated for a Best Actress statuette along with co-star Bette Davis in the Joseph Mankiewicz masterpiece about life in the American theater, *All About Eve*. When Davis, unhappy over the dual nominee status, complained that Baxter should have been nominated in the supporting category, she shrewdly shot back with one of the most famous one-liners in cinema annals, "The name of the picture is *All About Eve*, not *All About Margo*."

A SORT OF SEQUEL

Lang took another quick turn toward film noir under independent producer Bert Friedlob in the 1956 release, *While the City Sleeps*. By this time, McCarthy was no longer a major political force and would die one year after the film debuted, but Lang did not abandon his pursuit of his theme of moral ambiguity and the sinister web it weaves within the social fabric of modern society. In fact, absent the incrimination element which was so strongly represented in the frightened figure of Anne Baxter, directly allegorical with fifties McCarthyism, *While the City Sleeps* could be deemed a quasi-sequel to *The Blue Gardenia*. Central to the theme of Casey Robinson's screenplay was the steadily increasing influence of the media.

The film begins with Amos Kyne, ill and lying in bed. Playing Kyne is distinguished Broadway and film character actor Robert Warwick, who performed in a

Fritz Lang had a brilliantly evocative style with film noir, particularly for displaying the hypocrisies and moral ambiguities of humanity. His 1956 film *While the City Sleeps* exposes the opportunistic cynicism of employees of a New York media conglomerate. Vincent Price is cast as the playboy son who inherits the empire after his father, played by Robert Warrick, dies. His faithless wife, *femme fatale* Rhonda Fleming, uses her seductive charms to help her lover, James Craig, snag the organization's top post. Craig, reflective of Lang's biting cynicism, is also Price's "best friend."

role reminiscent of John Barrymore in *In a Lonely Place*. Head of a New York City media empire bearing his name, he articulates his fears to star television commentator and journalist Dana Andrews, a former Pulitzer Prize winner. In the process, he reveals the dichotomy facing media communicators, that of balancing the need to gain headlines to succeed competitively while serving the basic influence of informing the public. After stressing the importance of playing up the latest killing of a young woman, in which a message was written with lipstick on the wall with the message, "Ask mother," he suggests that the serial murderer be called "The Lipstick Killer," concluding that this will generate interest. Warwick then scales a loftier plane, exclaiming, "People need all the facts" as he philosophizes about the importance of maintaining a vigorous free press. Sensing that he is near death, Warwick expresses regret for spoiling his son, bemoaning "the polo ponies and especially the women." He clues the audience in on what will shortly unfold in the story.

Warwick promptly drops dead from a massive heart attack, which occurs just before Andrews is ready to go on the air. Andrews scraps his written script and ad-libs about the death of the last of a vanishing breed, a media giant interested in giving the public the facts. Andrews's tribute is comparable to a similar one made following the death of a media giant by commentator Peter Finch in the 1976 block-buster, *Network*.

With the elder Kyne now gone, his son Walter, played by Vincent Price, enters the picture. He calls in the leading figures of Kyne Enterprises and complains that the Lipstick Killer's latest murder is garnering more attention than the death of his father. Star writer and commentator Andrews as well as *The Sentinel's* experienced, hard-working editor, Thomas Mitchell, explain that the elder Kyne preferred it that way. Price realizes that Mitchell, along with Kyne wire service editor George Sanders and photo service editor James Craig all consider him an interloper without a shred of knowledge of the business, who is assuming the position through inheritance alone.

FEEDING FRENZY WITHIN FEEDING FRENZY

A central dramatic device skillfully employed in *The Blue Gardenia* was the feeding frenzy unleashed by columnist Richard Conte to find the female killer of Raymond Burr, which ultimately tormented Anne Baxter, who finally decided to meet him. A technique of a feeding frenzy within a feeding frenzy is incorporated into *While the City Sleeps*. This situation occurs when an angry Vincent Price, recognizing that the three leading figures in Kyne Enterprises, Mitchell, Sanders and Craig, have little respect for the son who has attained his lofty position through inheritance, unleashes a furious counter assault. He confides his plan to Andrews, whose expression reveals his distaste for the idea.

"I'll watch them cut each other into pieces," Price enthuses. He creates the position of executive director of Kyne Enterprises. The feeding frenzy for the top position is built around a comparable frenzy being artfully exploited through every Kyne outlet, that of locating the Lipstick Killer, who leaves a different clue following every brutal murder. The intense competition will be ultimately governed by which individual excels in the pursuit to obtain headlines, then hopefully lead police to the killer.

While Andrews openly professes a disinclination to move up in the power structure, he is anything but neutral in the competition, preferring hard-nosed newspaper editor Mitchell. In a bold attempt to draw the killer into the open, Andrews uses his television program to taunt the murderer. He calls him a "mamma's boy" and treats him as an immature child. The camera of Ernest Laszlo, who was also cinematographer on *D.O.A.*, closes in alternately on Andrews and the killer, played by John Barrymore Jr., who smirks when the commentator-columnist makes a particularly bruising remark. The by-play between the opportunistic commentator

Andrews and the angry response of killer Barrymore is akin to the taunting of a wild and frustrated animal. Once more, Lang's study of moral ambiguity is evident in the way that mass marketing commentator and journalist Andrews taunts his victim, enabling viewers to draw the conclusion that he is, in some ways, worse for taunting than the psychologically disturbed serial killer who reacts with wounded pride to the accurate barbs.

Barrymore, who dresses in black and works as a drugstore delivery boy, is greeted by his mother, Mae Marsh, after the program ends. She walks into his room and an argument ensues. It becomes quickly obvious that Andrews has analyzed his character traits unerringly. He mentions being an adopted son and loudly laments what he believes to be an unappreciated status. The casting of the younger Barrymore is interesting in that he appears in the same film with Robert Warwick, who was cast in a thinly disguised role of Barrymore's famous father in *In a Lonely Place*.

Andrews quickly reveals himself to be a figure of Lang moral ambiguity as he plots strategy to help Mitchell crack the case and win the grand prize of the executive director position. His plan is reminiscent of Richard Conte's letters to *The Blue Gardenia*. In that case, he created a feeding frenzy to draw in the young woman whose identity left an entire city speculating. Andrews has a bold game plan that involves none other than his fiancée, Sally Forrest, to goad an angry Barrymore. As a means of promoting an attack from Barrymore, Andrews sees that the announcement of his engagement to Forrest is displayed on the front page of *The Sentinel*.

THE PRINCE OF MORAL AMBIGUITY

Dana Andrews has earned a niche in sophisticated noir dramas as "The Prince of Moral Ambiguity" as the favorite leading man of the two directors specializing in dramas featuring that element. Otto Preminger brought Andrews to prominence by casting him in the challenging role of Detective Mark McPherson in *Laura*, holding fast to his convictions after Twentieth Century Fox studio boss, Darryl Zanuck, after viewing the film's early rushes, lamented that the actor lacked a certain toughness he sought. Zanuck's recommendation was that Andrews be replaced by John Hodiak. Preminger's creative instincts saw in Andrews just the right blend for the tortured detective who falls in love with what is at the time presumed to be a dead woman, Gene Tierney as Laura prior to resurfacing. Andrews possesses the proper blend of suave good looks coupled with intelligence to be convincing as a man grappling with moral difficulties. Andrews was well received opposite the hauntingly beautiful Tierney in *Laura*, so one year later, Preminger recast him opposite the Fox musical box office queen who was shifting in the direction of drama, Alice Faye, in *Fallen Angel* (1945). Preminger called on Andrews again to play opposite Joan Crawford in *Daisy Kenyon* (1947), where he was involved in a triangle with Henry Fonda, his competition. When Andrews was unavailable, Preminger cast Robert Mitchum in his place to star opposite Jean Simmons in the noir drama *Angel Face* (1953).

With Fritz Lang, as earlier noted, Andrews was his choice for columnist Casey Mayo in *The Blue Gardenia*; but when he was otherwise committed, Richard Conte received the role. Lang would use the veteran leading man, however, in the final two installments of his film noir trilogy dealing with moral ambiguity amid the pervasive influence of the modern media, starring Andrews in the subsequent *Beyond a Reasonable Doubt*, also released in 1956.

The sincere, clean-cut Forrest, who spends one night a week doing volunteer work at her local Red Cross, does her best to reform the heavy-drinking Andrews, who has also done his share of womanizing. While far from enthusiastic over being used as a decoy, she reluctantly agrees when her fiancé assures her that she will have a plainclothes detective following her every time she leaves her apartment, and that she will be "safer than you've ever been in your life."

FLEMING AS *FEMME FATALE*

In a film featuring double-dealings and cutthroat competition, sexy Rhonda Fleming emerges as an ideal *femme fatale*. While less lethal than gun toters such as Jane Greer, Barbara Stanwyck and Claire Trevor, Fleming nonetheless bares sharp claws, but they are used in a non-lethal, strategic manner. The stunning redhead, after being signed to a contract by David O. Selznick while still in her teens, received her first notable screen opportunity playing a nymphomaniacal mental patient in Alfred Hitchcock's *Spellbound* (1945). Two years later she emerged as a *femme fatale* in *Out of the Past*, playing Meta Carson, a San Francisco legal secretary who assists Kirk Douglas in killing her boss, who deeply loves her and is attempting to blackmail the syndicate head. When Robert Mitchum, realizing he is being used, clutches Fleming tightly, exclaiming, "I wanna come out of this in one piece," she has a ready answer. "Do you always go around leaving your fingerprints on women's arms?" she purrs. "Not that I mind. You have strong hands."

Fleming married spoiled rich man's son Price, who is so smitten with her he fails to recognize her disloyalty. Lang uses his naivete to create some rare humor, and that black. At one point, Price proudly grins that he met Fleming at the swimming pool of the Sands Hotel in Las Vegas, got a good look at her legs, and married her three days later. It makes viewers hearken back to the regret expressed by his father prior to his death about treating his son with too much kindness regarding his choices of women. She two-times him, spending much time in the apartment of the man supposed to be his best friend, James Craig, head of Kyne Enterprise's photo service. She chuckles to Craig about the excuse she perpetually makes of spending time with her mother. When she calls him from Craig's, Price growls irritably, "You sure have been spending a lot of time lately at Mother's!"

The wily Lang creates a sexy scene through innovation, displaying Fleming at her most alluring. The scene is the sun deck of Price's Upper East Side penthouse.

Initially a screen reveals a silhouette of Fleming, who is wearing a two-piece bathing suit and exercising while Price practices putting, notably missing shot after shot.

After the alluring silhouette shot, a primping Fleming stretches out on a chaise lounge, asking her always-attentive husband to rub tanning oil on her. As he does, she begins to pitch him on behalf of Craig for the top position, making certain to speak in a low-keyed, seemingly detached manner.

At a later meeting with Craig, Fleming lets him bluntly know that if she is responsible for him getting the executive director's post, he will be obligated to jump to her tune. A macho type, reminiscent of Clark Gable, the resemblance to whom prompted MGM to sign him, Craig's expression reveals his displeasure over Fleming attempting to assert control over him.

Lupino as Would-Be Seductress

Ida Lupino, during the pivotal decade of her creative powers, enters the picture as a would-be seductress to Andrews. Observing him as a man of seemingly relaxed will, George Sanders, playing the role of the manipulative cad which secured him an Oscar for Best Supporting Actor as acid-tongued drama critic Addison DeWitt in *All About Eve*, singles out Andrews for seduction by his own romantic interest, *Sentinel* columnist Ida Lupino.

An irony of the film is that Lupino, in seeking to seduce Andrews to win his support on behalf of Kyne Enterprises wire service editor Sanders for the coveted executive director position, is two-timing the sincere and upstanding Sally Forrest, someone with whom her own career is strongly linked. Lupino, the only prominent female director of the fifties following the tradition of Dorothy Arzner, whose films covered a period between 1927 and 1943, directed Forrest in her breakthrough role in RKO's *Hard, Fast and Beautiful* (1951), where she played a determined young tennis professional with Claire Trevor as her stoutly encouraging mother.

At the time she was working in *While the City Sleeps*, Lupino was starring with husband Howard Duff in the television series *Mr. Adams and Eve*. He appears in the film, but in no scenes with his wife, playing the detective lieutenant and boyhood friend of Andrews, who uses his assistance in getting helpful information on stories.

Lupino's seduction attempt begins in the Kyne Enterprises watering hole, a nearby bar, where Andrews has already imbibed generously by the time the attractive columnist arrives. She entices him to come to her apartment. The episode boomerangs for all concerned. Lupino concludes that Andrews won his Pulitzer Prize "for his writing" while Sanders's ploy backfires. As for Andrews, the torrent of office gossip that emerges prompts square shooter Forrest to terminate their engagement.

A Fast-Paced Conclusion

Lang and Robinson step up the story's pacing to reach a rousing conclusion. Despite Forrest's sudden loss of interest in Andrews, killer Barrymore remains

Robert Warrick, seated, playing mogul Amos Kyne, head of Kyne Enterprises, confers with top operatives, left to right, Thomas Mitchell, Dana Andrews and James Craig, as he approaches death in *While the City Sleeps*, German émigré director Fritz Lang's next to last American film, and one of his personal favorites. Warrick played an actor modeled along the lines of John Barrymore who befriends Humphrey Bogart in *In a Lonely Place*. As a Broadway actor, Warrick helped the young Bogart obtain stage roles. An irony is that the role of the serial killer in *While the City Sleeps* was played by John Drew Barrymore, son of the legendary actor Warrick's role in *In a Lonely Place* resembled.

aroused. When he attempts to break into her locked apartment, she immediately telephones the police. In the meantime Barrymore, observing Fleming in the apartment across the hall, which is tenanted by her love bauble Craig, spots her through the open door and emerges. Fleming proves tough in the clinches, fighting off his advances and forcing him to flee with the police in pursuit. After a brief subway battle in which a pursuing Andrews is involved, Barrymore is apprehended by police when he steps up to street level, prompting a confession to all crimes.

Lupino is summoned to the apartment building to interview a "Mrs. Smith" for a human-interest story concerning how she fought off The Lipstick Killer. When she finds Fleming as the alleged "Mrs. Smith" standing next to paramour Craig, Lupino realizes that she has the ingredients for far more than a newspaper story.

When Lupino and Craig emerge in the office, and the photo editor demands an immediate meeting in Price's office, a grinning Ida tells Mitchell and Sanders, "You both finished in a tie for second." The idea is that with Craig holding the goods on Price, the position will be his.

The Robinson script takes a surprise twist at the end, one which leaves some hope in an otherwise sea of murkiness in which Forrest was the only beacon of optimism. Andrews shows signs of character improvement by quitting his job, tired of life in the hornet's nest of Kyne Enterprises. With Forrest, who is still not speaking to him, sitting nearby, he issues a bitter denunciation against Price and his enterprise from his familiar stool at the all-too-familiar office watering hole. Price arrives in the midst of Andrews's monologue. When the former Pulitzer Prize winner pauses, Price exclaims, "Don't stop on my account." When he quickly concludes his lament and begins to leave, Forrest, seeing Andrews in a more favorable light, calls out, "Wait, I'm coming with you!"

The story ends in a Miami Beach hotel suite with Andrews and Forrest emerging after tying the marital knot. The bellboy offers a paper, which contains a story about the shakeup at Kyne Enterprises. Forrest reads the details. Craig has been sent on a two-year good will tour taking him to various points throughout the world. Merit wins out with hard-working Mitchell obtaining the executive director's post. Lupino has been given the position of special assistant under Price. Could she be his new love interest with faithless Fleming discarded? Or is he merely grateful for uncovering a sticky matter he wants to keep under wraps? Is Fleming still in the picture or out with Craig traveling the world? We are invited to use our imaginations.

As for Andrews, he receives the managing editor's position at *The Sentinel* just relinquished by Mitchell. The developing events display a Price who has received a rapid-fire, on-the-job media executive's training course. Displaying typical Andrews individualism, when the telephone rings and Forrest says, "That would be Walter Kyne," the new husband, desiring privacy above all else, places his hat over the telephone.

While the City Sleeps became one of Lang's favorite films. It helped bail out RKO at a time when Howard Hughes had produced a string of bombs. The bashful billionaire distributed the film and stayed out of the way, the best recipe for Hughes film success. While it is understandable why Lang was so fond of the film, given the bag of tricks displayed to show spirited and intelligent media people in intense professional conflict, against the backdrop of a serial killer's New York rampage, *The Blue Gardenia*, a film toward which he showed scant interest, perhaps because it was shot in a whirlwind ten days, displays a more solid and straightforward cinematic effort. The characters were sharply defined, and the story moved with steady forward momentum, focusing on the fears of a tormented young woman caught in the headlights of an onrushing media dominating an entire city. Despite its cleverness, *While the City Sleeps*, in its endeavor to portray clever tricks carried out by imaginative game players in combat, the constant character shift deprived viewers of the kind of dual by-play afforded by the Baxter-Conte relationship and the characters they represented.

Lang's next film in the media trilogy, *Beyond a Reasonable Doubt*, was his American finale. At the film's conclusion, the director stated, "I don't want to make any more films here. I don't want to die of a heart attack." His efforts on the film were complicated by two problems. The first was that his producer, Bert Friedlob, who had worked with him earlier on *While the City Sleeps*, was in great pain and dying of cancer. The second was that his agent failed to provide in the contract Lang's right to make script changes. With *Beyond a Reasonable Doubt*, this became a significant point since the screenplay of Douglas Morrow, who won a Best Story Screenplay Oscar for the Jimmy Stewart baseball film, *The Stratton Story* (1948), ends the drama in a manner contrary to Lang's wishes.

Dana Andrews agrees to involve himself in a scheme concocted by his prospective father-in-law, Sidney Blackmer, to demonstrate the flaws of circumstantial evidence in American jurisprudence. He agrees to fake a murder of nightclub dancer Barbara Nichols. As the trial nears its conclusion, the person with the evidence will surface to clear him, after which he will be able to marry Joan Fontaine and live happily ever after. The plan is spoiled when the person with the evidence dies in an automobile accident. Andrews is convicted and becomes a sympathetic victim until just before the film's surprise twist resolution, when it is learned that he was actually guilty of murder.

"I cannot, I said, make an audience love Dana Andrews for one hour and thirty-eight minutes and then in the last two minutes reveal that he's really a son of a bitch and that the whole thing is just a joke," Lang lamented. "But thanks to my agent's mistake I was contractually bound to shoot the producer's original script." The great director candidly stated, "I hate it (the film), but it was a great success. I don't know why."

In the manner of perfectionists like Lang, frequently when they are dissatisfied with the overall result, the public sharply disagrees. Despite his frustration over not being able to make a "second film against capital punishment like *M*," his talent to generate tight suspense and keep audiences riveted brought dividends.

Lang returned to his native Germany to direct three more films. He generated much attention in a starring role playing himself with Brigitte Bardot in Jean-Luc Godard's *Le Mepris* (*Contempt*) with the famous French director cast as his assistant director. Lang enjoyed the experience immensely, despite Godard's strong disposition toward improvisation, the antithesis of Lang's tightly organized structure from beginning to end.

His European concluding sojourn completed, Lang returned to America and an opulent mansion in Beverly Hills on Summit Ridge Drive set, appropriately enough, beside a canyon. This was the perfect spot for a Pygmalion director to look down on a world containing the moral ambiguity and other human foibles he depicted with such uncompromising fidelity in his long and productive career.

SIX

Armageddon Allegorical Noir

Keep away from the windows. Someone might blow you a kiss.
Kiss Me Deadly (1955)

The fifties was a decade known for McCarthyism and another element more potentially deadly, which would not go away until the end of the eighties, the Cold War, and its frightening potential for nuclear destruction. A Mickey Spillane novel, featuring detective Mike Hammer with plenty of violence created for a mass market audience of quick page-turners, would appear to be an unlikely subject for a film dealing with the dangers and incumbent fears regarding nuclear destruction, but *Kiss Me Deadly* offers just such an example.

The book by prolific author Spillane revolved around Hammer's quest to locate a valuable stash of drugs. The screenplay by A.I. Bezzerides changed the object to a radioactive isotope with destructive potential. The forbidden weapon was under the control of a mad scientist played by Albert Dekker, who shone in the role of Ava Gardner's syndicate boss husband in *The Killers*. Dekker was an ideal choice since the veteran character actor burst to prominence playing a mad scientist in the 1939 science fiction thriller, *Dr. Cyclops*, cast in the role of Dr. Thorkeld, who possesses the ability to shrink humans to doll size. In retaining the Spillane element invested in Hammer of the nihilistic, antisocial detective who will do anything to achieve his objective as contrasted by brilliant scientific vision which can be brought down to the level of anarchy at the expense of potential human extinction, scenarist Bezzerides and director Robert Aldrich served up an image of nuclear Armageddon, a vision of nihilistic forces unleashing the most scientifically destructive results which sophisticated creative minds have ever invented.

The teaming of director Robert Aldrich and screenwriter A.I. "Buzz" Bezzerides ensured a maximum of hard-hitting action. Aldrich looked the part of a man of action, and his films reflected that tendency. The director had the broad-shouldered, large-frame construction of the University of Virginia college football player he once was before graduation and his decision to spurn the business world, which his

129

prominent family wished for him. Instead his creative instincts turned Aldrich toward Hollywood. At Enterprise Studios, his experience was enhanced by working with top professionals such as John Garfield, Robert Rossen and Abraham Polonsky. He also worked with such major directors during his learning process as Charlie Chaplin, Lewis Milestone and Joseph Losey.

The year 1955, when *Kiss Me Deadly* was released, was a breakthrough year as another explosive Aldrich vehicle, *The Big Knife*, was released, which was a corrosive blast at traditional Hollywood and its destructive superficiality, with Jack Palance cast as a film star trying to live down a tragic drunk driving accident which cost a life, ending with his own suicide. The script was written by tough-minded Hollywood veteran Clifford Odets. The pull-no-punches style of Aldrich was evidenced in two other critical studies of Hollywood: the highly acclaimed 1962 black comedy, *Whatever Happened to Baby Jane?*, with a superstar tandem of Bette Davis and Joan Crawford, and the 1968 release, *The Legend of Lylah Claire*, starring Kim Novak, Peter Finch and Ernest Borgnine.

Aldrich tackled the challenging theme of mental illness treatment one year after *Kiss Me Deadly* and *The Big Knife* by presenting Cliff Robertson as a troubled young man who finds love with an older woman, played by screen legend Joan Crawford, in *Autumn Leaves*. He also chalked up a success with *The Dirty Dozen* (1967), a story about a group of misfits who develop into a tough WWII fighting force. *The Killing of Sister George* (1968) was a daring story set in London about lesbianism starring Beryl Reid, Susannah York and Coral Browne, which generated tremendous controversy and was ahead of its time. Aldrich also scored with the unconventional 1974 comedy, *The Longest Yard*, starring Burt Reynolds. Like *The Dirty Dozen*, the film dealt with reforming hard case criminals into a cohesive framework. In this instance, it was a group of prison inmates with former pro football star Reynolds playing quarterback, with the incentive of defeating an opposing team of prison guards.

Scriptwriter Bezzerides, who grew up in central California as the son of a trucker, entered the business as a young man. His rough-and-tumble early experiences resulted in a novel, *They Live by Night*, which became a successful 1940 Warners film directed by Raoul Walsh with a cast headed by perennial tough guys Humphrey Bogart and George Raft along with Ann Sheridan and Ida Lupino. Bogart and Raft play brother truck drivers battling against corrupt bosses.

Bezzerides returned to the same ground in adapting his own novel, *Thieves' Highway*, to the screen. Richard Conte won high marks in the 1949 release playing a son returning from the war who seeks justice after his father, played by celebrated Broadway actor Morris Carnovsky, loses both of his legs and his trucking business in a fight with corrupt racketeer Lee J. Cobb. This marked the last American film of director Jules Dassin, who fled to England after spurning the House Un-American Activities Committee's efforts to interrogate him. Bezzerides also turned in a solid effort for Nicholas Ray in the 1951 RKO release, *On Dangerous Ground*, in which burned-out New York cop Robert Ryan loses his hostile edge when he meets sensitive blind woman Ida Lupino.

Bezzerides's chief complaint about his screenwriting career was that he was frequently a writer for hire who did not get a chance to put his own creative stamp on his screenplays. He was delighted that the team of veteran British producer Victor Saville and director Aldrich, whose creative vision of tough action films coincided with his own propensities, gave him free rein with shaping the Spillane novel in his direction.

"The original book, *Kiss Me Deadly*, had nothing," Aldrich bluntly declared. "We just took the title and threw the book away. The scriptwriter, A.I. Bezzerides, did a marvelous job, contributing a great deal of inventiveness to the picture. That devilish box, for example—an obvious atom bomb symbol—was mostly his idea. We worked a long time to get the sound it made, the ticking and hissing. We finally used the sound of an airplane exhaust overdubbed with the sound made by human vocal cords when someone breathes out noisily, so that it became a subdued 'jet roar,' a sonic box type of thing."

"This is lousy.... I have to write something else," Bezzerides told Aldrich after reading *Kiss Me Deadly*. "So I went to work on it. I wrote it fast, because I had contempt for it. It was automatic writing. You get into a kind of stream and you can't stop. I get into psychic isolation sometimes when I'm writing."

The final Bezzerides script took an estimated three weeks to complete, during which the highly involved writer toiled night and day. What resulted was an adaptation of the natural brutality and nihilism of staple Spillane character Mike Hammer into the environment of a frightened nation during the height of McCarthy Cold War America. "I just heightened his (Hammer's) natural violence," Bezzerides explained. "I tell you, Spillane didn't like what I did with his book. I ran into him in a restaurant and, boy, he didn't like me."

PLOT QUICKLY ESTABLISHED

The film's inventiveness is quickly displayed by the credits being presented in an inverted manner, with viewers observing in an upward sweep. Ralph Meeker as Mike Hammer is driving in his swift, sleek sports car down a dark, deserted road. He quickly observes a figure in the distance. A beautiful blonde woman stands in the middle of the road wearing nothing but a trench coat. He is compelled to stop on a dime to avoid killing her, and does.

The sweep of activity reveals a good deal about the film and its characters. While most drivers would be extremely rattled by what Hammer has just experienced, what emerges is more of a gut curiosity than a hectic state. Hammer is a creature of his modern world, to which his sleek sports car bears testimony, but his unflappable nature coincides with his nihilistic side. He remains unflappable whatever the situation, even in exceptionally violent settings.

Hammer's surprise passenger is Cloris Leachman, making her film debut. A former Miss Chicago and runner-up in the Miss America Pageant, she would even-

Ralph Meeker, playing Mickey Spillane's two-fisted detective Mike Hammer in the 1955 release, *Kiss Me Deadly*, directed by Robert Aldrich, is cautioned by police detective Pat Chambers, played by Wesley Addy, along with secretary and lover Velda, played by Maxine Cooper, that he is getting in over his head in trying to bring down a powerful gang headed by a mad scientist played by Albert Dekker. This film appeared the same year as Robert Aldrich's hard-hitting expose of the Hollywood star system, *The Big Knife*, starring Jack Palance and Ida Lupino.

tually garner an Oscar for Best Supporting Actress in *The Last Picture Show* (1971). Meeker as Hammer has on his car radio, having listened to a rendition of Nat "King" Cole singing "Rather Have the Blues" before Leachman's appearance. He hears an announcement that a young woman has escaped from the local mental institution. The detective promptly covers for her when they are stopped by police, who are looking for the escapee, convincing them that she is his wife.

The dialogue between Meeker and Leachman reveals a lot about both of them. Leachman quickly pegs Meeker. She displays a liking for poetry, particularly the sonnets of Gabriella Rossetti, correctly ascertaining that Meeker would not be a poetry devotee. Leachman notes an absence of sensitivity, which would make him less open to mental communion with women. "You're self-indulgent," she notes. He does not dispute her analysis.

When Meeker pulls to a stop at a gas station, Leachman reveals more about her mystique, arousing his detective's curiosity. She hands a letter to the young gas station attendant and stresses the importance of mailing it. The station is located in Calabassas, situated just some two blocks west of the dividing line between it and Woodland Hills, where the Motion Picture Country Home is located.

There is a roadblock not far ahead, occurring just after Leachman's instruction as to where she wishes to be dropped off when they reach the San Fernando Valley. A gang of syndicate goons emerge, overpowering Meeker. In his groggy state, he observes a screaming Leachman hanging from the end of a rope by her neck. It is lights out for Leachman and almost for Meeker, as his sports car is pushed down a canyon with him still inside.

PLUNGED INTO ANOTHER WORLD

When Meeker barely escapes with his life after dangling on the precipice of death in critical condition, he receives a surprise which is linked to the mysterious stranger Leachman. A local Los Angeles detective, he is stunned to discover that the Interstate Crime Commission wants to speak with him. His meeting with them seated at a large table details much about his manner of making a living.

The term *unflappable* was earlier used to describe the rugged and nihilistic detective. It served him well in his meeting with the prominent crime commission members. With Meeker sitting silently, a commission member details information from his professional life, which is far from admirable. Meeker is described as a private detective who uses his attractive secretary as bait in divorce actions. The member explains that the secretary is employed to bait married men into affairs to provide ammunition for the wives who hire Meeker. When a curious member asks what happens when the reverse is the case, and a husband is seeking ammunition to use against a wife, he is informed that, in those situations, the detective himself seeks to draw the wives into extracurricular activity.

The commission member delivering the report as well as those listening intently display an overarching contempt for Meeker. Under identical circumstances, others might display great embarrassment for an obvious dressing-down from a high-level law enforcement agency. The detective responds with no more than a perfunctory sentence delivered in a bored monotone, "Okay, so I'm a stinker."

After Meeker is dismissed and he leaves the room, a commission member reveals his low regard for the detective and his business ethics with the cryptic comment, "Open a window." They appear as surprised as Meeker to discover that he has stumbled into a situation with such grave national and, as we will later learn, possible international ramifications.

Meeker's affluent apartment and elegant modern furnishings indicate that, while he is a neanderthal on the basic level, he is very much at home in modern society and knows how to live well. It is learned that he has a Crestview prefix and lives on Wilshire Boulevard, meaning an impressive Beverly Hills address for a detective who is nothing more than a successful domestic relations bedroom shakedown artist. His comely brunette secretary, Velda, played by Maxine Cooper, is leery about her lover moving out of his element into an unknown sinister world. "Keep away from the windows," she warns him at one point. "Someone might blow you a kiss."

A new innovation, which Bezzerides, a former engineer, inserts into the film, is a telephone answering machine, the first time the idea had been introduced on-screen. Making use of it is mad scientist Dekker, who issues a blunt warning to the detective to forget all about the meeting with Leachman or more violence will ensue.

Searching for Whatsit

What propels *Kiss Me Deadly* above the ranks of a regular film noir detective thriller is the Armageddon allegory inventively generated by Bezzerides and executed by Aldrich. Meeker's secretary and lover, Maxine Cooper, refers to the destructive atomic device as a "whatsit." While Meeker as a nihilistic detective is far from the kind of politically committed figure to dedicate himself to the proposition of finding the elusive device and solving the mystery behind Leachman's murder and the nearly successful effort to extinguish him, his makeup adds to the allegorical context of the story in an important way. His brutal preoccupation to find the truth is pitted against the murky world of global Cold War politics.

The Bezzerides allegory rests on the following foundation:

1) A destructive device which a mad scientist seeks to keep at all costs.

2) The determined countervailing force represented by Meeker as Mike Hammer, which could be said to represent society, unaware of the frightening potentials to be unharnessed and determined to prevent a cataclysmic Armageddon.

3) The dramatic interplay between the nihilistic and the orderly, between the realm of the known, which is kept secretive, and that of the curious unknown. An element used in the film to provide contrast is the playing of classical music in what would appear to be incongruous moments. As Meeker deals out pain to those holding out on supplying information, or as he is considering violent action, we are reminded of an orderly world of serenity and blissful knowledge through the playing of works by classical musical masters. Maxine Cooper exercises her trim figure to Strauss waltzes to retain the allure for potentially straying husbands, order contrasted with disorder.

4) Mike Hammer as contrasting symbols of balance and imbalance. Meeker plays Hammer as totally unflappable, a man who can shift gears even faster than his super speedy sports car. He lives in a fashionable apartment on Wilshire Boulevard in Beverly Hills with fine appointments, even including a telephone answering machine, an early scientific innovation. When the classical music is playing, one would conclude that the apartment's inhabitant is a mild-mannered, successful professional. We know how his income is derived and how his meeting with the Interstate Crime Commission ended with the comment, "Open the window," a succinct

manifestation of contempt by high-echelon crime fighters who are against everything Hammer represents. Their attitude is contrasted with the total absence of embarrassment or concern on Hammer's part when the bill of particulars is read concerning his unsavory means of livelihood.

While Hammer lives in an affluent apartment, he spends much of his time in the netherworld of Los Angeles, the shadowy hovels of small, dingy hotels. He never changes expression. The contrast is accepted, and he remains stony-faced and determined to obtain the information needed to help him crack his case. When he moves from passive to violent, there is not so much as a scowl or a raised tone of voice, only a tinge of impatient irritation. His swift acts of violence make any conversation superfluous. Those standing in his way know he means business, and to flout his objectives will be damaging, if not deadly. Through it all, he remains the man wearing the iron mask, the nihilist from the atomic age.

ANOTHER KILLING AND A KIDNAPPING

Meeker's code of justice, which exists despite the unsavory way he makes his living, is deeply aroused by the brutal killing of Cloris Leachman, though he only knew her for the last few minutes of her life. Two other events increase his relentless determination to resolve the mystery surrounding the mad scientist and the whatsit he values above everything.

The other friend and companion to the solitary private eye in addition to his secretary and lover, Maxine Cooper, is his mechanic Nick, played by Nick Dennis, who also assists him in his detective pursuits when asked. Dennis came to Hollywood to assume the same role he played on Broadway in the powerful Tennessee Williams drama directed by Elia Kazan, *A Streetcar Named Desire* (1951). He reprised the role of Marlon Brando's pal. Dennis plays a spirited Greek who enjoys imitating the sound of powerful automobile engines. After Meeker requests some snooping into the mad scientist case, Dennis is killed when a jack is removed and a car on which he is working crashes headlong into his body.

Incensed by the murder of his friend, Meeker finds additional motivation to hate the mad scientist after Maxine Cooper is kidnapped. The implosion of tragic events turns him into a whirling dervish of vengeance, albeit one with an icily calm exterior.

DETERMINED NOIR PURSUIT

Robert Aldrich in capable tandem with cameraman Ernest Laszlo combine to etch arresting noir portraits as Meeker doggedly pursues leads into the mad scientist and the destructive instrumentality he is determined to retain. Much of the action occurs in a lower middle-class section several blocks west of the heart of downtown Los Angeles, which was immortalized in literature by Raymond Chandler and mentioned in the earlier discussion of *Criss Cross*. This fascinating area is Bunker Hill, reachable by a trolley ride uphill from Third and Hill streets. The trolley line was called Angels Flight, the world's shortest railroad, which consisted of two cars. It was initially destroyed in 1969. Recently the tracks which had been destroyed were rebuilt, and activity recommenced.

The Bunker Hill that was exploited in mystery stories and noir films consisted of small, dilapidated hotels and apartment buildings, where individuals went in search of at least temporary anonymity, frequently due to fear of exposure from criminal activity. In the best noir tradition, the Aldrich-Laszlo tandem provides a voyeuristic look into the bleak world of people on the run living in dimly lit hotel rooms. As Meeker enters the ramshackle buildings, Laszlo shoots from above, providing dramatic angular down sweeps of a dark netherworld gone haywire. The approach is reminiscent of that of director Carol Reed and cinematographer Robert Krasker in *The Third Man* (1949), in which the intent of shooting at angles was meant to convey that something crooked was going on in post-war Vienna.

Meeker's imperturbable determination is evidenced at its most nihilistically cool and convincing as he visits an Italian opera lover who lives in a small hotel, with downtown Los Angeles observable below from the window. Classic opera is playing from the Italian's record player. When the man informs Meeker that he cannot help him with his inquiry, the detective calmly picks up a record and exclaims, "*Pagliacci* with (Enrico) Caruso! A valuable recording!" Before the Italian can do anymore than register quick assent, Meeker calmly breaks the record in two with his bare hands. The point is made. If cooperation is not quickly forthcoming, more violent behavior will quickly ensue. As answers are supplied, Meeker calmly walks over to the kitchen area, where a pot of pasta is simmering. The detective picks up a cooking spoon and helps himself.

Violence constantly follows Meeker as the battle of wits between scientist Dekker and the detective continues. On one occasion, his sports car is almost blown up. On another, after parking on the edge of downtown L.A. near the Mayflower Hotel, a man follows him in the darkness. Meeker stops at a corner and buys a bag of popcorn, continuing to walk. When the man stealthily approaches, ready to strike, Meeker wheels around and uses the popcorn as a surprise weapon, hurling it into the thug's face, then pummeling him and throwing him down a flight of concrete steps.

UNTAMED WOMEN AND THUGS

Noir stories frequently contain an interesting mix of untamed women and thugs. In the former category, Aldrich scored casting coups as four newcomers making their cinema debuts perform impressively. Two, Leachman and Cooper, have been mentioned. Completing the quartet are Gaby Rodgers and Leigh Snowden.

Rodgers is one of the pivotal figures of the drama. Masquerading as the roommate of the deceased Leachman, Meeker finds her in a bleak Bunker Hill hotel, expressing fear that she will meet the same fate as her friend. Meeker takes a liking to her and puts her up at his apartment for safety reasons, not realizing until informed by a police detective that Leachman's roommate had been killed by Dekker's gang and that Rodgers is none other than his mistress, selected to keep track of his actions. Despite his penchant for thinking quickly on his feet and ability to handle himself in violent situations, the detective remains all too fallible.

Snowden provides some needed comedic relief in the film. A beautiful nymphomaniac, she meets Meeker when he arrives at the palatial Beverly Hills estate of mobster Carl Evello, played by veteran character actor Paul Stewart. As Meeker enters the sprawling backyard area, Snowden jumps up from her chaise lounge next to the swimming pool and moves quickly toward him. After presenting a solid welcoming kiss, the sexy blonde delivers the memorable line, "You don't taste like anybody I know." Meeker remains as stolid in the face of impellent female attention as he does in response to violence. He even cautions her that she should be careful about expressing herself in such a robustly physical manner to just anybody.

When the brief kissing interlude with Snowden ends, Meeker goes back to work, entering the cabana behind the pool and snooping around. This draws the immediate attention of Stewart's forceful lieutenants, played by two notable film heavies named Jack, Lambert and Elam. Meeker's appearance at Stewart's estate is preceded by a scene in which Lambert and Elam are mentioned by an old contact of the detective's, a boxing manager. The meeting is the dramatic setting of Main Street Gym, where champions from Joe Louis to Muhammad Ali trained. Aldrich uses its effective ambience as Meeker is seen climbing the dusty stairs leading into the interior of the old building. When the manager gloats, confidently suggesting that Meeker wager money on his boxer, who is warming up prior to a major bout the following night, Meeker says bitingly, "Aren't you gonna sell him out like all the others?" When the manager answers in the negative, Meeker sarcastically intones, "You'd sell the gold in your mother's teeth."

Lambert and Elam are mentioned apprehensively by the manager. Meeker is there to quiz him about the murder of a former fighter, Kowalski, believed to know a great deal about Dekker's motivations. The manager grimly tells about the visit of the two toughs. "They said they were making me an offer I couldn't refuse." When Meeker inquires further, the manager explains, "They said they would let me breathe." The scene in the dusty old gym, sparked by crisply effective noir dialogue by Bezzerides, is one of the most evocative of the film relating to the genre.

When Meeker begins snooping on his own in the cabana, the inevitable confrontation occurs. Jack Lambert will be remembered as one of Albert Dekker's henchmen in *The Killers*. He is involved in the film's final climactic shootout, in which Lambert and Dekker both die.

Elam, one of the most natural-looking criminal types ever to appear in films and television, graduated from Santa Monica City College and worked successfully as an accountant following the war, numbering several important Hollywood stars among his clients. Having lost one eye in a childhood fight, which enhanced his unforgettably grim appearance, he feared that the demands of his profession could lead to the loss of his good eye. His swarthy visage, merciless glare, and wiry muscular construction prompted his film contacts to suggest he try acting. He made his screen debut in 1949 and worked steadily through the mid-nineties, when he was approaching the 80 mark. Elam had appeared one year earlier with Aldrich in *Vera Cruz*, a Western starring Burt Lancaster and Gary Cooper. He was also in Fritz Lang's offbeat western, *Rancho Notorious*, discussed earlier. The appearance as a contemporary villain in *Kiss Me Deadly* was less characteristic than the frequent activity he found in Westerns, including one comedic role in the 1969 Western spoof, *Support Your Local Sheriff!*, starring James Garner.

Lambert steps into the cabana first, intent on subduing Meeker. When he is quickly knocked unconscious for a period of two hours by a swift move from the ruthless detective, a wary Elam stares at Meeker with disbelief, moving away toward the pool area, electing not to do battle.

CODE OF HONOR

Meeker's explosive action in the cabana impresses Stewart. The two commence a serious discussion inside the mansion. The white-haired Stewart, frequently cast as a heavy, was more familiar in the role of a distinguished mob boss with brains who doles out the orders to the likes of a Lambert or Elam. The New York-born actor was already a young veteran when he joined Orson Welles's prestigious Mercury Theater group in 1938. He was one of the performers in the unforgettable radio drama adaptation of H.G. Wells's *War of the Worlds* and launched his film career in what has been termed by many the greatest film ever made, the powerful 1941 drama, *Citizen Kane*, starring, produced and directed by Orson Welles.

As a suave syndicate boss, it is no surprise when Stewart tempts Meeker to change sides and come over to the Dekker team. Meeker follows a tradition of detectives embracing a code of honor dating back to the first acknowledged film noir drama, John Huston's *The Maltese Falcon*. As the film moved to its dramatic conclusion, Humphrey Bogart, cast as Dashiell Hammet's famous detective, Sam Spade, had solved the murder of his partner, Jerome Cowan. He was tortured by the knowledge that the woman he had fallen in love with, his client, played by the aristocratically beautiful Mary Astor, had killed Cowan. She implored him not to turn her into the police, citing his love for her. Bogart reasoned that, even though he loved Astor and disliked Cowan that, "When someone kills your partner you're expected to do something about it."

Meeker followed identical reasoning after Stewart tempted him. Dekker had crossed the line with his conduct. Despite the fact that Meeker performed unethical services to make a living, seeking to tempt spouses toward disloyalty against their

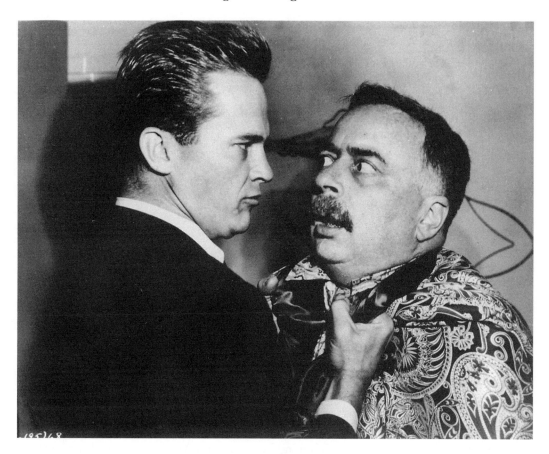

Detective Mike Hammer has tracked down art museum proprietor William Mist in a stirring scene from *Kiss Me Deadly*, but will be unable to extract any comment. In one of the most unusual scenes in film noir annals, Mist, anticipating Hammer's visit, has swallowed a fistful of sleeping pills and is already beginning to doze off as the determined detective confronts him. *Kiss Me Deadly* provided the one and only opportunity for Ralph Meeker, whose portrayal of Hammer received solid plaudits, to display his true greatness before the cameras. On stage he followed Marlon Brando in the lead of Tennessee Williams's dramatic classic, *A Streetcar Named Desire*. He followed that up by playing the male lead opposite Janice Rule in the Broadway production of William Inge's *Picnic*, but was overlooked for the starring role in the film version when Columbia studio head Harry Cohn opted instead for the more bankable William Holden.

mates to strengthen divorce actions, when it came to ruthless murder, he was not about to walk away from a steady path toward seeking resolution, despite the dangers involved and economic benefits to be obtained by joining the other side.

AN APOCALYPTIC RESOLUTION

Meeker is finally captured by Dekker's forces, beaten and pistol-whipped by Lambert and Elam, then taken to the Malibu beach cottage of the mad scientist located by the ocean's waters on the Pacific Coast Highway. Dekker implores him to assist his efforts, explaining that even though Meeker is ticketed for death, his secretary's life will be spared. In an attempt to coax information from Meeker, Dekker gives the detective a shot of Pentothal, stating his belief that the truth serum will produce results. Aldrich chooses to reveal Dekker's voice and not show his face until the film's climactic final scene. The camera reveals the mad scientist's black suit, showing a lot of his black shoes, leaving the audience to imagine what he looks like.

While Meeker lies in a semiconscious state in the bedroom, the sound of the television set in the next room can be heard. Sam Balter, longtime L.A. sports announcer, provides running commentary of a boxing match. His comments about the severe punishment one of the boxers is absorbing casts light on the plight of Meeker, who is destined for imminent death.

As Meeker is beginning to come to, Stewart arrives, seeking to obtain cooperation. Meeker asks him to come a little closer and he will whisper vital information to him. A cut is imposed to the next room, where Lambert and Elam sit. Lambert walks into the next room. After hearing a loud sound, Elam investigates, finding Stewart dead and Lambert unconscious. Elam's eyes observe an empty window, out of which Meeker made his escape. The sound of a car revving up is heard as Meeker drives off.

Meeker ultimately finds himself in a race with wily Dekker consort Gaby Rodgers for control of the mysterious box. When the detective returns to his apartment, Rodgers pleads with him to take her along on his fact-hunting foray, revealing that men showed up the night before at the door, and would be back to get her. He makes his critical mistake in taking her with him. An obsessed Meeker obtains the key which will enable him to find the mysterious box by removing it from the coroner, who had taken it out of the deceased Leachman's mouth. When he attempts to blackmail more money out of Meeker than he is willing to pay, the angered detective slams a desk drawer on the coroner's hand, making off with the key as his blackmailer writhes in pain.

A trusting Meeker leaves Rodgers in his car when he goes inside the private men's club with the newly acquired key, his most critical mistake. He is compelled to slap around the desk attendant to gain access to the locker. When he opens the box slightly, a flash of light is emitted and he is burned. Before leaving, Meeker warns the attendant to safeguard the box, realizing the potential danger of its contents.

When Meeker returns to the car, Rodgers has vanished. We soon learn that the mysterious box has been taken. A close-up reveals an open locker and the attendant lying dead next to it.

Finally Meeker learns the identity of a man running an art gallery who is linked to Dekker. After the detective, sensing he is nearing his objective, smashes a window and breaks into the gallery, its proprietor makes a move of his own. As Meeker moves quickly toward the living area adjoining the gallery, the man swallows sleeping pills and falls asleep shortly after Meeker has begun slapping him in his pursuit of answers. As his latest victim snores, Meeker observes the name on the bottle holding the sleeping pills—Dr. Soberin. He telephones the number of his office, where a woman answers, informing him that the doctor is seeing no one at the moment, suggesting that he might try to locate him at his beach cottage. That is all he needs to hear, having an intimate knowledge of the cottage being mentioned.

A MAD SCIENTIST AND *FEMME FATALE* EMERGE

The final scene begins before Meeker arrives. The Bezzerides script misleads the audience by showing Gaby Rodgers from Meeker's viewpoint. By deceiving Meeker, she has also deluded the audience as she parades as a seeming victim conveying a doe-eyed innocence and overt fear over being killed by Dekker's forces. Now we see Rodgers in her true image as a ruthless *femme fatale*. The ploy is unique in that *femmes fatale* are generally revealed long before the film's final scene.

Now that mad scientist Dekker has a name, Dr. Soberin, the audience gets its first full view of him, having previously been restricted to hearing his voice and observing his black suit and matching black shoes. Rodgers emerges as a shrewdly manipulative *femme fatale* who is Dekker's lover as well as partner in crime. Her curiosity alarms him as she asks, "What's in the box?"

Aldrich and Bezzerides finish the allegorical story element with a flourish as Dekker, an actor with prominent stage and film experience who speaks in mellow tones, sounds like a preacher warning of the coming apocalypse. He tells Rodgers that her curiosity can be destructive, mentioning the account of Pandora and the destruction reeked as a result of her overweening curiosity over the contents of a box. He then recounts the Sodom and Gomorrah biblical story and how Lot's wife, in turning back to look at the wicked city being destroyed, was turned into a pillar of salt. When Rodgers persists in her questioning, Dekker waxes allegorical again, mentioning that its contents contain the head of Medusa.

As a ruthless *femme fatale*, the irrepressible Gaby Rodgers is interested in material objects and not allegories from a silver-tongued mad scientist. She sees the box's contents as something of value. Dekker explains that he is going away on a trip and cannot take her with him. She returns to the subject of the box.

"I want half," she declares.

"The object of this box cannot be divided," Dekker responds.

"Then I'll take it all, if you don't mind," Rodgers states with steady resolve.

Rodgers backs up her demand with a revolver.

"Don't open the box," Dekker implores.

The warning represents Dr. Soberin's final words as Rodgers guns him down. At that point, Meeker enters the scene. She trains the gun on him and commands, "Kiss me."

Meeker approaches her diffidently. She fires on the detective, scoring a direct hit. He clutches his stomach and falls to the ground. He watches as she opens the box, letting out a shriek as she experiences pain. The ticking and hissing sounds are heard as the room becomes bathed in intense flashing light.

DOES MIKE HAMMER SURVIVE?

Finally able to make it to his feet, Meeker begins searching for his lover-secretary, calling out, "Velda." When he finds her in a bedroom, she cradles the badly injured Meeker and guides him out the back door. They reach the beach and watch as the ultimate explosion occurs, rocking the beach cottage, which erupts into flames.

The aforementioned finale is the one highlighted in current DVD and VHS versions of *Kiss Me Deadly*. It is followed after a written explanation with the version that was shown predominantly when the film was shown in theaters. In this version, the explosion occurs while Meeker and Cooper are trapped inside the cottage.

Historians, reviewers and interested viewers of *Kiss Me Deadly* speculate on whether Mike Hammer survived. In the earlier predominantly shown version, there is no question that he as well as Velda perish in the explosion and resulting flames. In the version where Hammer makes it outside, with his girlfriend pulling him toward the beach's waters where they watch the apocalyptic cataclysm, the detective is badly slumped over, and from all appearances, Rodgers scored a direct hit in his stomach. It is doubtful if he could have survived such a wound, or whether he could be transported to a hospital emergency room with the prospect of overcoming his wound.

Based on the apocalyptic thrust of Bezzerides's screenplay, the logical symmetrical result would be for Hammer and his secretary to die. Hammer was a major player, as were Leachman, Stewart, Dekker and Rodgers. Death would appear to be the symbolically fitting result for the detective. Due to his secretary's close links to him, her death would appear to befit the directional story structure as well.

In a story replete with symbols, the name of the mad scientist bears scrutiny. Dr. Soberin is close to sober and sobering. Nuclear technology was a truly sobering experience to citizens of the fifties.

DEKKER'S STRANGE END

Albert Dekker's film career in some ways embodied a walk on the wild side, encapsulating the very apocalyptic overtones revealed so graphically in *Kiss Me Deadly*. His starring role which brought him the most attention, *Dr. Cyclops*, revealed a scientific genius gone mad, using his talents for evil purposes. *The Killers* displayed Dekker as a cunning mob boss who uses wife Ava Gardner to pull off a sting on his criminal cohorts, enabling him to both walk off with all of the booty as well as humiliate his dreaded enemy and rival for Gardner's affections, Burt Lancaster. Eventually, however, the investigative efforts of Edmond O'Brien cause the brilliant maneuver to be uncovered. Dekker dies a quick death after a gun battle in his home with Jack Lambert, who also tastes death. The third tier of the Dekker cinema apocalypse occurs with his demise in *Kiss Me Deadly*, as he falls victim to the woman, Gaby Rodgers, on whom he felt he could depend.

Albert Dekker's strange demise on May 5, 1968, in his Hollywood apartment, located at 1731 N. Normandie, just north of Hollywood Boulevard, was deemed highly puzzling. He was found in the bathroom of his apartment hanging by his neck at the end of a rope, which was tied to the shower curtain rod. The rope, knotted tightly around his neck, was also wrapped around both of his legs and one of his arms. His hands were bound with a pair of handcuffs while two hypodermic needles were stuck in his body. Obscenities were scrawled all over the corpse, at one point leading some to conclude that the actor might have been killed in the course of rough sex. Police originally listed his peculiarly grotesque death as a suicide. Several days later, the L.A. County Coroner's Office ruled Dekker's death to be "accidental." The accompanying statement indicated, "We have no information that Mr. Dekker planned to take his own life."

According to movie historian Ken Schlessler, "Dekker left a bizarre trail of death behind him – over 20 actors and actresses who had appeared in movies with him, died tragic deaths, either by suicide, murder or unusual circumstances. His only son committed suicide in 1957, and his girlfriend's daughter killed herself."

Dekker could readily relate to the Cold War fifties' allegorical symbolism pervading Bezzerides's clever script. A political activist, Dekker was elected to the California State Assembly in 1944, serving his Hollywood district. As the fifties beckoned, the actor spoke out emphatically against the excesses of Senator Joseph McCarthy. In doing so, he suffered the consequences of many others in the film community, difficulty in locating work. He resolved the problem by returning to the venue where he had performed prior to moving west to Hollywood, the Broadway stage. Dekker had launched his Broadway career years earlier by performing in Eugene O'Neill's *Marco's Millions*. The New York stage offered the actor, who performed in over 100 films, an opportunity to gain employment when movie roles were more difficult to obtain.

HARD-LUCK ACTOR

The good news for leading man Ralph Meeker was that Aldrich in *Kiss Me Deadly* gave the Northwestern University graduate and Broadway star an opportunity to showcase his uniquely physical talent, that of a volcano ready to explode through the exertion of inward tension. The bad news was that this was the one and only opportunity, playing macho Mickey Spillane detective Mike Hammer, that Meeker had to appear in such a favorable vehicle.

Meeker arrived on Broadway as the Method school of acting was beginning to take hold. His first role was as Stanley Kowalski in *A Streetcar Named Desire*, taking over from Marlon Brando. Some felt that he came closer to fulfilling the image of playwright Tennessee Williams's hot-blooded lead character than Brando. He assumed the lead in another role calling for a dynamic physical presence as he played the role of ex-college football star and roustabout Hal Caner in William Inge's *Picnic*, playing opposite Paul Newman, who was cast in the role of his former collegiate friend Alan. In the case of *Streetcar*, the actor who preceded him in the Broadway role, Marlon Brando, surged to film stardom as Stanley Kowalski. When it came time to cast the coveted role of Hal in the film, Columbia boss Harry Cohn bypassed Meeker for William Holden. Two reasons loom large. Holden was a more bankable commodity bearing a screen name. Also, with the role of Madge going to Kim Novak, the voluptuous blonde Cohn intended to assume the role of studio goddess Rita Hayworth, the studio boss was more than likely hedging his bets by placing a semi-veteran Hollywood leading man opposite a promising performer with only a few roles under her belt.

Early in his film career, Meeker received an opportunity to play a role suited to his physical style, appearing as a boxer in the Raoul Walsh 1952 release, *Glory Alley*, which also featured the jazz music of Jack Teagarden and others, reflective of the movie's New Orleans setting. Not long after his triumph in *Kiss Me Deadly*, Meeker was tapped by director Stanley Kubrick to perform in the sensitive role of a condemned army private in the highly acclaimed *Paths of Glory*. In 1959 he starred as army investigator Steve Dekker in the television series *Not for Hire*.

Aldrich's deft director's hand was at work in his skilled use of no less than four lovely actresses making their film debuts, each performing in a tailored setting different from the others. Cloris Leachman was believable and engrossing as a young woman who escapes from a mental institution, but turns out to be anything but mentally troubled, and is instead the victim of the ruthless Dekker-Stewart syndicate. Maxine Cooper is appropriately sexy and efficient as Meeker's secretary-love interest, not necessarily in that order, while Gaby Rodgers is superb in her role as someone purporting to be in mortal danger who ultimately turns into a conniving *femme fatale*, fooling both Meeker and Dekker. The performance of Leigh Snowden as a seductive blonde nymphomaniac served as a needed smooth touch of comic relief in a highly serious film, playing her heated aggressiveness against the coolness of unflappable detective Meeker.

In many respects, *Kiss Me Deadly* was a Greek tragedy rich in allegory transported to the ideological exigencies of the fifties' nuclear age. The concern over the prospect of impending destruction is articulately voiced by the police detective who is there to greet Meeker when he exits the hospital after his brush with death early in the picture after meeting the ill-fated Cloris Leachman. Wesley Addy exhibits disgust with Meeker over his lone wolf investigating tactics, occurring outside the ambit of the police. Addy, cast as Pat Chambers, replies to a colleague who asks what should be done with the recalcitrant Meeker. He responds with blunt anger,

"Let him go to hell!" The film ends for Meeker in a modern version of a flame-filled hell replete with intense light along with hissing and ticking sounds. Addy spells out for Meeker why he should have left the investigating to the authorities, revealing the ominous names of the Manhattan Project, Los Alamos and Trinity.

The nihilistic, hard-headed Meeker as Mike Hammer symbolically reflected an overwhelmed public helpless to deal with the destructive advent of modern science and its potential for an apocalyptic Armageddon cataclysm. Any semblance of order was ultimately supplanted by greedy nihilism and the crushing finality of nuclear destruction.

SEVEN

Kubrick's Ticket
to the Big Time

What's the difference?

The Killing (1956)

"What's the difference?" Johnny Clay asks fatalistically. With shrugging acceptance he watches as two plainclothes officers walk slowly toward him at Fadeout. His fiancée Fay stands next to him, knowing that the fate she had previously hated and feared a repetition of awaits her again—loneliness.

Tall, muscular, sandy-haired Sterling Hayden was ideally cast as a rebel seeking to win but seemingly destined to lose. His convincing role as such a figure in John Huston's noir masterpiece, *The Asphalt Jungle* (1950), made him a perfect candidate for the pivotal character Johnny Clay in *The Killing*, the first major league film triumph of a fresh and dynamic young talent from the East who had come west to direct the low budget heist film.

Stanley Kubrick, from the release of *The Killing* in 1956 until his death in the picturesque town of St. Albans in Hertfordshire, England, just north of London, on March 7, 1999, would command the attention of scores of movie enthusiasts around the world. It took little time for a cult to develop around him. As was the case with Greta Garbo, long associated with the phrase "I want to be alone," the more frequently that Garbo and Kubrick projected propensities toward privacy, the more intense the waves of interest to learn more about them. At a time when Kubrick could have been the toast of Hollywood, he left for England, where he would reside until his death.

The precocious son of a Bronx doctor, Kubrick was born July 26, 1928. Encouraged by his father to take up photography, he became a staff photographer for *Look* magazine at 17, having made an impression through a photograph he took the day President Franklin Delano Roosevelt died. From the outset, he was captivated by movies. While working at *Look*, Kubrick attended film screenings at the Museum

146

of Modern Art. He later said that seeing so many bad films gave him the confidence to do better. "I was aware that I didn't know anything about making films, but I believed I couldn't make them any worse than the majority of films I was seeing," Kubrick once said. "Bad films gave me the courage to try making a movie."

He decided to take the big plunge in 1950. Kubrick quit his job at *Look* and made his first film, a 16-minute documentary, *Day of the Fight*, encompassing the activities of New York middleweight boxer Walter Cartier on the day of combat. He sold the film to RKO-Pathe and his career was launched.

Kubrick did two more documentary shorts before making his feature debut in 1953 with *Fear and Desire*, a low budget film financed with family money, which he wrote, directed, photographed and edited. Following his second feature, the 1955 release *Killer's Kiss*, he formed a production company with producer James B. Harris and optioned rights to a novel that would serve as his springboard to fame. The book was *Clean Break* by Lionel White, the story of a daring racetrack robbery. To enhance Kubrick's screenplay with the kind of tough, succinct edge it needed, crime novelist Jim Thompson was enlisted to provide dialogue and authenticity.

Kubrick's first two features were made with minuscule budgets of about $40,000 each, perhaps making the $320,000 budget of *The Killing* look significant to the 27-year-old filmmaker. It was very tight by major league standards. In the manner of noir craftsmen, he stretched his money by emphasizing cramped spaces, the scenic claustrophobia of the world of darkness, inhabited by losers, a place where the sun will not shine even at high noon. Kubrick later revealed he was influenced by French director Max Ophuls. His camera work was fluid, including many medium setups to include most of the main characters and reinforce the image of the gang involved in the daring heist.

CLUES TO THE FUTURE

The New York Times obituary story by Stephen Holden carried in its headline a reference to Kubrick as "a Film Director with a Bleak Vision." For Kubrick devotees, a careful viewing of *The Killing* is every bit as indispensable as reading *Of Mice and Men* and *The Grapes of Wrath* for John Steinbeck admirers. The bristling cynicism of the characters and situations embodied in *The Killing* alert one to Malcom McDowell warbling "Singin' in the Rain" while delivering a brutal beating in Kubrick's haunting portrayal of sadistic future shock in *A Clockwork Orange* (1971).

Kubrick and producer Harris exercised shrewdness in casting, garnering maximum "bang for bucks" by securing a stellar contingent of character performers who delivered memorable efforts at reasonable cost. A little better than 12% of the overall budget was expended on the lead character, gang leader Johnny Clay, played by veteran performer Sterling Hayden, for $40,000. When James Harris was negotiating for the actor's services, Hayden's agent, who had never heard of the youthful Stanley Kubrick, asked, "Are you sure you're not talking about Stanley Kramer?"

Hayden was in many ways a real-life version of Johnny Clay, an intense loner who valued his privacy. On the allied subjects of privacy and independence, Hayden also had a lot in common with Stanley Kubrick. Born in 1916, Hayden quit school and left his Montclair, New Jersey, roots to become a mate on a schooner. In the manner of Humphrey Bogart, Hayden had a lifelong love for the sea. Unlike Bogart, Hayden never particularly liked the acting life, launching a modeling career as a means of buying his own boat. In 1940 he received Hollywood recognition, being signed that year to a contract by Paramount. He began in starring roles with *Virginia* in 1941 and *Bahama Passage* one year later. While Paramount trumpeted Hayden as a "Blonde Viking God," he married one of the most beautiful blondes in films, British actress Madeleine Carroll.

Following WWII service in the U.S. Marines, Hayden returned to the cinema capital, and his career was re-launched. In 1949 he appeared in a John Wayne western, *El Paso*, and a film noir, *Manhandled*, playing an insurance investigator seeking to locate missing jewels. Having accustomed himself to film noir, Hayden's career took a quantum leap the following year.

THE BURNETT TRIO

The Asphalt Jungle has been referred to by many as a high budget *The Killing*. The basic story premise is the same for each film, a lifelong quest for the gold ring by a team of life's losers intent on changing things through one daring robbery. John Huston, who launched his directing career with what has been classified by cinema historians as the first noir triumph, *The Maltese Falcon*, collaborated for a second time with his writing partner from *High Sierra*, W.R. Burnett. Novelist Burnett had three of his works adapted to the screen in respective decades, with *Little Caesar*, a Mervyn LeRoy triumph in 1930, in which Edward G. Robinson delivered an unforgettable performance as a mobster, and Raoul Walsh's *High Sierra*, in which Humphrey Bogart stars as a holdup artist on the run. *Asphalt Jungle* completed the three-decade cycle with its 1950 release. Huston and Ben Maddow crafted the Burnett novel into screenplay form. Huston won the New York Film Critics Circle Award as Best Director while the movie triumphed in the Best Film category. Distinguished character actor Sam Jaffe, earlier mentioned as the longtime agent of Humphrey Bogart, won in the Best Actor category at the Venice Film Festival. *Asphalt Jungle* also copped Best Film honors at the British Academy Awards.

In the manner of *The Killing*, *Asphalt Jungle* is a probing study of a group of people revealing their inner selves against the backdrop of a tense robbery that will make them rich or break them. The group converges on Cincinnati for the big caper. Sam Jaffe is the brains of the operation, the organizer, a master criminal recently paroled from prison. Louis Calhern is a crooked attorney who will act as fence once that the jewels are acquired, agreeing to pay Jaffe and cohorts a cool million dollars. Sterling Hayden plays an impoverished hood hoping his cut of the robbery will enable him to buy back his father's Kentucky horse ranch. James Whitmore is a tough-as-nails professional thief who runs a diner. He agrees to assist safecracker Anthony Caruso in the heist as his driver. Marc Lawrence is a nervous bookie who doles out cash for the operation at Calhern's behest. Hayden notices Lawrence's profuse sweating as he counts out bills, inquiring about it. Lawrence replies, "I always sweat when I handle money."

While in *The Killing*, the robbery initially succeeds with a double cross and shootout ultimately foiling a well-planned effort, in *The Asphalt Jungle*, a security guard is able to wound Caruso after he has blown the safe open. He is rushed home by Whitmore and dies in front of his sobbing Italian family.

Lawrence, who sweats when he counts money, appears to be a weak link and is, cracking under the interrogation and ultimate beating by corrupt cop Barry Kelley, who has been extorting money from him and is angry over being left out of the caper. The effort produces results, as the hapless Lawrence reveals the facts and principals involved in the theft.

The operation then becomes thoroughly unglued. While the police are en route to Calhern's home to confront him, Jaffe and Hayden arrive with the stolen gems, demanding their money. They are received by Calhern and private detective accomplice Brad Dexter. Calhern does not have the money, having squandered it on a stylish blonde mistress, played by Marilyn Monroe in her first major dramatic effort. A gun battle ensues as Dexter is killed and Hayden wounded. Hayden urges Jaffe to flee, doing so himself.

The police arrive at Calhern's and begin interrogating him. He excuses himself momentarily, stepping into another room and blowing his brains out.

All principals suffer an ill fate. Whitmore is arrested and the dragnet closes on Jaffe. The irony is that the brainy planner is undone by his libido as he tarries too long watching a buxom teenager jitterbugging in front of a jukebox, foiling his opportunity to escape to Cleveland with the help of a cab driver as he is promptly arrested.

A critically wounded Hayden is the final gang member at large, gaining extended freedom in the midst of rapidly diminishing life. With his longtime mistress Jean Hagen at his side, he drives furiously toward Kentucky and the ranch of his father he fervently desired to acquire. By the time he reaches it, he is delirious, collapsing and dying as he staggers through the gate.

CONSPICUOUS PARALLELS

The Killing and *The Asphalt Jungle* are excellently plotted noir gems with conspicuous story parallels:

1) A group of outsiders, in many respects life's losers, drawn together in a common enterprise, a daring robbery, which will catapult them sharply upward to a new economic status.

2) A leader who has recently left prison, a hardened criminal of great experience, Sterling Hayden in *The Killing* and Sam Jaffe in *The Asphalt Jungle*.

3) The presence of a moneyman stating a willingness to stake the operation, with Jay C. Flippen a solid presence in *The Killing* and Louis Calhern problematical as he fails to come through in *The Asphalt Jungle*.

4) A weak link whose untimely release of information foils the enterprise, Elisha Cook Jr. in *The Killing* and Marc Lawrence in *The Asphalt Jungle*.

5) A crooked police officer, Ted de Corsia in *The Killing* and Barry Kelley in *The Asphalt Jungle*.

6) Fatal shootouts, two in *The Asphalt Jungle* and one in *The Killing*, which proves so fatal that it eliminates all gang members and double-crossers with the exception of lone survivor Hayden, who surrenders in fatalistic fashion.

7) Women who foil the enterprise, Marilyn Monroe in *The Asphalt Jungle*, whose high living breaks attorney Louis Calhern so he is unable to honor his part of the bargain, and Marie Windsor in *The Killing*, who treacherously undercuts husband Elisha Cook Jr. by revealing details of the robbery to boyfriend Vince Edwards.

8) Two long-suffering women looking for stability, both with Sterling Hayden, Coleen Gray in *The Killing* and Jean Hagen in *The Asphalt Jungle*.

The aforementioned similarities encompass a solid blueprint for a noir heist story with Sterling Hayden occupying pivotal positions in each film. In *The Killing*, he is the brains of the operation, while in *The Asphalt Jungle*, he functions as a hapless gun toter looking for money to buy his father's ranch. His loner image in *The Killing* was not only taken from real life but also sharpened considerably two years earlier in Nicholas Ray's symbol-loaded Western, *Johnny Guitar*, opposite Joan Crawford.

A major element of *The Killing* was that the team Hayden assembled to rob a racetrack on the day of its biggest race was a group of forlorn figures outside the mainstream of criminal enterprise. Hayden combs the ranks of the professionals only to secure freelance services in two vital areas he will not trust to amateurs, and those individuals are paid only for their specialized jobs and told nothing about the theft they are aiding.

A Perfect Team

One important quality that separates top directors from the rest of the pack is the ability to intelligently cast parts. One of the most familiar faces in gangster film folklore is that of Elisha Cook Jr. Born into a show business family in San Francisco, Cook was performing in vaudeville and stock by the time he was 14. The big-eyed, forlorn expression he carried made him perfect for vulnerable types. He will be remembered as the member of Sydney Greenstreet's colorful entourage who is slapped around and belittled as "the gunsel" by Humphrey Bogart in *The Maltese Falcon*. At film's end, obscure desk clerk Cook is revealed as the murderer of Carole Landis in *I Wake Up Screaming* (1941). In Robert Siodmak's *Phantom Lady* (1944), Cook plays a hard-luck drummer who is seduced by Ella Raines for information, then brutally strangled by serial killer Franchot Tone. Appearing opposite Bogart again in *The Big Sleep*, he evokes sympathy as a murder victim of professional executioner Bob Steele. More sympathy is evoked as he is victimized by another expert gunman, Jack Palance, in George Stevens's Western classic, *Shane* (1953), starring Alan Ladd.

Kubrick provided Cook with a role of great substance and meaning in *The Killing* as henpecked husband George Peatty. Those huge pleading eyes continued to get him cast as a long-suffering victim type, particularly within the dramatic scheme of a gangster film, but now that he had acquired some maturity, adding lines of care in his face, he was no longer the seemingly eternal youngster of the earlier Cook years. Now he was ready for a role of more complex scope and dimension. Cook's brilliant portrayal is reliant on the carefully orchestrated teamwork involving his ruthless wife Sherry, played with appropriate harshness and treacherous opportunism by Marie Windsor.

Marie Windsor was born Marie Bertelsen on December 11, 1922, in Marysvale, Utah, a farming community of about 200 residents. At 5-9, she was the tallest girl in her class and captain of her high school's basketball team. By the time she was 11, her parents were driving her 30 miles to Richfield for drama lessons. In 1939 Windsor entered and won first place in a "Queen of Covered Wagon Days" contest. In Marysvale the chamber of commerce "unofficially" gave Marie that year's "Miss Utah" title. That enabled her to enter and ultimately win the Jesse Lasky Radio Talent Show in Salt Lake City. Her prize in the annual "Gateway to Hollywood" contest was $100.

Marie's parents drove her to Hollywood in 1940. She was interviewed and accepted as a student by prominent Russian character actress and drama coach Maria Ouspenskaya. Her parents returned to Marysvale, and Marie first stayed with family friends, then moved to the famous Hollywood Studio Club, whose other residents included Marilyn Monroe, Donna Reed and Ruth Roman.

Being an expert horsewoman aided Windsor in securing numerous Western roles. Her statuesque demeanor hindered her in obtaining parts opposite some of the industry's shorter leading men. In addition to Westerns, Windsor found a niche in film noir. She played the wife of John Garfield's gangster partner in *Force of Evil*, where she tempts Garfield into an affair but fails.

A major breakthrough role for Windsor came in a low budget RKO vehicle under young director Richard Fleischer in *The Narrow Margin* (1952). She appeared opposite RKO contract player Charles McGraw, who would surge to later fame as Rick, the role made famous by Humphrey Bogart, in the television series version of the Warners film classic *Casablanca* (1942). Windsor plays a tart-tongued woman said to be the widow of a gangster killed by the mob. McGraw is the no-nonsense cop entrusted to deliver her safely by train from Chicago to testify at a grand jury hearing in Los Angeles. Despite his best efforts, Windsor is killed, after which he learns she was actually a police decoy, leaving McGraw with the task of finding the real widow and bringing her to the courthouse safe and sound. Jacqueline White, a woman toward whom McGraw became attracted on the train, turns out to be the actual gangster's widow, shocking the policeman. The low budget RKO gem enabled Fleischer to vault into higher-budget sweepstakes and eventual triumphs such as *The Vikings* (1958), *Compulsion* (1959*)*, *The Boston Strangler* (1968) and *10 Rillington Place* (1970).

Windsor was good-humored about her height costing her roles. In this case, opposite the wiry and diminutive Cook, the contrast was exploited effectively by director Kubrick and his talented veteran cameraman, Lucien Ballard, who had worked early in his career with Joseph von Sternberg, had shot several films with his glamorous actress wife Merle Oberon, and had specialized in lush color Westerns with Henry Hathaway, Sam Peckinpah and Budd Boetticher.

The Kubrick-Ballard chemistry was never better utilized than in an early sequence of the film, just after an important meeting presided over by Hayden, in which Cook had been provided with information concerning the upcoming racetrack heist. Windsor's towering presence, along with the falling shadows and claustrophobic setting of the small living room of a cheerless apartment, conveys the impression of a world closing in on all sides of Cook, being dwarfed by his wife and suffering a hapless fate as an unloved husband. When her vicious tongue lashes out at him repeatedly, meeting each kind and timid comment with a piercing retort, Cook asks in exasperation; "Sherry, why did you ever marry me anyway?" At one point, she says icily, "If people didn't have headaches what would happen to the aspirin business?"

Windsor begins waxing friendly when Cook informs her he is onto something, a deal that will make him rich. Initially she waxes more sarcasm, asking her verbally abused husband if he ordered up his wish at the North Pole. When his steadfastness convinces her that this is no idle talk, her manifestations of kindness prompt him to reveal that he is going to an important meeting that night concerning a racetrack heist. To any detached observer, her kind demeanor would be no more than an effort to obtain information from Cook, reflecting no genuine feeling. The thoroughly frustrated husband, however, filled with inferiority feelings, is a man with a parched throat wandering the desert in search of water. He seeks desperately to believe that the woman hurling tart invective in reality cares for him. When he is not looking, she snoops and discovers the address where the meeting will be held.

The next scene reveals the treacherous nature of Windsor. She arrives at the apartment of her lover, Val Cannon, played by Vince Edwards. The formfitting black, short-sleeved shirt reveals Edwards as a beefcake pursued by a woman in search of sexual thrills. Edwards, who attended Ohio State University on an athletic scholarship before pursuing an acting career, was ideally cast in the hunk-type role he played frequently during that period, before he became famous in the sixties as television's *Doctor Ben Casey*. Windsor, who mistreats as well as cheats on Cook, immediately questions Edwards on why she could not reach him by phone

one evening earlier. "I guess I was goofing off at a movie," he responds flippantly. He concedes, "I step out once in awhile." Windsor presses her point, explaining she wants an exclusive relationship. Initially Edwards balks, but becomes increasingly attentive when the *femme fatale* begins telling him about her husband being involved in a potentially big-money operation. "That meatball?" Edwards asks incredulously. When Windsor explains the plan for a racetrack robbery, Edwards exclaims, "That's crazy! It's never been done before!" Those were the same ominous words delivered frequently in *Criss Cross*. As Windsor reveals more and more, Edwards becomes increasingly interested.

Edwards demonstrates an even more greedy nature than Windsor. While she plots to get Cook's share of the proposed job away from him, whereupon she can live happily thereafter with Edwards, he sees the big picture. Cook will only be receiving a portion of what figures to be a huge payoff. He urges Windsor to find out more so he can undercut the fortune seekers and rob them of their entire booty.

AFFECTION FOR JOHNNY

Sterling Hayden as Johnny Clay lacks the sadistic cruelty or wise guy demeanor demonstrated by many criminal types, such as Edwards's Val Cannon. He resembles a gentle giant on the one hand, a man of engaging sensitivity, while additionally inspiring confidence as a take-charge individual who knows his way around. One derives the feeling that, had a few breaks gone in a different direction, he might well be heading his own company rather than scrapping for an existence in the underworld.

Two characters in the film hold profound love and admiration for Johnny Clay, seeking different types of relationships with him. Jay C. Flippen, who performed brilliantly in *They Live by Night*, plays Marvin Unger, a bookkeeper with the opportunity to secure the payoff money needed to give Johnny's scheme viability. A lonely, solitary figure who lives in a small, dark apartment on Olive Street in a run-down section of downtown Los Angeles, Unger has worked at the same boring job for 10 drab years and loves Johnny Clay like a son, admiring his resourceful confidence and desire to get ahead.

Flippen has provided Hayden with a key to his apartment and permits it to be used as the gang's meeting place. Shortly before the meeting, Hayden puts the apartment to use for lovemaking with Fay, his girl extending back to his youth, played by Coleen Gray. In 1947, the slender brunette, while under contract at Twentieth Century Fox, had the female lead in *Kiss of Death* and received tributes as the honest and faithful girlfriend of shifty con artist Tyrone Power in the highly acclaimed 1947 noir film directed by Edmund Goulding, *Nightmare Alley*. Gray's expressive eyes conveyed a sincerity of purpose and vulnerability that made her perfectly cast as the fearful, highly dependent girlfriend of Hayden in *The Killing*. Gray recently commented on director Kubrick and her role in the film.

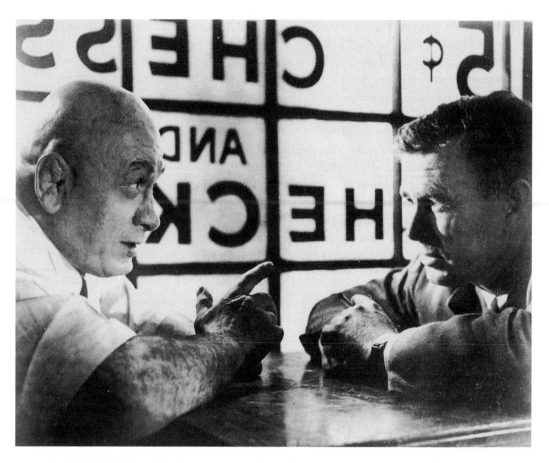

Sterling Hayden, right, plays a role similar to the one he had six years earlier in John Huston's *The Asphalt Jungle*, that of a criminal hoping to hit the big time with one big heist,
in Stanley Kubrick's *The Killing*. He is seen enlisting the help of strong-arm man Kola
Kwariani, whose job will be to start a fight and distract attention so that Hayden can rob
a major racetrack of its cash earnings on the day of its biggest race. Kwariani, a professional wrestler, was a chess-playing friend of Kubrick's. The success of the low budget
sleeper propelled Kubrick, then in his late twenties, into filmdom's top ranks.

"He was this small man wearing army fatigues and clodhopper shoes, and had
bushy hair and was very quiet" Gray recalled. "I kept waiting for him to direct and
nothing happened. 'When's he going to tell me what to do?' He never did, which
made me insecure. He seemed extremely preoccupied. Maybe the fact that I felt insecure was fine for the part—that girl *was* insecure."

Gray's Fay was insecure, and Kubrick's directorial instincts more than likely told
him he needed to do nothing with the talented actress, who was investing the kind
of clinging dependence into her role, which was needed. After their lovemaking,
Gray expresses her feeling for Hayden, empathizing with the painful frustration he
bore while doing a five-year prison stretch at Alcatraz. She tells Hayden soulfully
that she has always followed him "from the time we were kids." Gray explains how

difficult it had been away from him during his prison stretch. As the camera closes in on her, Fay reveals her insecurity: "I'm not good for anybody else. I'm not very pretty and not very smart so don't leave me alone again, Johnny." A coolly dispassionate Johnny Clay instructs Fay to quit her job at the end of the week and reveal nothing other than that she is quitting to get married. He will next see her at the airport on Saturday night, after the job has been completed and all money divided. They will then board a plane for Boston and a new life.

Flippen makes his own pitch for enjoying a new life with the man he admires as a successful son. When Hayden visits his apartment early the Saturday morning of the racetrack heist, expressing his thanks and saying his heartfelt good-byes, the older man bares his soul. Telling Hayden that the fortune he will receive will open up a new world for him, where he will meet many people of substance, he tells Hayden that he thinks of him as a son, is skeptical about him marrying, and wonders aloud how nice it would be for the two of them to travel and watch the world turn. Hayden seeks to let him down easily, grinning and suggesting he get some more rest since it is early.

AN UNCONVENTIONAL GROUP

The major plot element separating *The Killing* from the similarly plotted *The Asphalt Jungle* is that the latter draws from losers and malcontents from the criminal world, while Johnny Clay deliberately seeks operatives among the citizenry pool's disaffected, the exceptions being two specialized jobs to be mentioned shortly. Clay finds his civilian brigade more manageable, and when he does seek professionals for specialized jobs, he is careful to reveal no more than the necessary particulars of the jobs for which they have been recruited. The unconventional nature of the group gives the Kubrick drama a special twist, differentiating it from more familiar cops and robbers melodramas.

In addition to moneyman Flippen and pitiable henpecked Cook, Joe Sawyer as Mike O'Reilly is also a sympathetic figure in the gang. While Cook functions as a cashier at Lansdowne Racetrack, Sawyer is employed as a bartender in the area where Cook operates his window. The door nearby Cook's window is the direct route to the upstairs room where cash proceeds, other than what cashiers and vendors need to make change, are kept. Sawyer, an uncomplicated easy-going type, is nursing a sick wife. He hopes the big payoff will enable them to buy a home and secure good doctors who will nurse his spouse back to health.

The unpleasant member of the gang is Randy Kennan, portrayed by screen heavy Ted de Corsia. While engaging in crooked activities, he does so as a uniformed officer of the Los Angeles Police Department. De Corsia played the killer ultimately tracked down by New York policemen Barry Fitzgerald and Don Taylor in the Gotham-set melodrama, *The Naked City*. In the Jules Dassin noir classic, de Corsia was cast as a professional wrestler who throws his weight around. In *The Killing*, he is a cocky and sometimes pugnacious officer using his position to tiptoe outside the law's confines and make deals.

De Corsia's motivation for joining the enterprise is quickly revealed as he enters a bar, where he is well known to patrons. The darkened atmosphere, with a table lamp supplying the light, conveys a strong noir essence, as does his conversation with local mobster Leo, played by Jay Adler, brother of Luther, the suave gang leader of *D.O.A.* and Nazi executioner of *Cornered*. The emerging dialogue between the mobster and crooked policeman is couched in the blunt yet diplomatic manner in which underworld figures warn those who owe them money. Adler begins by telling de Corsia that he likes to live well, as attested by his nice apartment and car. "So I like to live well," de Corsia responds. "Any objections?" Adler rejoins, "None, as long as you don't overlook your financial obligations." The details are so obvious to both men that they are overlooked to the very end. De Corsia explains that he is unable to pay Adler at the moment, but that he has a deal going and should be able to deliver soon. When pressed by an eager Adler for details, de Corsia clams up, but explains that he will be able to pay him off "within two weeks." Stressing the importance of payment, Adler concludes by giving the debtor extra time, after which he expects $2,600 plus $400 in interest. When asked if the terms are satisfactory, de Corsia grimly replies, "I don't have any other choice."

HIRED HANDS

Hayden has had five years to plot strategy. He explained to girlfriend Gray that he intends to shoot for big stakes since they can put you in prison just as easy for a two-bit job. At the meeting in Flippen's small Olive Street apartment, he explains the need for two hired professionals to perform strategically important tasks. Flippen is the moneyman who will divert funds from his company's books to pay the criminal specialists, earning him an equal share with the others.

Recognizing the importance of distraction to achieve his goal of robbing the second-floor room where the money is kept at Lansdowne Racetrack, Hayden hires two seasoned professionals in an ingenious scheme to divert attention from his activities. He seeks to enhance the prospect of pulling off his daring grand theft, which he reveals should result in a windfall of approximately $2 million.

Timothy Carey is cast as sharpshooter Nikki Arane, who lives on a small farm outside the city. He supplies Hayden with the detachable machine gun with which he will pull off the big job that Saturday afternoon. Hayden then hires him to exercise his rifleman's marksmanship in the Lansdowne Stakes, the $100,000 handicap. Reasoning that the runaway favorite, Red Lightning, will be in the lead, Hayden offers Carey $5,000 to kill the horse as it moves into the far turn heading into the stretch. A curious Carey seeks to learn more, but Hayden coolly informs him that the generous price being paid includes not asking questions as well as performing the job requested. Besides, Hayden explains, knowing nothing about the overall plan will protect Carey if anything goes wrong.

For the part of professional ruffian Maurice Oboukhoff, Kubrick cast a personal friend. Kola Kwariani, a professional wrestler during the fifties, became a crony of Kubrick's when he and the young director frequented the same chess parlor on New York's Forty-Second Street. Kwariani plays a cerebral muscle man who hangs out at The Academy of Chess and Checkers. As a seasoned professional criminal with a shrewd mind, he does not place Johnny Clay on the same pedestal as do his gang members. "Johnny my boy, you were never very bright but I love you anyway," he tells the gang's mastermind. Kwariani thinks of Hayden in the same endearing terms as Flippen does, as a son. The shrewd veteran expresses surprise when Hayden offers him $2,500 to start a fight at the racetrack bar during the crucial seventh race, when the job is being pulled. He tells Hayden that he could find a thug to perform the same job for as little as $100. Hayden replies that he is buying both Kwariani's professionalism and confidence that he will say nothing when placed in captivity. Repeating what he told Carey, knowing nothing more than the details of his own job will protect him, and he should do no more than 60 days in jail on a disorderly conduct charge.

THE WEAK LINK

By revealing information to his faithless wife, Cook becomes the gang's weak link, whose actions, combined with his wife's perfidy, ultimately defeats the effort. Spurred on by her lover Edwards, Windsor is caught by de Corsia and knocked out when he finds her spying in the hallway while her husband and the remaining members of the gang plot strategy in Flippen's apartment. When de Corsia drags Windsor into the apartment, he asks if anyone knows the identity of the eavesdropper. When Cook excitedly jumps to his feet, revealing that she is his wife, de Corsia punches him while a cool but determined Hayden demands immediate answers.

A nervous Cook replies that Windsor must have entertained suspicions that he was involved with another woman and followed him there. Hayden tells de Corsia and Sawyer to drive Cook home. He will deal with Windsor personally. As she is beginning to regain consciousness, he tells Flippen he will not kill her and intends to "just slap that pretty face into hamburger meat. That's all." As he makes his brutal threat, however, he winks at Flippen.

Hayden prefers dealing with Windsor alone, asking Flippen to go out and see a movie while he deals with the gang's emerging problem. When Windsor awakens, she plays off of her husband's implausible line, that she was jealous he might be seeing another woman. Hayden responds sarcastically that she would not be concerned if he were seeing someone else. Windsor seeks to use her feminine wiles by playing up romantically to Hayden, knowing she is in danger. He is having none of it, responding with cold calculation: "You'd sell out your own mother for a piece of fudge. You've got a dollar sign where other people have a heart, but you're smart."

The approach of the gang leader is to convince Windsor that plenty of money will be in her hands if she lets well enough alone, reasoning that Cook "will spend all of his money on you anyway." If there is anymore suspicious activity, Hayden warns, the job will be called off and she will realize nothing.

Some sterner mob hands would simply rub out Windsor as a potentially fatal risk. Instead Hayden concludes that by appealing to her overriding greed, he will obtain her silence until the job can be successfully completed. His erroneous calculation is based on the degree of cunning and greed that Windsor possesses. By sharing information with hoodlum lover Edwards, she is opting for much higher stakes than the mere share husband Cook is slated to receive.

THE DARING PLAN

Put in perspective, the Johnny Clay game plan consisted of the following:

1) Having Maurice start a fight at the racetrack bar by calling bartender Mike O'Reilly "a stupid-looking Irish pig," punching the bartender when he objects to the burly man's manner, as the paid riot starter holds off the inevitable subduing as long as possible, stretching time for Clay and his enterprise while drawing as many policemen as possible to make Clay's effort easier.

2) Hired rifleman Nicki Arane scoring a bull's-eye on favored horse Red Lightning, creating more confusion and diversion as Clay goes into action.

3) Through the prolonged distraction of Maurice's diverting riot expertise, track cashier George Peatty sneaks away from his post and opens the door for Clay to enter, after which he goes to Mike O'Reilly's locker and opens it, pulling out the flower box the bartender obtained from the locker Clay had rented at a bus station, which he tells his co-workers contains flowers for his wife. It actually contains the disassembled weapon built by Nicky as well as a Halloween mask he puts on, along with a large duffel bag.

4) Moving upstairs and entering the room where the money is stored after the last contingent of officers has left for downstairs to break up the riot Maurice started.

5) Once the job has been completed and the track employees are ordered into an adjoining room under threat of immediate death, Johnny Clay throws his weapon along with his Halloween mask, his coat and hat into the duffel bag, which he hurls, along with the $2 million in bills that it contains, out the window. It lands on the ground and is picked up by Randy Kennan, who puts it into his police patrol car and whisks it away to the run-down motel where Clay has been staying, to be picked up later by Clay, who puts on dark glasses to further disguise his appearance and leaves the track.

An inventive technique is employed by Kubrick to show the independent actions of gang members. Kubrick uses a replay technique to cover identical periods of time. Another ploy, which gives the film a flavor of a rapidly paced documentary, is using

Elisha Cook Jr. secured a mark as one of the most memorable character performers in Hollywood history, with a long career of portraying losers, often in the criminal realm. He had an enduring feature role in John Huston's *The Maltese Falcon*, which historians cited as the first noir film. Pictured here in a scene with Marie Windsor from Stanley Kubrick's 1956 classic, *The Killing*, Cook plays a henpecked husband whose love for wife Windsor is unreciprocated. Windsor two-times him as she romances handsome hunk Vince Edwards. Cooke and Windsor each received rave notices playing a married couple existing at staggering cross-purposes.

a narrative technique. This technique was employed in *The Naked City*. More recently linked to 1955, when *The Killing* was filmed, the narrative technique with its documentary flavor was successfully employed by Jack Webb, who served as narrator and lead performer Sergeant Joe Friday of the L.A. Police in the long-running *Dragnet* television series. Kubrick's narrative technique coupled with his replays of key events relating to the various gang participants gave the film the same kind of "You are there" flavor, which helped popularize *Dragnet*.

THE FIRST GANG CASUALTY

The first gang casualty was Timothy Carey, who arrives early at the racetrack and is compelled to convince parking lot attendant James Edwards to allow him to park his convertible in a facility not then open. He is concerned about acquiring space in the front row leading into the far turn to facilitate shooting the prize thoroughbred Red Lightning. Initially the going is tough, but when Carey convinces Edwards that he is a paraplegic who sustained his injury in the Battle of the Bulge, the attendant replies that he was also wounded in WWII and has a bad leg, allowing him access. Edwards at first refuses the money Carey is willing to pay him for the privilege, only taking it at Carey's insistence.

James Edwards was in reality a wounded veteran of WWII who received his break playing a soldier during that conflict as he starred in the 1949 Mark Robson war drama, *Home of the Brave*. The film focused daringly on the abuse Edwards, an African American, received from his fellow soldiers. The Kubrick-Thompson script plays intelligently off of the racial theme as Edwards registers delight that Carey has treated him so kindly. Early in the afternoon, he visits him long enough to provide a free program. Trouble ensues eventually when his next trip, just before the start of the seventh race, in which he brings Carey a horseshoe for good luck, makes the gunman feel nervous since the race will soon begin. Noticing Carey's suddenly cold manner, Edwards asks if anything is wrong. Carey tersely replies, "You're wrong, nigger! Get lost!"

His harsh manner evokes suspicion from Edwards. After killing Red Lightning on the far turn, a uniformed security policeman immediately surfaces, demanding that Carey halt. One shot from the policeman pierces a front tire, which goes flat, after which Carey is then gunned down by the officer. A shrewd close-up is employed showing the horseshoe that Edwards angrily discarded on the ground and the prostate body of Carey in the front seat of his car.

Hayden experiences an anxious moment after the robbery. He opens the same door that Cook had earlier opened for him, planning to make an immediate exit from the track. An armed track security policeman asks him to halt. Here he receives a boost from Flippen. Hayden had urged his father-like friend to stay away from the track and take in a movie, limiting his involvement, but Flippen cannot resist being on the scene. Seeing that potential trouble looms, Flippen bumps into the security policeman just hard enough to disrupt his concentration. Hayden then delivers a well-timed right to the jaw, knocking the officer out. In the confusion, Hayden's act is not even observed as he walks unobtrusively toward the nearest exit.

The swiftly paced action shifts next to the crucial meeting at Flippen's apartment, where the cash will be divided up and the participants will go their separate ways. Hayden had gone immediately to the motel room and picked up the duffel bag containing the cash left by de Corsia, but heavy track traffic has delayed his arrival at Flippen's apartment.

As expected, the edgiest member of the team is its most vulnerable member, Elisha Cook Jr. That morning, having awakened early and looking nervous, a shrewd Windsor gets up to fix him coffee. Her kindness, as always, holds the same ulterior motive, crass self-interest. She seeks to extract information from him that the job is being planned for that day. Initially he resists her inquiry, but ultimately he is worn down when Windsor makes things personal and emotional, suggesting that Cook holds more feeling for gang boss Hayden than for his wife. That prompts him to divulge the important information.

As the gang sits and waits, a sound is heard at the elevator. Eyes brighten and Hayden is expected. A nervous Cook had stepped into another room momentarily. Instead of Hayden, Windsor's lover Edwards and an accomplice arrive. De Corsia responds to the guns pointed at the group by saying, "Somebody's given you a bum steer, buddy." Edwards knows better, replying that he has been listening to all kinds of interesting information on the radio, meaning the periodic reports of the daring Lansdowne Racetrack robbery. Observing that Cook is missing, Edwards snarls, "Where's the jerk?"

Cook has had the last grain of beach sand thrown in his face. As a precautionary measure, he had taken a loaded revolver to the track with him. Suffering the humiliation of condescension from his wife's lover, Cook quickly reappears. "The jerk's right here," he replies, opening fire on Edwards and killing him instantly. This triggers a quick and thoroughly destructive gun battle in which everyone but Cook is killed. Cook has been wounded, but does not seek immediate help. In the manner of a kicked dog, he returns to the one place he knows as home and the one person, despite consistent mistreatment, whom he loves above everyone else.

Despite needing immediate medical attention, Cook is compelled to see Windsor. As he enters the apartment, she is making final preparations to leave with Edwards. He mentions the name of "Val," which prompts her to coldly dismiss him, telling her husband that he had better leave before her lover arrives, unaware that her cuckolded marital partner has disposed of him. He asks her to call him an ambulance, explaining that he is not feeling well. Windsor coldly orders him to leave, suggesting he call a cab. Her curt dismissal is the final blow. Cook fires one fatal shot at Windsor. She drops to the ground, clutching her stomach, incredulous that he would summon the requisite nerve to kill her. "George, you're the only real husband I ever had," she says weakly. Moments after she drops to the floor dead, Cook does the same. All that can be heard is their talking bird in its cage.

The Cook-Windsor teaming was one of the brilliant casting strokes of film noir annals, with a high dramatic peak being scaled through the interaction of opposites, a castrated husband with less-than-zero self-esteem and a sharp-tongued, sadistic wife who derives joy by crushing a tortured soul who desperately loves her, the only man who loves her unselfishly. She spurns Cook for the handsome but narcissistic Edwards, whose sole concern is himself. Recognizing their contributions to absorbing film drama, Cook and Windsor enjoy large fan followings. Cook, a reclusive type who lived in Big Pine, California, and was contacted by Hollywood studios via courier, was frequently sought for interviews by film historians and reporters up to his death in 1995 at the age of 88. Windsor remained a popular figure at film festivals, which she regularly frequented until her death on December 10, 2000, just one day short of what would have been her 78th birthday. Several years ago, the Turner Classic Movies cable network featured Windsor in a film noir tribute as an interview subject with Coleen Gray, Jane Greer and Audrey Totter.

Windsor commented not long before her death on Kubrick and working with him in *The Killing:*

"Stanley was an introverted person. He was very quiet and while on the set I never heard him yell at the crew or anybody. When he had some idea for me to do or change, he would wiggle his finger and we would go away from the action and he would tell me what he wanted or didn't want. One time when I was sitting on the bed reading a magazine, he came up and said, 'I want you to move your eyes when you're reading.' He was only in his 20's but you just had a sense of his having pure confidence in himself."

FROM DOLORES TO SEBASTIAN

Hayden barely misses the shootout, arriving at the Olive Street location as Cook staggers out the door toward his car. Once he sees an approaching police car, the meticulous Hayden realizes it is time to incorporate the gang's backup plan, which calls for him to hang onto the money until it can later be distributed. He is unaware that, after Cook's swift demise, he remains the lone survivor with over $2 million.

Once Hayden drives away just as the police car is arriving at the Olive Street scene, he goes to a pawnshop and secures the largest suitcase he can find. He then drives to a wilderness location, where he removes the bills from the duffel bag and stuffs them into the suitcase.

Hayden's next stop is the airport, where he meets Gray. Since he had checked in all other baggage in the morning for that evening's flight to Boston, his only remaining luggage is the suitcase bulging with some $2 million in bills. He encounters a problem when the airline clerk explains that the suitcase is too large to carry by hand aboard the plane and will need to be checked in with other luggage. When the supervisor supports his employee's decision, an increasingly nervous Hayden agrees to let the suitcase be checked in with the other luggage.

The plane that Hayden and Gray hope will soon spirit them to freedom and a new life of riches will be boarding soon, so they watch as the luggage cart is transported toward the plane. Standing near them is a woman holding a small white poodle she refers to affectionately as Sebastian. While Hayden and Gray watch the large suitcase bulging with bills being transported toward the plane, the mischievous Sebastian jumps out of the woman's arms. The dog darts toward the cart. The cart driver is compelled to cut sharply to avoid hitting Sebastian. In the process, the bulging suitcase, already swaying back and forth, falls to the ground and flies open. While Hayden and Gray watch helplessly, the bills float through the air, resembling at a distance a convoy of ducks.

Sebastian becomes one of two film canines who assist in providing fascinating closing plot twists in film noir classics. One year after Sebastian inadvertently disrupts the carefully laid plans of Sterling Hayden in *The Killing*, Scotland Yard detective Bernard Lee uses canine Dolores as bait to entice Rod Steiger "across the bridge" for capture in the Ken Annakin film of the same name. The inventive twists cap resourceful and highly unconventional suspense dramas.

Hayden and Gray move promptly toward the airport exit. The supervisor receives a call. He immediately concludes, due to the request by Hayden and the fact that he is departing just as boarding is to be announced for his flight, that there is a connection between the money and the tall, sandy-haired man. Gray unsuccessfully seeks to hail a cab while Hayden stands in helpless defeat, his bills having vanished in a dark Los Angeles evening sky.

When the supervisor speaks with two plainclothes officers standing at the door, they move toward Johnny Clay, guns drawn. The loyal Fay implores him to make a run for it.

"What's the difference," he responds fatalistically, watching as the arresting officers move toward him at Fade Out.

Prior to its general 1956 release, *The Killing* had a New York unveiling at the Mayfair Theater. In a May 21, 1955, review, A.H. Weiler of *The New York Times* wrote:

"Mr. Kubrick has kept things moving at a lively clip as the plotting is revealed in timetable fashion. Sterling Hayden makes a restrained but hard and efficient leader. His Johnny Clay is a tough citizen who knows the dangers his boys will face and he takes no chances. Elisha Cook does well by the role of a Caspar Milquetoast of a racetrack cashier who is willing to risk his neck to buy the love of his wife. As that two-timer, Marie Windsor is properly cheap, brassy and decorative."

While crediting youthful director Kubrick with superb pacing, Weiler found the film reminiscent of "but not nearly as imaginative as *The Asphalt Jungle*." A better indication of Kubrick's meteoric success story was reflected across the Atlantic. Impressed by the story's brisk pacing, its hard-boiled mold, along with the superb dark settings illuminated frequently only by a lamp, not to mention the superb racetrack photography at Bay Meadows near San Francisco, British critics eagerly embraced *The Killing*. Kubrick received the first of many honors as *The Killing* was named Best Film at the British Academy Awards. The land of brooding drama, the nation of Shakespeare and Marlowe, saluted a new genius on the film horizon, Stanley Kubrick, someone who would a few years later be making his home in England.

KEY REPRISE PERFORMERS

Timothy Carey and Sterling Hayden would reprise in two future highly acclaimed Kubrick films. Carey surfaced as condemned prisoner Private Ferol in Kubrick's next effort with producer partner James Harris after *The Killing*. Crime author Jim Thompson joined the Kubrick team again to adapt the Humphrey Cobb war novel, *Paths of Glory*. While now acknowledged as one of the greatest anti-war films ever made, the major studios rejected the project until Kirk Douglas agreed to star. The film was shot in Germany and released in 1957. *Paths of Glory* won Best Film honors at the British Academy Awards, Kubrick's second in as many years following *The Killing*. His future wife Christiane Harlan, whom he would marry in 1958 and live with the rest of his life, played a cabaret singer who appears near the end of the film.

Sterling Hayden would play a major role in a black comedy satirizing the military and its vast industrial complex in Kubrick's 1964 blockbuster, *Dr. Strangelove or How I Learned to Stop Worrying and Love the Bomb*, adapted from a Peter George novel. The versatile Peter Sellers played three roles in the film, the President of the United States, mad scientist Dr. Strangelove, and a British captain. Hayden's key role contained a strong note of personal irony. A former U.S. Communist Party member who left the party and cooperated as a friendly witness with the House Un-American Activities Committee (HUAC), naming Abraham Polonsky among others, Hayden returned to films after a six-year absence and was reunited with Kubrick in *Strangelove*, playing the mad, war-hungry U.S. general who triggers a nuclear conflict with the Soviet Union.

Just one year before his return to films, Hayden's autobiography, *The Wanderer*, was published. The reclusive actor focused on two areas of his life, his ocean adventures and profound regret for cooperating with the HUAC. In one revealing paragraph, Hayden candidly denounced himself as a "stoolie" for his friendly witness role:

"Not often does a man find himself eulogized for having behaved in a manner that he himself despises. I subscribed to a press-clipping service. They sent me two thousand clips from papers east and west, large and small, and from dozens of magazines. Most had nothing but praise for my one-shot stoolie show. Only a handful—led by *The New York Times*—denounced this abrogation of constitutional freedoms whereby the stoolie could gain status in a land of frightened people."

A MAJOR PINCH HIT ROLE

Kubrick's next major career break after *The Killing* and *Paths of Glory* came in a pinch-hit role. In 1959 he replaced Anthony Mann as director of *Spartacus*, a lavish historical epic in which he was reunited with *Paths of Glory* star Kirk Douglas. The all-star cast also included Laurence Olivier, Charles Laughton, Jean Simmons, Peter Ustinov and Tony Curtis. It was the most costly Hollywood film to that point with a budget exceeding $12 million. Released in 1960, *Spartacus* was a major success and received a Golden Globe for Best Picture.

The director resurfaced soon thereafter with an adaptation of one of the century's most controversial novels. Russian author Vladimir Nabokov adapted his story about the obsession of a middle-aged professor for a young girl, whose age was moved from 12 to14 to at least partially placate censors, who nonetheless would wax apoplectic upon the 1962 release of *Lolita*. James Mason played the love-struck professor with Sue Lyon making her screen debut as Lolita, the object of his spellbound fascination. Peter Sellers as competition for Lyon's love and Shelley Winters as her mother supplied brilliant satirical comedic touches. Due to financial and legal difficulties, Kubrick shot the film in England. When the film was completed, the director never left, making England his home for the rest of his life.

In December 1965, Kubrick began what would become his milestone cinematic achievement, working with British science fiction author Arthur C. Clarke in adapting his story, *The Sentinel*, a project eventuating in the 1968 release, *2001: A Space Odyssey*. Kubrick's quest for exploring the unconventional in the most innovative manner was realized in a futuristic tale in which a computer named Hal rebels against astronauts Keir Dullea and Gary Lockwood, jeopardizing their craft in space. The only Academy Award ever bestowed on a Kubrick film was conveyed in the Best Visual Effects category. The mind-boggling effects surpassed anything previously seen in Hollywood.

"I was always aware that he knew exactly what he wanted," Keir Dullea reminisced about Kubrick. "He would invite Gary Lockwood and myself to have dinner at his beautiful home. And he would invite a lot of other people from all walks of life and different disciplines—art historians, authors and intellectuals. And he was as informed as anybody about their disciplines. He was like an onion—every layer you peeled off there were two new ones to be exposed."

After the success of *2001*, Kubrick's next venture was set in a futuristic world, that of violent anarchy, in the 1971 adaptation of the Anthony Burgess novel, *A Clockwork Orange*, starring Malcolm McDowell. While a satire, the film's pronounced savagery prompted criticism that it glorified violence. As Stephen Holden wrote in his obituary of Kubrick in *The New York Times*, "Kubrick withdrew the film from distribution in Britain after it was said to have inspired copycat crimes. But if Kubrick's misanthropy prompted some critics to accuse him of coldness and inhumanity, others saw his pessimism as an uncompromisingly Swiftian vision of human absurdity."

Kubrick's next effort was a costume drama set in the eighteenth century, an adaptation of the William Makepeace Thackeray novel, *Barry Lyndon*. The 1975 road-show release starred Ryan O'Neal as an Irish rogue who achieves meteoric success followed by a sharp downturn. Kubrick took great pains to evoke lighting and imagery commensurate with the period. The costly movie took 300 shooting days to complete and fared only modestly at the box office.

Five years later, Kubrick was back in the news with the release of *The Shining*, based on a novel by horror story master Stephen King. Jack Nicholson stars as a writer who holes up with his family in a Colorado hotel and goes berserk.

In 1987, the director completed a three-picture cycle about the savagery and insanity of military conflict. He began in 1957 with *Paths of Glory*, his next film following *The Killing*. Kubrick moved from a strong anti-war dramatic statement to brilliant satire with his tour de force *Dr. Strangelove* in 1964. The horrors about America's most controversial military adventure, the Vietnam War, were the focus of Kubrick's 1987 film, *Full Metal Jacket*. Adapted from a Gustav Hasford novel, *The Short-Timers*, the film, which starred Matthew Modine, is divided into two parts, a harrowing look at Marine basic training in Parris Island, South Carolina, and the Vietnam conflict.

Stanley Kubrick had just completed editing his final film, *Eyes Wide Shut*, before his death. The adaptation of the Arthur Schnitzler novel, *Dream Story*, was a venture into the psychosexual as exemplified by a Manhattan yuppie couple played by real-life husband and wife duo Tom Cruise and Nicole Kidman. As Stephen Holden related, "Filmed in Britain in an atmosphere of military secrecy, it took 15 months to shoot." Controversy would swirl around Kubrick even in death as, to placate censors and allay distribution fears, digitized computer figures were used to block sexual activities at a masked orgy occurring at a mansion outside New York City attended by some of the city's most prominent and highly disguised citizens. The edited version played in America, and the original in international release.

While much was written about Kubrick's concern for privacy, Tom Cruise and Nicole Kidman, who formed close bonds with the director, insisted that he was no recluse. The same position was taken by Sydney Pollack, a featured actor in the film. Pollack, the distinguished director of such major films as *They Shoot Horses, Don't They?* (1969), *The Way We Were* (1973) and *Tootsie* (1982), delivered the following appraisal of Kubrick shortly after his death:

"I always think of Stanley literally on the edge of a smile. His eyes always had mischief in them. He always had this sense of the devil in him while he was very calmly asking questions. He read everything, and knew absolutely all aspects of the business, including literally what the box-office receipts to every theater in the world were over the past few years."

Frederic Raphael, who co-wrote *Eyes Wide Shut* with Kubrick, penned a memoir of his working experience with the famous director, *Eyes Wide Open*. Maintaining a professional relationship largely through fax exchanges, the Academy Award-winning scenarist of *Darling* (1965) said regarding Kubrick:

"Perhaps he is an enigma without a secret, a man who has abandoned motives: there is no sense in trying to divine the psychological makeup of someone who is no longer interested in himself. He limits self-knowledge to having inflexible ambitions. I have to hope that making this film is still one of them."

Raphael's conception of a self-immersed creator in a self-created cocoon appears to be in contrast to what Cruise, Kidman and Pollack have stated, but it must be remembered that they dealt with Kubrick on a different level than did his co-screenwriter. More than likely, the complex Kubrick had many layers. One thing appeared certain about him. In the manner of Greta Garbo and Howard Hughes, the more tenaciously he shunned publicity, the more insatiable the curiosity about him.

In 1997 Kubrick received two of the film's highest honors. He was given the D.W. Griffith Award from the Director's Guild of America and the Golden Lion

Award at the 54th Venice International Film Festival. Kubrick received prestigious Best Director honors three times by the New York Film Critics, always in tandem with similarly awarded Best Picture recognition. The films were *Dr. Strangelove*, *A Clockwork Orange* and *Barry Lyndon*. He received Best Director and Best Film honors at the British Academy Awards for *Barry Lyndon*. The director who left America to reside in England was highly acclaimed in Britain. Six of his movies secured Best Film honors at the British Academy Awards.

Kubrick's eclectic film output was one of the most fascinating ever. His momentum surge propelling him into cinema's big time began with a sharply crafted film noir epic, *The Killing*, which conclusively demonstrated that in the world of suspense drama, less can be more with a smaller budget and money wisely utilized.

EIGHT

All About Water and Power

'Course I'm respectable. I'm old. Politicians, ugly buildings and whores all get
respectable if they last long enough.

Chinatown (1974)

Once color television was invented and the necessity of using the color process
in filmmaking became pronounced, the leaner and claustrophobic black and white
dramas such as *D.O.A.* and *The Killing* became as extinct in a cinematic sense as the
passing of the wild buffalo on the American frontier. With the focus on color, a new
dimension surfaced on the film noir scene, leading to one more of those apparent
oxymorons that really does make sense once it is explained.

In the era of Vietnam and Watergate, a breakthrough film was released to audiences in 1974, which demonstrated the kind of imaginative film noir that could be
achieved in the world of color filmmaking. *Chinatown* combined a sharply focused,
biting script with a showcase performance by one of the cinema's leading anti-heroes
along with taut direction. Just as the brilliant Abraham Polonsky film, *Force of Evil*
(1948), used a small budget and black and white photography to present Manhattan in a claustrophobic setting, *Chinatown* covered a sprawling Los Angeles in 1937,
focusing on its torrid heat and bright, intense sunshine. The point is repeatedly
made to the audience that Los Angeles is a desert. In fact, the names of the respective directors varied only by two letters, with Roman Polanski the director of *Chinatown*.

Chinatown bore the ring of searing reality, due in no small measure to the fact
that it is based on true-life incidents bearing heavily on the history of Los Angeles. The city that spawned the film capital is presented in the sprawled-out fashion
of an extended area representing recently arrived residents from all over the globe.
Just as the presentation of darkness and confined quarters depicted film noir in the
black and white era, now the use of color and the emphasis of exhausting heat and
its enervating result of diminished energy levels and angry behavior served as the
Great American West's antidote to the mean streets of New York depicted by the

likes of Abraham Polonsky. The noir battleground was moved from the city at night to the enervating heat of day.

Just as Los Angeles represented the great microcosm of a city in perpetual transition, invaded by increasing numbers of people from other places, Florida was explored in the 1980 release *Body Heat*, directed by Lawrence Kasdan in his debut. Filmed in Lake Worth, neighbor to the south of affluent Palm Beach, *Body Heat* is set in the midst of a torrid Florida summer heat wave. In addition to shortening tempers, the excessive heat can also propel libidos to the thermometer breaking point, which occurs in the case of the film's male protagonist, played by William Hurt. He becomes manipulated by a scorpion-like *femme fatale* reminiscent of the Stanwycks, Greers and Trevors of yesteryear, played by Kathleen Turner in a brilliant showcase role.

In the manner of artistic shapers and movers, Robert Towne was a product of his time. He came into the industry, as did his frequent partner Jack Nicholson, with an early boost from horror film director Roger Corman. The sixties, when Towne entered the industry, were marked by Vietnam and sexual experimentation. Nicholson, who began as an outsider, starred in two of the defining films of the sixties, *Easy Rider* (1969) and *Five Easy Pieces* (1970). A rebel with the kind of expression which revealed that he was both shrewd enough to understand society's foibles and cynical enough to laugh at them at the same time, he quickly found his metier and parlayed it into extended success in the seventies. As for Towne, his writing career received a significant forward thrust with help from Nicholson. In 1973 Nicholson played a Navy Shore Patrol guard of a prisoner headed for prison for a long stretch in *The Last Detail* (1973). Showing both his compassionate and rebellious sides, Nicholson displays feeling toward the young prisoner and treats him to a night on the town before incarceration. Towne wrote the screenplay, and the following year marked the release of the epochal film starring Nicholson that was a hallmark of his celebrated career and won Towne a Best Original Screenplay Oscar for *Chinatown*.

Audiences and critics alike found something refreshingly honest and creatively outreaching about *Chinatown*, a blending of rebel actor Nicholson and an imaginative screenplay stressing the helplessness of the common citizen to cope with circumstances beyond his or her control dominated by powerful and unstoppable forces. Director Polanski kept the action moving at a swift pace while seeing that the broad expansiveness of Los Angeles was emphasized through sweeping views, the reverse noir side of the dark, confining claustrophobia of an Edward Dmytryk or Abraham Polonsky. Polanski's artistic vision, cohering alongside that of Towne, was one man's untiring effort to portray a sprawling area consisting of people from all walks of life, who tug in disparate directions. Exhausted by the vortex of the perpetual head-turning tennis match was Jack Nicholson as Jake Gittes.

A brilliant casting stroke involved the selection of the economic colossus who balances 1937 Los Angeles in his hand in the manner that King Kong did to Fay Wray. Noah Cross admits that he has no idea how much money he is worth. In response to a question from Jake Gittes as to what propels him unceasingly forward, the quick response is "The future, Mr. Gittes, the future." In that, *Chinatown* was a badly needed trip back to the world of film noir, it was poetic justice that the larger-than-life Hollywood figure chosen to play the controlling octopus was John Huston, director of such classics from the dark side as *The Maltese Falcon, The Asphalt Jungle* and *Key Largo.* Huston as Noah Cross supplies the appropriate mix of cocky irreverence and unflinching control of a man accustomed to bulldozing everyone who stands in his way and getting away with it.

Gittes is a voice in the wilderness attempting single-handedly to turn back a tidal wave in the person of Cross along with the vast machine he controls, a perfect cinema vehicle for the seventies. Just as film noir had surged to the fore at the close of WWII, with audiences prepared to look beyond conventional happy endings to a realistic look at a planet in which a tyrannical megalomaniac named Hitler was almost able to assert dominant control, by the mid-seventies, a technocratic revolution was in full swing, making the individual feel increasingly dwarfed. The most controversial American military conflict in the nation's 200-year history, the Vietnam War, was concluding in a manner that made Americans realize that victory was not an inevitable concomitant to the commitment of large numbers of U.S. troops and significant military budget allocations. This was also the period of Watergate, which made Americans feel increasingly vulnerable to a government able to function beyond its control irrespective of what happened at the polls and after the votes were counted. In August 1974, the first U.S. president in the nation's history, Richard M. Nixon, would resign from office in the wake of the threat that he could not only be impeached, but perhaps would even be sentenced to a stretch in federal prison, a fate endured by the Hollywood Ten one generation earlier after refusing to name names on a committee on which then-California Congressman Nixon served.

A frequently repeated Hollywood saying regarding perfect casting is that the actor "owned the role." If the role of private detective Jake Gittes appeared to be made to order for Jack Nicholson, it was due to the fact that it was. Nicholson was Robert Towne's oldest Hollywood friend. The two met in 1960 as aspiring actors in the popular workshop run by drama instructor and veteran character actor Jeff Corey. Roger Corman was also in the class, providing Nicholson and Towne with work in some of his early horror films. Towne did a little acting for Corman, but quickly found his niche as a scenarist.

Eventually Towne would become renowned in Hollywood as a great script doctor, a job he performed with remarkable skill on *Bonnie and Clyde,* starring another close friend of Towne's, Warren Beatty, with whom he would collaborate on the script of *Shampoo* (1975). Towne credits *Bonnie and Clyde* (1967) director Arthur Penn with teaching him a lot about filmmaking.

When *Chinatown* was no more than an idea in his mind, Towne discussed his project with the film's eventual producer, Robert Evans, who was then married to Ali MacGraw. Evans was interested in *Chinatown* as a starring role for MacGraw. The female lead would ultimately go to Faye Dunaway. When Towne was asked if he had written the script with MacGraw in mind, he replied, "I wasn't writing the girl (Evelyn Mulwray) for any actress in particular. I was just writing that one part for Jack."

In view of the closeness of his association with Nicholson, it is doubtful that anyone has a clearer understanding of the actor's professional repertoire than his former roommate, who recalls being impressed by his skills from improvisations he gave at Corey's workshop. Towne's familiarity with Nicholson's unique skills gave him a distinct advantage over any other writer attempting to capture the actor's dramatic essence.

"His improvisations were inventive," Towne recollected of the early Nicholson. "When he was given a situation, he would not improvise on the nose. He'd talk around the problem, and good writing is the same way: It's not explicit."

Nicholson's puckish grin demonstrates a street-smart man's sardonic awareness of the injustices, anarchistic underpinnings, and inequities representing the worst facets of modern American life. Beyond the grin lies a man who will also, in the manner of Robert Mitchum in *Out of the Past*, battle potent, inevitably indomitable forces as cunningly and determinedly as possible, a survivor who thrusts out his chin and dares you to knock him down. As Mitchum said, if death is inevitable, he remains determined to "die last."

When Nicholson as Jake Gittes begins investigating suspicious activities relating to the city's water supply against a backdrop of periodic mysterious deaths and overriding corruption, the cunning individual and controlling element he ultimately confronts is Noah Cross, played with relentless confidence by John Huston. At his initial meeting with Huston, Nicholson is provided with the same kind of warning by a powerful force that Dick Powell received in *Murder, My Sweet* and subtly conveyed to John Garfield and Edmond O'Brien in *Force of Evil* and *D.O.A.*, respectively. While Nicholson sits and dines with Huston at the Albacore Club, which the latter owns, Huston warns, "You may think you know what you're dealing with— but believe me, you don't." Huston also reveals his cynical outlook, but from a varying perspective from Nicholson's. Nicholson's cynicism is that of the outsider looking in; Huston's is that of the definitive insider controlling events. "'Course I'm respectable," Huston responds to Nicholson. "I'm old. Politicians, ugly buildings and whores all get respectable if they last long enough." Huston's response to Nicholson is typical of the power broker. He hires Nicholson's services but is ultimately crossed up by the detective, who refuses to be put in his place by a wealthy man content to control him through frequent payments.

Towne regarded the first meeting of Gittes and Cross as a pivotal educational experience for the younger man. "Gittes thinks he understands people's limitations," Towne explained, "and then he comes up against a monster, Noah Cross, who will do *everything*. There is *nothing* he won't do. Man *has* no limits. That was the point of the confrontation scene, which Gittes didn't understand: Cross tells him that some people have *no* limitations. At a given place and a given time, people are capable of anything. Gittes' cynicism, by comparison, is petty, naive, and almost sweet."

A Well-Organized Process

Towne's *Chinatown* screenplay is notable for its succinct organization and the manner in which the story conflicts and character nuances are revealed. Noted screenwriting instructor Syd Field was so impressed with the symmetry and compelling storytelling of Towne's script that he used it as a model for study at the Sherwood Experimental College in the seventies, where the likes of Paul Newman, Dustin Hoffman, Martin Scorsese and Sidney Lumet conducted classes on their respective crafts in a workshop setting in Sherman Oaks in the San Fernando Valley. Field was particularly impressed by the manner in which Towne laid out the plot and conflict of his story in the first 20 pages, informing viewers about private detective Jake Gittes, revealing his foibles and mannerisms in setting the stage for his suspense drama.

The shrewdly constructed first scene of *Chinatown* displays Gittes in his professional environs dealing with a client under delicate circumstances. Some grainy photographs are displayed showing a couple in the throes of lovemaking. While Gittes sits coolly at his desk, his client Curly, played by Burt Young, is reacting with the rage and torture of a cuckolded husband. Before one word of dialogue is spoken, Towne has revealed two important elements of the story: 1) Gittes, with a large and well-appointed office, is making a good living as a private detective snooping on the citizenry's bedroom conduct, and 2) his cool, unruffled demeanor demonstrates that he has been at his job long enough to anticipate rage and desperation from his clients.

After Curly, a San Pedro fisherman, has slammed his fists against the walls, kicked a wastepaper basket, and caused some autographed pictures of movie stars hanging on the walls to sag, Gittes coolly responds before the deceived husband causes any property damage. A totally distraught and heavily weeping Curly sinks to his knees in such torment that he begins biting the blinds. At this point, Gittes delivers his first dialogue in the film:

GITTES: All right, enough is enough—you can't eat the Venetian blinds, Curly. I just had 'em installed on Wednesday.

The next clue concerning Gittes's makeup is so subtle that it is likely to be discerned only by keen-eyed bartenders. A careful perusal indicates that the detective, as he reaches into the cupboard, actually removes a cheaper bottle of bourbon near the back rather than one of the more impressive brands in the front. After a long sip, Curly begins relaxing a little as the following exchange occurs:

CURLY: She's just no good.
GITTES: What can I tell you, Kid? You're right. When you're right, you're right, and you're right.

Once more Gittes reveals his expertise, knowing how to soothingly agree and provide opportunity for a deceived marital partner to release steam. After telling Gittes he will not give his wife another thought, Curly, in the unpredictable pattern of wounded spouses, promptly turns violent in his thoughts. "I think I'll kill her," Curly tells the detective. The fisherman explains that "They don't kill a guy" for killing his wife over infidelity, what is commonly referred to as "the unwritten law."

Gittes feels a need to take charge over a man who has emotionally run amok and threatens to do the same physically. Gittes's sagacity is revealed, as is the basic point made in *Chinatown*. It is regrettable that in later versions for television, DVD and VHS, this essential piece of dialogue has been clipped because it forms the guiding principle which ultimately dooms Gittes's pursuit of justice at the near expense of his life. Gittes pounds the photos of the lovemaking on his desk and shouts:

GITTES: I'll tell you the unwritten law, you dumb son of a bitch, you gotta be rich to kill somebody, anybody, and get away with it. You think you got that kind of dough, you think you got that kind of class?

Gittes's emotional response illustrates the difference between citizens such as himself and Curly contrasted with the Noah Cross figures of the world who control society and get away with murder. Gittes further illustrates his point to Curly regarding his lack of funds by reminding him, "You can't even pay me off." Curly apologizes for not being able to pay Gittes as the detective, who has other business, is easing him out of his office. After Curly's embarrassed explanation over how tough times have been lately on his fishing boat, Gittes replies, "Forget it. I only mention it to illustrate a point. I don't want your last dime. What kind of a guy do you think I am?"

As Curly is escorted out the door by Gittes, he is impressed by the detective's folksy "Call me Jake" manner along with his reluctance to apply pressure for money. While Gittes displays himself as a man of compassion who is not scraping for the last dollar of a hard-working fisherman, his relationship with Curly will later reveal a crafty side of the detective.

With Curly, Towne employs the technique of introducing a character early in the film, then, as the film moves to a dramatic climax, using him again. At a later pressure point, when Gittes is in the clutches of the law, he uses Curly to help free him from his predicament in a manner that frustrates the police.

As soon as Curly makes his exit, Diane Ladd surfaces. She identifies herself deceitfully, as events will prove, as Mrs. Mulwray. As in the earlier instance with Curly, Gittes shows he is not out for the last dollar. When Mrs. Mulwray sadly explains that her husband, whom she loves, is romantically involved with another woman, the detective who makes his living investigating such activities tells her to "go home and forget it," adding, "I'm sure he loves you, too. You know the expression, let sleeping dogs lie? You're better off not knowing."

The determined intensity displayed by the woman convinces Gittes to take the case. When he matter-of-factly asks her husband's first name, she replies, "Hollis. Hollis Mulwray." A visibly surprised Gittes replies, "Water and Power?"

Diane Ladd as the woman posing as Mrs. Mulwray confirms that her alleged husband is chief engineer of the department, making the detective aware that he is dealing with a powerful figure in local circles. In the next scene, Gittes surfaces at L.A. City Hall for a meeting at council chambers concerning the proposed Alto Vallejo Dam and Reservoir, at which Chief Engineer Mulwray will be speaking. Initially a bored Gittes is thumbing through a *Racing Form* prominently displaying a picture and story about the thoroughbred champion of the thirties, Seabiscuit. Former Mayor Sam Bagby, in his emotional plea for passage of the bond initiative, underscores the critical need for water:

"Gentlemen, today you can walk out that door, turn right, hop on a streetcar and in twenty-five minutes end up smack in the Pacific Ocean. Now you can swim in it, you can fish in it, you can sail in it—but you can't drink it, you can't water your lawns with it, you can't irrigate an orange grove with it. Remember—we live next door to the ocean but we also live on the edge of the desert. Los Angeles is a desert community. Beneath this building, beneath every street there's a desert. Without water the dust will rise up and cover us as though we'd never existed." He pauses long enough for the message to sink in, then concludes. "The Alto Vallejo can save us from that, and I respectfully suggest that eight and a half million dollars is a fair price to pay to keep the desert from our streets—and not on top of them."

When Hollis Mulwray is called upon to speak about the proposal, Gittes demonstrates interest, putting down his *Racing Form*. A conflict is presented after Bagby, speaking for prominent local economic interests, is challenged by Chief Engineer Mulwray:

"In case you've forgotten, gentlemen, over five hundred lives were lost when the Van der Lip Dam gave way—core samples have shown that beneath this bedrock is shale similar to the permeable shale in the Van der Lip disaster. It couldn't withstand that kind of pressure there. Now you propose yet another dirt banked terminus dam with slopes of two and one half to one, one hundred twelve feet high and a twelve thousand-acre water surface. Well, it won't hold. I won't build it. It's not that simple—I am not making that kind of mistake twice. Thank you, gentlemen."

Mulwray's emphatic declaration prompts an indignant response from a red-faced farmer who leads into council chambers several scrawny, bleating sheep. This prompts a grin from an intrigued Gittes. The council president angrily demands that the farmer remove his sheep, to which he briskly retorts, "Tell me where to take them! You don't have an answer for that so quick, do you? You steal the water from the valley, ruin the grazing, starve my livestock—who's paying you to do that, Mr. Mulwray, that's what I want to know!"

The farmer's angry question remains utmost in viewers' minds with a dramatic shift to a dry Los Angeles River, which manifests the desperation of city residents caught in a drought. Gittes watches in the distance through binoculars as Mulwray, played by Darrell Zwerling, stands in the dry riverbed and has a conversation with a young Mexican boy wearing a sombrero who sits on a swaybacked horse. While this vigil is in process, Gittes gets a surprise as some water trickles in his direction from a nearby out-fall. Soon he is standing in a puddle of water.

Without one word of dialogue, viewers are able to contrast the desperate spectacle of the angry farmer and his water-starved sheep in the Los Angeles City Council Chambers alongside obvious runoff. Something crooked seems to be happening. With water so precious, where is the runoff coming from and, even more importantly, why?

The next day, Gittes's emissary Walsh tracks Mulwray, who visits three reservoirs and becomes involved in a loud argument outside the Pig'n Whistle restaurant in Hollywood. Walsh has pictures. The other man is Huston, someone beyond Gittes's recognition at the moment. Soon a strong connection will emerge.

While Gittes confers with Walsh, he receives a call from his other colleague, Duffy, who is tailing Mulwray. He reports that the city's chief engineer is rowing in Echo Park near downtown Los Angeles with a young blonde woman. Gittes arrives on the scene with Walsh, taking pictures of Mulwray and the unidentified young woman as they row past him. To avoid suspicion, he gives the impression he is taking Walsh's picture.

The Gittes stakeout of Mulwray and the girl next leads him to the El Macando Apartments. From the vantage point of a nearby ledge, he observes Mulwray and the girl talking in the backyard. From outward appearances, the woman claiming to be Mrs. Mulwray is correct and the city water department's chief engineer appears to be actively pursuing a younger woman.

THE DOUBLE CROSS

Towne astutely plays with the audience's imagination by crossing it up just when it appears that a major story element has been exposed. Jake Gittes is victimized by a shrewd double cross, which exposes him to ridicule. The plot twist is visually revealed as Gittes sits in a barbershop getting a shave. A newspaper headline focuses on a story about a love nest being operated by the Department of Water and Power's chief engineer at the El Macando Apartments at city expense. Barney the barber tells him, "Face it. You're practically a movie star." Gittes stares outside. The heat wave and intense drought are once more exposed as a man stands helplessly in the street, the hood of his car up, watching his radiator boiling over. "Heat's murder," Barney says solemnly.

No sooner has the intense heat been mentioned than more comes from a different direction as a near fight erupts. The man in the adjoining chair begins denouncing Gittes for the story in the paper, telling him, "You got a hell of a way to make a living." Anger quickly escalates as the man, when asked by Gittes how he makes his living, replies that he works in the Mortgage Department of First

National Bank. Gittes responds that issuing foreclosures is not his way of making a living. Barney seeks to restrain Gittes, who issues a challenge to the banker to step outside and "talk this over." He hotly defends his livelihood: "Look, pal—I make an honest living. People don't come to me unless they're miserable and I help 'em out of a bad situation. I don't kick them out of their homes like you jerks who work in the bank."

Barney pulls Gittes away and averts trouble by starting to tell him a risqué joke about how Chinese men approach intercourse. Before listening to Barney, a still-rattled Gittes declares, "I don't know how that got in the paper as a matter of fact —it surprised me it was so quick. I make an honest living."

A Speedy Transition and Major Career Trouble

Gittes shows himself to be a man who can change moods quickly. By the time he returns to the office, he is all smiles, the reason being the joke about Chinese intercourse habits, which Barney finished telling him. He is so determined to tell the joke to his aides Walsh and Duffy that he dismisses his secretary to go to the "little girl's room." As he tells a crude men's locker room joke, an elegantly dressed, beautiful, extremely solemn-appearing woman stands behind him, unknown to Gittes. His emissaries seek to tip Gittes off, but he is undeterred, refusing to be interrupted. A small, gray-haired man stands next to her.

The detective receives a profound shock when he finishes the story and observes the elegant woman with the high cheekbones and classic features standing in his office. He realizes why Walsh and Duffy were so intent on interrupting him. The woman is so stunning that he is almost gasping, as well as feeling embarrassment over the fact that she has overheard the joke. She is the real Evelyn Mulwray portrayed by Faye Dunaway. Her anger is cold and measured as she asks if they have ever met. "I think I—I would've remembered," a stunned Gittes blurts. When she reveals she is Evelyn Mulwray, Gittes responds, "Not that Mulwray?" She quickly apprises him that since he apparently likes publicity, he is going to get it, which leads to the following exchange:

GITTES: Now wait a minute, Mrs. Mulwray. There's some misunderstanding here. It's not going to do any good to get tough with me.
EVELYN: I don't get tough with anybody, Mr. Gittes. My lawyer does.

Evelyn Mulwray stalks out of Gittes's office as the gray-haired man reveals the reason for his presence, handing the detective a summons and complaint. A stunned Gittes stands and contemplates his fate amid a flood tide of events. Now his very livelihood is in jeopardy. The legal action could ultimately result in his private detective's license being lifted by the state.

Jack Nicholson enjoys a rare quiet moment with Faye Dunnaway in Roman Polanski's 1974 noir blockbuster, *Chinatown*. Detective Nicholson is targeted for murder when he investigates the corrupt influence of John Huston, a multimillionaire seeking to control Los Angeles's water supply and waltz off with $30 million after buying up real estate at a cheap price and selling it after water is made available in the areas involved. Robert Towne secured an Oscar for Best Original Screenplay by adapting to the screen a real-life incident involving Los Angeles pioneer William Mulholland.

Filmmaking is a combination of pictures and character conflict. Robert Towne during the first 20 pages of *Chinatown* has carefully set out the following scenario with minimal dialogue:

1) Detective Jake Gittes is revealed as a detective hired to spy on those suspected of cheating on their spouses, displaying a similarity to Mike Hammer in *Kiss Me Deadly*. His modus operandi as well as his personal characteristics are revealed in his meeting with Curly. While telling his client not to worry about the money he owes him, the wily Gittes will put Curly to work in an important capacity late in the film.

2) A woman proclaiming herself to be Evelyn Mulwray next appears, hiring Gittes to engage in his specialty, spying on a presumed disloyal spouse, in this case the powerful Chief Engineer of the Los Angeles Department of Water and Power.

3) Gittes's investigation propels him into the heart of the burning political controversy of the city, a ballot measure allocating taxpayer money to build a dam to bring needed water to Los Angeles, which is in the midst of a drought. Hollis Mulwray is a formidable obstacle, believing that the proposed dam is unsafe to build.

4) Gittes is subjected to a double cross after the pictures he has taken of Mulwray with a young woman at Echo Park and the El Macando Apartments are leaked to a local newspaper, which runs a highly sensationalized story about the discovery replete with photos.

5) Gittes is confronted by the real Mrs. Mulwray who, in a cold fury, informs him he will be getting plenty of publicity before he is through, the clear inference being that his career will be in tatters. She exits a few steps ahead of the process server, who politely serves Gittes and leaves.

BASED ON HISTORY

The political controversy which plagued Gittes in *Chinatown* was rooted in fact. A major crisis rocked Los Angeles—not in 1937, as in the Towne script, but in 1903. The city had reached the 100,000 mark when the Los Angeles River went bone dry. A new water supply was vitally needed. A man of vision went to work to realize that objective.

William Mulholland was a self-made man in the strictest sense of the term. Born in Ireland, he arrived in the United States toward the end of the nineteenth century and settled in Los Angeles. While he never finished grade school, the self-educated Mulholland read Shakespeare and engineering manuals. In the manner of Hollis Mulwray of *Chinatown*, he became a one-man information library on the subject of water resources and was able to carry the water plan of the entire city around in his head. Mulholland in the early twentieth century served in the same capacity as Mulwray some three decades later.

Mulholland's vision for a fresh water source for Los Angeles was shared by the city's business and community leaders. The proposed source was the Owens Valley, located some 200 miles north of Los Angeles. Mulholland visited there in 1904. It was a rugged two-week journey, and stories abounded that Mulholland and his party left a trail of discarded empty whiskey bottles.

The result of Mulholland's efforts was the building of an aqueduct which bears his name. The effort prior to the actual vote by the Los Angeles citizenry was conducted in secrecy for good reason. Former Los Angeles Mayor Fred Eaton bought the only dam site for himself, the companion figure to Sam Bagby in the film, who argued vociferously on behalf of the project. Harrison Gray Otis and Harry Chandler, publishers of the *Los Angeles Times*, supported the project in secrecy, gloating over the artifice and chicanery involved.

The secrecy involved keeping the public in the dark regarding what was happening in the San Fernando Valley, which was not a part of Los Angeles at the time. The water from the proposed aqueduct would pass through the valley, tremendously enhancing the value of land there, and acreage was purchased on a wide scale by a major real estate syndicate. "The investors comprised an old boy network," *Chinatown* scenarist Towne revealed. "It was a WASP network."

A central element of the film was the $30 million profit realized by Noah Cross. In order to provide the San Fernando Valley with the benefits of the rich water supply, it was necessary for the valley to be incorporated into the city. With major elements from the business and political communities solidly supporting the incorporation, the result was easily accomplished.

Solid support for the aqueduct proposal was provided by none other than President Theodore Roosevelt, known as "the great conservationist." Roosevelt assured a hands-off policy for the entire area surrounding the proposed aqueduct by declaring it a national forest and thereby off-limits to anything other than conservationist activity. The irony is that with its desert composition, the forest consisted of but a few trees.

"Los Angeles never had a reason to be there," Marc Reisner, author of the book *Cadillac Desert*, exclaimed. "Above all it lacked water."

If the water stopped flowing, the thriving city of Los Angeles would become a desert overnight, which made a compelling argument to voters who turned out to decide whether William Mulholland's dream would become reality. Los Angeles voters approved the Mulholland Aqueduct by a margin of 10 to 1. A total of 100,000 workers toiled on the project. The reason for the large number was the necessity of frequently replacing workers enduring 110-degree heat to create what was referred to as "the world's largest garden."

A prideful and buoyant William Mulholland presided over the Mulholland Aqueduct dedication ceremony when the vast project was completed in 1913. As the first surge of water broke through the aqueduct and became visible to the joyous onlookers, Mulholland exclaimed, "There it is! Take it!" Though a full program of entertainment had been planned, including music, it was soon canceled upon the realization that the only true star of the occasion apart from the man after whom the aqueduct was named was the water itself. All entertainment ceased as the onlookers sprinted toward the new aqueduct, drinking the cascading water as they became a part of an important moment of city history.

At the time the Mulholland Aqueduct was initially functioning, it had the capacity to supply four times more than what the city's present population required. Unlimited potential was created and land speculators enjoyed a tremendous boom. The desert was turned into a blooming Garden of Eden as the city's population increased by leaps and bounds. The head of the Los Angeles Chamber of Commerce visited cities throughout the United States, extolling the virtues of the new Eden created in the middle of the desert. A major emigration catalyst was the weather, a shirtsleeve climate virtually the entire year without the presence of the air pollution that would later plague Los Angeles and surrounding areas. "The air was wonderful," Robert Towne said. "It has an ideal mean temperature all year around. You can walk around with almost no clothing. The air was like an extension of your own skin."

The year that the Mulholland Aqueduct was opened some enterprising pioneers who would become the first moguls of an exciting new industry arrived. According to Kevin Starr, California State Librarian, "The first movie moguls D.W. Griffith and Cecil B. DeMille came to Los Angeles in 1913, just a few months after the water had come." Scores of others joined them from all parts of the country and other parts of the world. By 1920 Los Angeles became the nation's leading agricultural center. By 1932 the city had one million residents.

Following the tremendous population upheaval, the original Owens Valley water source was insufficient to handle increasing demand. Water was siphoned from the Owens River into the dam, precipitating great anger from residents of Bishop, who saw their water supply jeopardized. At one point, the aqueduct was dynamited as local resistance increased. Today citizens who participated in the resistance effort are saluted as heroes by their descendants and other residents. Bishop is located near the town of Bridgeport, where Robert Mitchum relocated and opened a gas station in *Out of the Past* after being left by Jane Greer. (The scenes in the film were actually shot at Lake Arrowhead, between Los Angeles and Palm Springs, much closer to RKO Studios.)

William Mulholland sent a contingent of 600 heavily armed policemen to the Owens Valley to restore order, and while he was able to quell that disturbance, a major tragedy occurred that destroyed his life and prompted his early demise. The Saint Francis Dam broke, flooding entire communities and causing the worst natural disaster the state had encountered up to that time along with the San Francisco earthquake. Mulholland had examined the dam shortly before the disaster and supplied his approval. "There was talk of the father of the city being indicted," Kevin Starr said.

To that point, William Mulholland had been an exuberant man with an energy and appearance belying his chronological years. After the Saint Francis Dam tragedy, he shortly became old beyond his years and died, never able to shake the trauma of the tragedy and loss of life. When Hollis Mulwray responds to former Mayor Bagby in *Chinatown*, stating emphatically that he will not build the proposed Alto Vallejo Dam, the chief engineer's allusion to the Van der Lip Dam and the tragedy that resulted is mindful of the Saint Francis Dam episode from local history.

As noted, while incidents such as those described in *Chinatown* had predecessors in fact, they occurred a full generation before the Depression year of 1937 in which the film is set. The question arises as to why Towne did not set his story in the actual period in which the events described occurred.

FLEMISH ART AND A HISTORICAL SHIFT

Syd Field, as earlier noted, was so impressed by the brilliant story thrust and mechanics of Towne's *Chinatown* script that he used it as a model for his students. While he was teaching a screenwriting course in Brussels, having taken Towne's script with him to serve as an instructive example, one weekend Field traveled to Bruges, a fifteenth-century city filled with great architecture and canals located one hour from the Belgian capital by train. He visited a museum featuring early Flemish art. A friend remarked that a custom of early Flemish painters was to visit Italy to sharpen their skills. They sketched and painted Italian landscapes, then returned to Brussels or Antwerp. When they painted their patrons, they used those landscapes as backdrops for their work. As Field stood and observed the beautiful paintings featuring the Italian backdrops, a connection surfaced: "That's when the light bulb flashed, and suddenly I understood *Chinatown*! I finally understood what had been nagging me about the film. Robert Towne took a scandal that occurred at the turn of the century and used it as the backdrop for a screenplay that takes place in 1937! That's what the Flemish painters did!"

There was sound reasoning behind Towne's historical transposition. At the turn of the century, Los Angeles was in more of a pioneering stage, and the vast migration and development characterizing it as it existed one generation later, where Towne set his story, made it a more fascinating place to write about as well as a more scenic city. By setting the film in 1937, Towne enabled director Polanski and cinematographer John A. Alonzo to shoot locations such as Echo Park, City Hall and Chinatown itself as they existed at the culmination of comprehensive development contrasted with the turn-of-the-century city in which Mulholland lobbied assiduously to bring his aqueduct dream to reality.

Film historians and critics have focused on the detective character Towne etched, Jake Gittes, and observed influences from the two hard-boiled California detective writers credited with sparking the film noir movement, Dashiell Hammett and Raymond Chandler. An analysis of Gittes as well as the film's subject matter demonstrates that Chandler was far more of an influence. It will be recalled that Hammett described Sam Spade, as faithfully portrayed by Humphrey Bogart in John Huston's *The Maltese Falcon*, as a man noted for taking charge of things, of being able to stay one jump ahead of his foes, capable of outthinking or outfighting them depending upon the occasion. The unforgettable scenes in which Bogart bats the ears and generally humiliates a hapless Elisha Cook Jr. are reflective of Sam Spade as a detective in command.

The Jake Gittes character brilliantly delineated by Jack Nicholson is reflective of the Vietnam-Watergate period in which Towne wrote the screenplay and when the film was initially released. Nicholson as Gittes comes much closer to Dick Powell in his unforgettable portrayal of Chandler's detective, Philip Marlowe, in *Murder, My Sweet* (1944). By that point in the forties, with the world at war, traditional hero concepts were being discarded for more realistic cinema portrayals of protagonists bucking vast machines. Otto Kruger with his penthouse suite at the Sunset Towers, with his money enabling him to hurl considerable weight, is reminiscent of John Huston holding court at the Albacore Club in *Chinatown*, where he seeks to casually buy off Nicholson in a manner to which the corrupt millionaire has become all too accustomed. Nicholson, like Powell before him, is a determined detective forced to surmount powerful obstacles to arrive at the truth, always mindful of how formidable the opposition is as well as his own limitations.

Syd Field interviewed Towne at Sherwood while Field was conducting his screenwriting class there. Towne explained his point of view in approaching *Chinatown* by saying, "Some crimes are punished because they can be punished. If you kill somebody, rob or rape somebody, you'll be caught and thrown into jail. But crimes against an entire community you can't really punish, so you end up rewarding them. You know, those people who get their names on streets and plaques at City Hall. And that's the basic point of the story."

Towne made his point crystal clear in the first scene of the film after Curly, in despairing humiliation, contemplates aloud killing his wife, mentioning the "unwritten law" he perceives will protect him. A case-hardened Gittes, who has experienced firsthand the power of money and the control it buys, brings Curly in prompt touch with reality as he shouts, "You gotta be rich to kill somebody, anybody, and get away with it. You think you got that kind of dough, you think you got that kind of class?"

A NATIVE SON'S VIEW

The Los Angeles of 1937 graphically depicted by Robert Towne combined a solid research eye with a native son status. He grew up in San Pedro, the merchant fishing community he depicts through the cuckolded Curly. Towne, like Curly, worked as a young man as a commercial fisherman.

"I grew up amidst fishermen, Mexicans, chief petty officers in the merchant marine with three-day growths of beard who would come up and *wheeeeze* on you," Towne recalled. He described his boyhood neighborhood as "rather polyglot," adding, "I was the only Jew on the block, I think." Towne expressed the belief that "Every writer has to use the world he lives in as source material, I think, though it shouldn't impose restrictions or limitations on what you write. You have to be able to get into the worlds, the fantasies of people outside yourself as well."

Towne reflected on William Mulholland's "There it is, take it" statement regarding the cascading water at the Mulholland Aqueduct opening, extending it well beyond that epochal Los Angeles moment. He saw Mulholland's statement as representing a local attitude.

"'There it is, take it.' That's what the attitude had always been out here about everything," Towne exclaimed. "L.A. has never been viewed as a city, but as a place where hustlers come. It's like a mine, and everyone's trying to hit the main vein and get it out, then leave…. It's never viewed as a city. Never has been. It's a place where you just Get Yours, then get out. It doesn't matter what happens to the land, the air or any of its natural beauty. That's the attitude."

Towne researched thirties' Los Angeles by speaking to local residents who were there during that period. He discovered a pattern of discrimination heightened by the fact that so many people came from elsewhere. A conformity pattern developed in which traditional Anglo-Saxon Americanism was stressed. The lewd joke about the sex pattern of Chinese men that Gittes hears in the barbershop and repeats in his office was told to him by a native Angeleno who had lived in the city during the thirties and heard it then.

Later in the film, Towne focuses on discriminatory restrictions often excluding all but traditional WASP types. The topic of restrictive covenants in real estate transactions, which were not declared unconstitutional by the U.S. Supreme Court until 1949, and notoriously in country clubs, is broached by Towne when Nicholson and Dunaway, while in the process of snooping for information, visit a rest home for seniors. He chides the home's manager by asking if individuals of the "Jewish persuasion" are permitted.

A CHANDLER RING

The similarity between Chandler's Marlowe and Towne's Gittes becomes discernible when Gittes visits the office of Hollis Mulwray at City Hall and is directed to the chief engineer's assistant, Russ Yelburton, played by John Hillerman, who exudes an oily smoothness, appearing to cooperate with the detective when the street-smart Gittes knows he is covering up. After Yelburton and Gittes finish talking, the detective observes a familiar face standing in front of the elevators in the hallway, Claude Mulvihill, played by Roy Jenson. The following Chandleresque exchange occurs:

GITTES: Mulvihill, what are you doing here?
MULVIHILL: They shut my water off, what's it to you?
GITTES: How'd you find out? You don't drink it, you don't take a bath in it, maybe they sent you a letter. Ah, but then you'd have to be able to read.

An angry Mulvihill moves toward Gittes. "Relax, Mulvihill, glad to see you," Gittes responds. The biting dialogue is reminiscent of Chandler. There is more of the same after Yelburton reveals to Gittes that Mulvihill is working for the department. Before Gittes steps on the elevator, he tells Yelburton he is in luck since Mulvihill is a good choice to aid in water conservation. Gittes deadpans that when Mulvihill was sheriff of Ventura County, he saw to it that bootleggers during Prohibition were able to transport rum into Mulvihill's bailiwick without one drop being lost.

Intent upon restoring his reputation in place of being "a local joke," Gittes visits the home of Mulwray. Instead he has his second meeting with Mrs. Mulwray, who informs him her husband is not there. Over iced tea, she agrees to drop her lawsuit. Gittes expresses concern that the young blonde woman he observed with Mulwray has vanished. She refuses to be drawn into "personal" matters, informing Gittes that her husband might possibly be at Oak Pass Reservoir.

DEATH AND A GRIM REMINDER

In order to gain access to Oak Pass Reservoir, which has been sealed off by police, Gittes pulls a Philip Marlowe-type move. On his visit to the Department of Water and Power, he had taken some cards from Deputy Chief Yelburton. To gain entrance, Gittes hands a uniformed officer a card and successfully passes himself off as Yelburton. When he arrives in the restricted area, he encounters Lieutenant Luis Escobar, a sleek-looking man in his thirties with a no-nonsense manner and expression, portrayed by Perry Lopez. One sees diffidence on the part of Gittes, especially when he learns that Escobar has been promoted to lieutenant. He is immediately needled by his assistant, Loach, reminiscent of Chandler and Marlowe's recurring difficulties with policemen, especially in Bay City.

As is so frequent in drama, tension emerges not from the spoken word but through what remains unsaid. Gittes knew Escobar from Chinatown, where the private detective functioned as a policeman working as an investigator for the Los Angeles District Attorney and the lieutenant worked as an officer there in his earlier days on the way up. One sees a painful expression of "what might have been" when Gittes learns about Escobar's promotion. *Chinatown* is a highly symbolic title, shorthand for what is wrong with the system as well as Gittes's personal Waterloo. Forces far more powerful than Gittes were responsible for bringing him down when it was believed that he was standing in their way. The actual circumstances are never revealed, but mere mention of the word resurrects a painful syndrome within Gittes. Early in their conversation, Gittes asks, "You still throw Chinamen into jail for spitting on the laundry?" Escobar immediately replies, "You're behind the times, Jake—they've got steam irons now—(smiles) And I'm out of Chinatown."

The Chinatown colloquy ends and Gittes expresses a desire to talk to Hollis

Mulwray, asking Escobar if he has seen him. Escobar responds grimly, "You're welcome to try. There he is." Gittes looks down into the reservoir, observing two men using poles with hooks as they ultimately pull up and out of the water a dead man, who is Mulwray.

It takes little time for Gittes to be drawn ever tighter into the developing web. When Evelyn Mulwray is questioned by Lieutenant Escobar, she discloses that Gittes had been representing her. The self-serving claim is untrue, since the closest he came to representing a Mulwray was when an imposter, played by Diane Ladd, came to his office and hired him. Gittes, a man who professionally lives on the edge, recognizes the potential danger of the widow's claim. Earlier he had been concerned about professional ridicule and the prospect of losing his license resulting from a lawsuit pursued by an influential wife of an important city official. Now another danger stems from the same source, Evelyn Mulwray, in her false claim that Gittes had been representing her.

Gittes does not believe that Mulwray committed suicide or died from an accidental fall. His instincts, honed from his bitter Chinatown days, tell him that the chief engineer was murdered and that important influences are involved, those seeking to control the destiny of the city through the crucial issue of water. If Evelyn Mulwray can be found to be linked in any way to her husband's death Gittes can be prosecuted for withholding information from the police and as an accessory in the water chief's murder.

Luis Escobar tells Gittes that the police will declare Mulwray's death an accident out of respect for his position, but Gittes's detective's instincts will believe none of it. Mulwray was murdered in his mind, and a visit to the county morgue confirms his suspicion. A local drunk who had been living in one of the downtown storm drains was said to have drowned through passing out in an intoxicated state at the bottom of the riverbed in the Los Angeles River under Hollenbeck Bridge. The following dialogue ensues between Gittes and the coroner's assistant:

GITTES: It's bone dry, Morty.
MORTY: It's not completely dry.
GITTES: Yeah, well he ain't gonna drown in a damp riverbed either, I don't care how soused he was. That's like drowning in a teaspoon.
MORTY: We got water out of him, Jake. He drowned.

Gittes's increasing suspicions prompt him back to the riverbed of the Los Angeles River. He finds the same Mexican boy riding on his swaybacked horse to whom Hollis Mulwray had been speaking while Gittes had been following the now deceased water chief. Gittes asks about the subject of the conversation with Mulwray. The boy replies that he told him about the water "when it comes." Gittes asks what the young Mexican boy had told Mulwray. "Comes in different parts of the river," the boy responds. "Every night a different part."

A Hellish Marathon

Another element of *Chinatown* reminiscent of *Murder, My Sweet* is the effective use of the hellish marathon ordeal in each film. In *Murder, My Sweet*, Powell almost tastes death after he visits the Sunset Towers penthouse suite of smooth-talking mobster Otto Kruger. When Powell asks tough questions of Kruger, the detective eventually punches him, after which the mobster knocks him out with the butt of his revolver. The ensuing nightmarish sequence in which brilliant montage photography is used finds Powell alternately dropping off into deep sleep and awakening amid tremors and heavy sweating. He is the captive of a merciless quack doctor in a supposed hospital on a residential street of Hollywood, which is actually a drug operation. Powell's ordeal continues after he finally breaks out of the phony hospital, having to confront once more the dogged presence of the homicidal Moose Malloy, played by Mike Mazurki. Eventually Powell reaches the home of Anne Shirley, having gone a full day without food or sleep. Just as he is experiencing some badly needed peace and quiet and Shirley is preparing him some food, two policemen arrive on the scene and interrogate him.

Such marathon sequences are effective for several reasons: 1) Action has been sustained for a long period of time; 2) sympathy and empathy build toward the detective as a victim, having had to endure such a nightmarish period; 3) the ordeal underscores the traumas of the private detective; and 4) in the resulting conflict, the respective determination of the detective, along with that of the powerful forces arrayed against him, are dramatically displayed.

The hellish marathon of Jake Gittes ensues as he climbs a fence and trespasses into Oak Pass Reservoir. As he conducts his silent inspection, illuminated by one overhead light amid the humming of high-tension wires, he hears gunshot sounds. He dives into the flood control channel. Eventually he loses the men pursuing him, but it is not long before he is overrun by an avalanche of water, which carries him down the channel. He finally pulls himself out of the water by clutching at the fence. He curses the loss of a Florsheim shoe, but before he can reflect further, his old nemesis Mulvihill emerges with a small man carrying a switchblade knife.

Never in the long and distinguished career of Alfred Hitchcock did his famous brief appearances before the camera in his films contain the symbolic meaning of the role played by *Chinatown's* director Roman Polanski playing the small man brandishing the knife. Mulvihill punches Gittes, then pulls his coat down and pins his arms, making him vulnerable prey for the knife-wielding small man.

A street lamp overhead displays the silvery knife with a luminous gleam. The symbolism is abundantly clear as Polanski exclaims, "You are a very nosy fellow, kitty cat.... You know what happens to nosy fellows?" With a quick flick, the small man, steaming with rage, illustrates his point by splitting Gittes's nostril. He tells the detective that nosy people lose their noses, issuing a warning: "Next time you lose the whole thing, kitty cat. I'll cut it off and feed it to my goldfish, understand?" Gittes is compelled to reply that he understands, after which he grovels on the ground as blood spurts from his nose. The scene ends with his tormentor pushing him to the ground with his shoe.

Gittes, his nose bandaged, is seen the next day at his office. His associates Duffy and Walsh discuss the possibility of suing Mulvihill for his attack on Gittes. The savvy detective replies that he wants to nail "the big boys that are making the payoffs." Walsh brings the discussion back to the central focus of Towne's script: the ability to flout the law through financial might. "Sue people like that, they're liable to be having dinner with the judge who's trying the suit," Walsh exclaims.

Gittes's discussion with his colleagues is interrupted by a telephone call from an Ida Sessions, who explains that she was the woman who had come to his office and impersonated Evelyn Mulwray. She explains she was put up to the job but refuses to meet with Gittes. Instead she passes along a tip that he can find "one of those people ... in the obituary column of today's *Times*." Before a puzzled Gittes can follow up, Ida Sessions hangs up.

Gittes continues moving at the same brisk pace. He is next seen having lunch with Evelyn Mulwray. Gittes mentions having received a generous check from her. He strongly doubts that the check was motivated by concern over her proposed lawsuit against him and the professional difficulty she might have caused him. When she reveals that she learned about her husband's affair and was actually grateful to receive the information, Gittes exclaims that this runs counter to his experience as a professional who is paid to check up on the misbehavior of spouses. He implores her to cooperate with him and reveal all she knows.

The detective then proceeds along Wilshire Boulevard to City Hall and the office of the chief engineer, a position now being assumed by former assistant Russ Yelburton. While Gittes waits in an outer office, unable to be discouraged from sticking around by Yelburton's secretary, who tells him he will be tied up for a long time, he observes pictures of the late Hollis Mulwray with Noah Cross. He immediately makes a connection. He had learned for the first time at lunch that Evelyn Mulwray's maiden name had been Cross. The secretary, angry over Gittes's stubborn determination to see her boss, is questioned about the connection between Mulwray and Cross. She tartly responds that they owned the department together as partners.

Annoyed by Gittes's refusal to leave and the questions he poses, the secretary finally confers briefly with Yelburton, then reveals that the chief engineer will see him. Yelburton notices Gittes's bandaged nose. Gittes tells him he cut himself shaving. When Yelburton says, "That must really smart," Gittes delivers a Chandleresque one-liner, "Only when I breathe."

That turns out to be the only humor in an otherwise tense discussion. The detective launches a frontal assault:

GITTES: Well, look at it this way, Mr. Yelburton. Mulwray didn't want to build a dam—and he had a reputation that was hard to get around, so you decided to ruin it. Then he found out that you were dumping water every night—then he—was drowned.

When Yelburton coolly denounces the charge as "outrageous," Gittes gets up and walks toward the door, telling him "Whitey Merholtz over at the *Times*" would like to know about gallons of water being dumped "down the toilet in the middle of a drought," which prompts a concerned Yelburton to ask him to sit down. He explains that the runoff was designed to benefit some of the badly hit farmers in the northwest San Fernando Valley.

Gittes's pace is unyielding. He next speaks with Evelyn Mulwray in his office. She wishes to hire him, and he seeks answers. As she peruses and prepares to sign the detective's standard representation form, he quizzes her about Noah Cross and Hollis Mulwray. She becomes so nervous that at one point, she forgets she is smoking one cigarette and lights another, being reminded by Gittes that she already has one going. Conceding that she is indeed the daughter of Noah Cross, Evelyn tells Gittes that the two men had a falling out after the Van der Lip Dam tragedy, which Mulwray had opposed building. Mulwray also believed that the public should own the city's water supply, a position Cross did not share. When Evelyn Mulwray explains that the two men had a falling out over the dam tragedy and had not spoken since, Gittes spots an inconsistency, recalling the pictures Walsh took of the furious argument the two men had outside the Pig'n Whistle in Hollywood. When he asks her about whether she gets along with her father, Gittes's newest client refuses to answer at all!

The peripatetic detective is next seen having breakfast with Noah Cross at the Albacore Club. The frantic pacing reveals the determination of Gittes to get to the bottom of a dangerous continuing dilemma encompassing an entire city and the vortex in which he finds himself, having had the end of his nose taken off for being "nosey" and threatened with much worse.

John Huston's portrayal of Noah Cross is sheer perfection. The bravado and air of supreme confidence befits a mogul at the peak of his power, an un-elected kingpin of an important and rapidly developing city. His proposal that Gittes represent him is typical of a wealthy power broker accustomed to controlling people through his potent purse. Cross questions Gittes on whether he is sleeping with his daughter, then inquires about Lieutenant Lou Escobar. When Cross asks if Escobar is honest, Gittes reveals his cynically pragmatic side: "Far as it goes—of course he has to swim in the same water we all do." Cross refers to his daughter as a disturbed woman who has lost her husband. When Cross exclaims, "You may think you know what you're dealing with—but believe me, you don't," he is stopped short by the detective's expression of amusement. It leads to the following dialogue:

CROSS: Why is that funny?
GITTES: It's what the D.A. used to tell me about Chinatown.
CROSS: Was he right?

Gittes responds with a noncommittal shrug. Once more that influential code word from Gittes's darkest past is disclosed to codify the subterranean world of double-dealings, back alley transactions, as well as those in which Cross and influential operatives are involved, particularly the bureaucrats controlled by the mogul.

Cross then displays the cynicism of the puppet master after Gittes uses the word "respectable" in connection with him. "'Course I'm respectable," Cross concurs, adding acidly, "I'm old. Politicians, ugly buildings and whores all get respectable if they last long enough. I'll double whatever your fees are—and I'll pay you ten thousand dollars if you can find Hollis' girlfriend."

Gittes is not bowled over by the prospect of quick money. Instead he stubbornly seeks answers, informing Cross that if he still wants to hire him, it is imperative that he learn why he and Mulwray were arguing at the Pig'n Whistle.

TACKLING THE BUREAUCRACY

Nicholson is at his dramatic best conveying a shrewd cynicism. At a point when the pacing has been consistently rapid and the facts have been revealed in the manner of shotgun blasts, some humor is needed in the story, along with a brief change of gears. In one scene, Gittes speaks with a *force majeure* who controls bureaucrats. In the following scene at the Hall of Records, Gittes deals with a young clerk who serves as perfect comedic foil in the detective's quest for information. While John Huston manifested the powerful creator and controller of bureaucrats, Allan Warnick as the clerk at the Hall of Records demonstrates the frustration of a minor bureaucrat as a small cog in a large machine who, nonetheless, demonstrates the small power he possesses by unleashing inner discontent, creating difficulty for those he is paid to serve.

Gittes asks a simple question, where he might find the plat books for the northwest valley. The young clerk demonstrates his petulance by informing Gittes that part of the northwest valley is in Los Angeles County and the rest is in Ventura County. "We don't have Ventura County in our Hall of Records," the clerk says tartly.

The clerk informs Gittes where he can find the L.A. County records. Gittes's interest is aroused by all the new names posted in the plat book. He is told that the new names signify recent sales. "But that means that most of the valley's been sold in the last few months," Gittes exclaims. After being curtly told that "this is not a lending library," the resourceful detective borrows a ruler, explaining that he left his glasses at home and wanted to be able to read the fine print. Gittes coughs loudly, then uses the ruler to tear off the information he requires.

After a brief respite from the wars, Gittes is then flung into a combat zone as he visits the avocado orchards in the northwest valley, investigating Chief Engineer Yelburton's claim that water had been diverted to assist farmers in that area. He is greeted with hostility and suspicion by a red-faced farmer on horseback and two other farmers, who search Gittes. The farmer on horseback asks if Gittes has been sent by the water department or the real estate office. When Gittes explains that he is investigating on behalf of a client whether or not the water department has been irrigating the farmer's land, he explodes, "Irrigating my land? The water department's been sending you people to blow up my water tanks! They threw poison down three of my wells! I call that a funny way to irrigate—who'd hire you for a thing like that?"

When Gittes reveals his client's name, Evelyn Mulray, a big farmer nearby accuses Mulray of having orchestrated the campaign against them. When an angry, thoroughly frustrated Gittes replies sharply, "Mulwray's dead—you don't know what you're talking about, you dumb Okie," a brief but furious fight ensues as the farmers attack and Gittes is subdued. Gittes awakens from his temporary unconscious state. Evelyn Mulwray is there to pick him up. The red-faced farmer and farming colleagues appear contrite over what they perceive as a misunderstanding. The red-faced farmer called Mrs. Mulwray after locating her card in Gittes's wallet.

The detective's marathon session of scrapes with death and bodily injury continues as Evelyn Mulwray drives him away in her cream-colored Packard. His car might have been damaged in the scrape with the farmers, he might be bruised and bloodied, but his brain continues to click as he pieces together the information he has amassed during better than a day without sleep. As Evelyn drives, Gittes informs her that the dam her husband opposed is a con job, that the facility L.A. voters were being duped into supporting will result in the water going to the San Fernando Valley rather than the city. "Yeah—they've been blowing these farmers out of here and buying their land for peanuts," Gittes explains. "Have any idea what this land'll be worth with a steady water supply? About thirty million more than they paid."

Gittes has been mulling over the list of names obtained from the Hall of Records. One name stands out in his mind, that of a Jasper Lamar Crabb who was recorded as having purchased 25,000 acres of valley land. He pulls out his wallet, retrieving the obituary column he had ripped out of the *Times* after receiving the call from Ida Sessions. He learns that a memorial service was held at Mar Vista Inn for Jasper Lamar Crabb, who had died three weeks earlier, meaning the land he was registered as having purchased occurred one week after his demise.

ANOTHER BRUSH WITH DEATH

Jake and Evelyn pose as husband and wife when they arrive at Mar Vista Inn and Rest Home. A Mr. Palmer greets them as Gittes tells him they are interested in finding a residence for his father. He twits Palmer and reveals the widespread discrimination in effect in thirties Los Angeles by asking his host with an expression of mock seriousness if Mar Vista accepts anyone of "the Jewish persuasion." An embarrassed Palmer replies, "I'm sorry—we don't." A cynical Gittes replies with feigned smoothness, "Don't be sorry, neither does Dad. Wanted to make sure though, didn't we, honey?" Jake looks at a stunned Evelyn.

Gittes is rebuffed on grounds of confidentiality when he asks to see a list of Mar Vista's patients, but Palmer agrees to allow them to have a look around. For Jake, the Mar Vista excursion is the latest in a cram course on the treachery and

corruption of Noah Cross and his octopus-like machine, where the shadow of imminent death remains paramount. It takes little time to tie the Mar Vista operation
to Cross. He tells Evelyn, "You're looking at the owners of a 50,000 acre empire."
Jake seeks out an Emma Dill, a listed recent purchaser of valley acreage, who embar-
rassedly explains that her late husband once owned some Long Beach beach property, "but we lost it." The detective notices that the material from the quilts on
which Emma and a group of other women are working bears the "AC" symbol of
Cross's Albacore Club. A disgusted Palmer then reenters, explaining, "We're a sort
of unofficial charity of theirs, Mr. Gittes. Would you care to come this way? Someone wants to see you."

Jake and Evelyn accompany Palmer to the entrance hall, where Mulvihill hov-
ers. The Cross operative explains, "I want you to meet somebody, Gittes." Evelyn
seeks to remain, but Jake talks her into leaving and getting into her car. It is a calculation that will save his life. As Mulvihill walks ahead of Gittes toward the door,
Jake makes a swift move, kicking the Cross enforcer in the groin, then pummeling
him to the ground, returning the favor for the last time they met. At one point, Mulvihill's gun falls out and Palmer makes a quick move to retrieve it, but the detective kicks it away, then promptly leaves. As Jake finishes exiting Mar Vista, he
observes the smaller man who extracted a piece of his nose along with an accomplice moving menacingly toward him. The strategy of asking Evelyn to return to
the car bears fruit as the cream-colored Packard roars toward him, forcing Gittes's
pursuers to step aside. She brings the car to a screeching halt and Gittes enters. They
speed away as two shots are fired.

LOVE AND HYDROGEN PEROXIDE

At long last Gittes has achieved some peace and quiet at Ellen Mulwray's home.
Having observed the hazardous and breakneck pace of activity Jake has endured
over the course of the afternoon and evening in which Evelyn accompanied him,
she remarks, "Well, I'm only judging on the basis of one afternoon and an evening,
but if that's how you go about your work, I'd say you're lucky to get through a whole
day." When Gittes replies that he has encountered nothing like the day he has just
endured "in some time," he is pressed for details. She has to press hard before he
ultimately reveals that the last time he endured comparable circumstances was in
Chinatown working for the district attorney, where he was told to do "as little as
possible," a key phrase that will resurface at the climax of the film. When a startled
Evelyn queries, "The district attorney gives his men advice like that?" the detective's
reply is swift and on point, "They do in Chinatown."

When Gittes asks if Evelyn has any hydrogen peroxide, she administers to him
and, at close range, two people who have endured close calls together and have
become much closer acquainted, enter the pre-intimacy stage during her ministra-
tions, as she ultimately removes the bandage from Jake's nose, concluding that the

doctor did a nice job. *Chinatown* analyst Syd Field calls the scene one of his favorites. Following the hectic eighteen hours of dangerously hellish nonstop activity of Jake Gittes, the pacing switch to a tender love scene makes thematic sense. Two people who have endured tragedy together get to know each other in a new intimate way. They make love after he notices an imperfection, an iris in Evelyn's eye. It is interesting to note just how much Towne has working for him in one scene: 1) The opportunity, through ministering to a wounded detective, an opportunity for Jake and Evelyn to know each other in a way not previously possible when they were immersed in tragedy and escaping disaster; 2) Evelyn probing curiously for details about Jake's past and his highly sensitive reluctance to talk about his Chinatown experiences; 3) The revelations she extracts about regretful instances from Jake's past; 4) His confidence in generating a romantic involvement based on noticing a flaw in the iris of one of Evelyn's eyes; and 5) The culmination of the scene in lovemaking.

Gittes's stated helplessness in influencing events in Chinatown stemmed from a conversation Robert Towne had with a policeman who had formerly worked the vice beat there. "Down there we never do anything," Towne related that the officer told him. "We don't know all the dialects, and they say don't do anything, because you could make a mistake. You don't know who's a crook and who isn't a crook. You don't know who you're helping and who you're hurting. So in Chinatown they say just don't do a goddamn thing." Towne found the notion intriguing and elaborated on it, turning it into an important metaphor. "Chinatown is the place where Gittes fucked up," Towne explained, "and Evelyn is a *person* where he fucked up. That was the idea. But ultimately, I think Chinatown—where if you're smart you do nothing—suggests the futility of good intentions."

Before Jake and Evelyn share intimacies, she is able to extract from him an admission that he left Chinatown due to a painful tragedy that will be thematically repeated at the end of the film. "I thought I was keeping someone from being hurt and actually I ended up making sure they were hurt," the detective explains with sad reluctance. Towne shrewdly works in the discovery by Jake of Evelyn's flaw in her iris, an imperfection, to invest him with the confidence to romance her in the wake of his earlier conception of her as someone who thinks she is better than the likes of himself. Towne delineated the perception of Gittes:

"So Gittes comes up against this woman who is infuriatingly correct, and everything about her is an insult to this lower-class guy who monograms everything and is made to feel ... crude ... and finally: He sees a flaw in the iris. It's emblematic at that moment of her vulnerability. If you've ever seen such eyes, you know they are very pretty. To me it was also emblematic of the fact that she is psychologically flawed. The fact that she was shot in the eye later is a coincidental echo."

"The postcoital love scene ... was improvised on the set," Towne revealed. In the earlier Towne script draft, Evelyn, who had professed to neurotic sex reactions, was ignoring Gittes, who was misconstruing her concern for the other lover the detective believes exists, a notion she encouraged to keep secret her relationship with Mulwray and the appearance of the young blonde thought to be the water chief's mistress. Towne attributes the change to the deeply rooted beliefs of director Roman Polanski.

"I don't think Roman Polanski could be interested in a woman who is involved with somebody else, or, in this case, a hero who would *worry* (about) his lover," Towne explained. "And it was Roman's identification with the hero that was making the film work. It has to be unqualified involvement with him. As with the love scene."

In earlier drafts of the screenplay, Towne revealed Jake Gittes as a great admirer of the leading racehorse of the thirties, Seabiscuit. Initially the near-fight in the barber shop, occurring due to another customer's accusation that Gittes is a cheap sensationalist who played up the suspected involvement of Mulwray with the young blonde, instead related to another comment that "Seabiscuit folded in the stretch" of a recent race. Jake's admiration of Seabiscuit was a thematic device of Towne to demonstrate the detective's appreciation of a top-line thoroughbred, which correlated with his feelings toward Evelyn Mulwray. In the final shooting script, Gittes's awkwardness toward the higher-bred, better-educated woman is conveyed through his frequent apologies after making crude comments from his former policeman's and current detective's demeanor through use of the word "broad" and other earthy expressions.

Chinatown is a story of intricately connected threads, some of which are delineated sharply during the few moments of intimacy Jake and Evelyn share after making love. Evelyn curiously probes for more information about Jake's Chinatown years, even commenting, "You must have looked cute in your uniform." After much probing, she finally wiggles it out of the detective that a woman was involved in the tragedy occurring in Chinatown, one he failed to protect. The incident was so upsetting that he left the police force as a result. It is his contemporary and current pursuer, Luis Escobar, who has won some begrudging admiration by making lieutenant rather than Jake Gittes.

Once the scene of tender sensitivity concludes, a detective's relentless chase for the truth promptly resumes. The couple's intimate conversation is interrupted by the shrill ring of the telephone. After some hurried words, Evelyn asks Jake to "trust her" and refuses to tell him where she is going. While she hurriedly dresses, Gittes reveals that he met her father that morning. "I want you to listen to me," she warns. "My father is a very dangerous man. You don't know how dangerous. You don't know how crazy." She repeats the succinct warning Noah Cross articulated at his meeting with Gittes at the Albacore Club: "You may think you know what's going on, but you don't."

SHIFTING INTO THE FINAL PHASE

A paramount reason screenwriting instructor Syd Field gave for selecting the *Chinatown* script for analysis in his classes was for its thematic organization. According to Field, the first 30 minutes of a script, constituting an equal number of minutes, consists of seizing viewer interest, introducing characters, and launching the story. Field, who also worked as a script editor at Cinemobile, contends that most viewers make up their minds in the first 10 minutes of a film, while an editor often does the same in the first 10 pages. At or around the half-hour mark, a dramatic event occurs, which spins the story toward the next hour or 60 pages, which consists of conflict. At or around page 90, the story takes a second spin with another dramatic event, leading it toward final resolution at roughly page 120 or the two-hour mark, the time frame of the average American film. Ernest Lehman, veteran scenarist with such major films as *Sweet Smell of Success, North by Northwest* (1959) and *The Sound of Music* (1965), believes in the approach of classifying the three basic segments in the manner of a playwright, with Act One, Two and Three. The death of Hollis Mulwray occurs at about the 30-minute mark of the film, propelling Towne's story into the conflict as private detective Gittes realizes he is dealing with potent forces embodying a "take no prisoners" philosophy. The intervening pages leading up to the 90-minute mark encompass Gittes's explorations, his near brushes with death, and his developing relationship with Evelyn Mulwray. At about the 90-minute mark, following sex between the film's two leading performers, Jack Nicholson and Faye Dunaway, the story pivots into its concluding phase.

The intricately constructed *Chinatown* screenplay exists on two levels: 1) The machinations of Noah Cross and connected associates and beneficiaries to control the vital water supply of a rapidly developing city, and whether Hollis Mulwray on behalf of the people or Cross will control it; and 2) the developing personal relationship between Jake Gittes and Evelyn Mulwray. The two-tiered drama cleverly intersects. The dark secrets of the Cross family are uncovered by Jake commensurate with his understanding of the business machinations of the ruthless empire builder. Too great an emphasis by Towne in recreating a key historical period of Los Angeles history could tend to make *Chinatown* too top-heavily documentary to generate audience empathy. The romantic element and the detective's interest in Evelyn Mulwray the person, who also happens to be the daughter of the film's chief villain, Noah Cross, personalizes the story and enhances dramatic potential.

As the film spins into its concluding phase, Jake begins unraveling the mystery surrounding Evelyn and the mysterious young blonde thought to be her late husband's mistress. He borrows her late husband's Buick and follows her cream-colored Packard along winding mountain roads in the darkness of late evening to a small house. He observes through a window the tear-stained face of the blonde woman along with Evelyn and her Chinese butler.

When Evelyn leaves the house and enters her car, Gittes is sitting on the passenger side. He expresses concern that the young woman is being held against her will, which Evelyn emphatically denies. All the same, she will not agree to allow him to go inside and talk to her. She implores Gittes to leave the young woman alone, explaining that she is her sister and is very upset about the death of Mulwray. "Take is easy," Gittes responds. "If it's your sister it's your sister.... Why all the secrecy?" The skeptical detective explores the deep hidden dimensions of the mystery by asking if the secrecy relates to the girl seeing Mulwray. The conversation concludes with Evelyn emotionally telling Jake that she would never harm Hollis, who had "put up with more from me than you'll ever know."

He knows there is much more to be investigated concerning the mysterious young blonde in the house as he parts company with Evelyn to go home and hopefully obtain some badly needed sleep. The fates, however, appear to be stacked against Gittes ever sleeping. No sooner does he finish a relaxing shower, put on his pajamas, and climb into bed than the telephone rings. A man's voice solemnly informs him that Ida Sessions is eager to see him. He tells the man that she can call him at his office. The persistent caller phones again, providing an Echo Park address, reiterating the importance of him seeing the woman who had posed as Evelyn Mulwray. "She begged me to call you," the man informs. "She's waiting for you."

ANOTHER TRAGIC DEATH AND INCREASING SUSPICION

As morning dawns on Los Angeles, Jake Gittes confronts the dark midnight of death. The door is open, and he enters the small apartment set in the courtyard of small bungalows so typical of Los Angeles during the thirties. He discovers the body of Ida Sessions lying on the kitchen floor. Groceries from a broken bag lie next to her, some spilled vegetables and melted ice cream.

"Find anything interesting, Gittes?" Escobar asks as he and his assistant, Loach, suddenly emerge. Gittes denies knowing Ida Sessions, explaining he had simply responded to a telephone call. The lieutenant points to Gittes's phone number written on the kitchen wall. The following tense dialogue ensues, again sounding straight out of Raymond Chandler:

ESCOBAR: Isn't that your number?
GITTES: Is it? I forgot. I don't call myself that often.
ESCOBAR: Just to be on the safe side, we had Loach here give you a ring.

Tension erupts between Gittes and Loach, who plainly dislike each other, when Escobar's partner asks him what happened to his nose, suggesting he got it closing a window. Gittes responds with a barb about Loach's wife closing her legs prematurely in sex with him, culminating with a sarcastically delivered, "Know what I mean, pal?" Loach lurches forward and Gittes tenses, preparing to commence battle, when Escobar steps in and restrains the angry enemies.

Escobar's suspicions toward Gittes are revealed as he shows the detective the pictures he took of Mulwray and the blonde girl in the boat at Echo Park and at the El Macando Apartments hideaway. Escobar demands the rest of the pictures. "This broad hired you, Gittes," Escobar concludes, "not Evelyn Mulwray." Escobar reveals that Mulwray had salt water in his lungs. He wants to know how the deceased water chief could have died by accident in a freshwater reservoir. A tense exchange occurs. Escobar concludes that Gittes saw Evelyn kill Mulwray, and that "she's been paying you off like a slot machine ever since her husband died." Jake bristles at the accusation of extortion: "I'd never extort a nickel out of my worst enemy, that's where I draw the line, Escobar."

Jake bristles at what he perceives as an illogical conclusion, that Evelyn Mulwray would kill her husband at the beach, then drag him to Oak Pass Reservoir. His own conclusion, based on dangerous personal experience, is that Mulwray was murdered after discovering runoff into the ocean, then moved to the reservoir to alleviate suspicion. Escobar puts his theory to the test by accompanying him to the ocean. His suspicion increases as only a trickle of water drops into the ocean and the drainpipe is empty. Lieutenant Escobar is unimpressed by Gittes's explanation that they arrived too late. "They only dump the water at night," Jake explains.

A uniformed policeman arrives to tell Escobar that Chief Engineer Yelburton has been contacted by phone. Yelburton tells the police the same story Gittes had heard earlier, that a little runoff results after efforts to irrigate the valley to help farmers there. Loach presses Escobar to swear out a warrant for Evelyn Mulwray's arrest. His patience exhausted, Escobar stares hatefully at Gittes and barks, "Have your client in my office in two hours—and remember: I don't have to let you go. I've got you for withholding evidence right now."

In the manner of solidly constructed mystery stories, clues and accompanying results burst forth as the film reaches its finale; but in the case of private investigator Jake Gittes, his motivation to tie the messy details of a tragic Los Angeles scandal into a neat bundle stems from a desire to maintain his detective's license and avoid exchanging his tailored suits for drab prison grays. A seething Escobar, suspecting him of extortion and withholding evidence as well as being an accessory after the fact regarding Mulwray's murder, gives him only a brief reprieve prior to booking him. Jake's first stop, logically enough, is the mansion of Evelyn Mulwray. He finds a Chinese maid in the process of closing things up, informing him that everyone has gone.

As he steps outside, he sees the same Japanese gardener with whom he has exchanged past pleasantries. The story device of resolution through eliminating misunderstanding is effectively employed. The gardener speaks poor English. He repeats something Gittes heard before as he works by the pond. "Bad for glass," he repeats what he told Gittes on a past visit. "Bad for glass," Jake politely replies. This time he learns much more as the gardener points toward the lawn, explaining, "Salt water velly bad for glass."

Gittes recognizes that the gardener had been trying to tell him about the salt water in the pond and its negative impact on the grass. As his focus shifts toward the pond, he observes an object shimmering in the light. The gardener fetches the item for him as he realizes the significance of the bifocals he holds.

The trigger mechanism is now in place for the vital final 20 minutes of film as events move at an ever brisker pace. Jake immediately calls Cross, reminding him of the agreement they made at their meeting. He tells the mogul to meet him at the Mulwray residence, concluding with "Just bring your checkbook."

PRESSURING EVELYN AND CURLY'S RETURN

Realizing the importance of locating Evelyn, Gittes drives to the house where the young woman was being held. He observes that clothes are being packed, and Evelyn explains that they have a 4:30 train to catch. The girl is upstairs, and the Chinese butler is assisting in departure preparations. As the butler goes upstairs to watch over the girl, an angry and exasperated Jake, feeling he has been used and seeking to protect his reputation, promptly telephones Lieutenant Escobar, curtly informing the widowed Mrs. Mulwray that she is going to miss her train.

Jake has clearly reached the end of the road and will not extend himself for Evelyn any further as the ever-shortening arm of the law looms closer. While Evelyn protests, seeking to leave, Gittes asks if she knows any criminal lawyers. "Don't worry—I can recommend a couple," he tells her. "They're expensive but you can afford it." Evelyn demands to know what is going on, and Gittes produces the glasses from the pond, adding that the coroner's report revealed that Mulwray had salt water in his lungs. "Now I want to know what happened and why," he demands. "I want to know before Escobar gets here because I want to hang onto my license."

While Evelyn becomes increasingly rattled from Jake's disclosures, his temper accelerates until he is on the verge of rage, seeing himself trapped in the vise of her problems, which she refuses to share with him. He presents a defense: She fought with her husband in a state of jealousy and he fell, hitting his head. She did not have the stomach to harm the girl and provided her with hush money instead. Evelyn promptly rejects Gittes's suggested defense.

Now Gittes is rigidly determined to learn the truth promptly, knowing that Escobar is on his way and that he as well as Evelyn may end up in handcuffs. He demands to know the identity of the girl, disclosing that she is not Evelyn's sister because she does not have one, revealing that he has been checking up on her. Evelyn promises to tell the truth and reveals the girl's name is Katherine. Jake begins to feel that perhaps events are finally moving on the right track, until a sour note is hit and he erupts in rage.

"She's my daughter," Evelyn reveals. Gittes stares at her in disbelief, then slaps her. "She's my sister," Evelyn sobs. He slaps her again. The process is repeated as she alternately asserts that Katherine is her sister and her daughter. Eventually he hits her hard enough to knock her into the sofa, where a cheap Chinese vase is smashed in the process. The loud commotion prompts her butler to run down the stairs in her defense. A tearful Evelyn tells the butler to go back upstairs and watch Katherine.

Finally Jake understands as Evelyn painfully reveals, "My father and I, understand, or is it too tough for you?" A crestfallen Gittes, his rage expended, is silent. The painful truth is finally disclosed by a humiliated woman dealing with a painful past. She was 15 when Katherine was born. She ran away to Mexico. It was Hollis Mulwray who came to take care of her as well as her daughter after the girl was born. Her plan is to once more travel to Mexico, but a now firmly supportive Gittes tells her that Escobar's men will be watching the train station as well as the airport. He volunteers to take care of things, meaning providing her with an escape. He is then jolted by her disclosure that the glasses he retrieved from the pond did not belong to Hollis, who did not wear bifocals. Once more an obstacle is hurled in the detective's path when he believes he has solved a case.

It is finally decided that Gittes will provide transportation for Evelyn and Katherine. She gives the address where she will be—1712 Alameda. The camera closes in on the detective, revealing an ominous look. He calls his office, instructing Walsh that Escobar will be booking him in five minutes. "Wait in the office for two hours," he tells Walsh. "If you don't hear from me, you and Duffy meet me at 1712 Alameda." Walsh's tone is as ominous as Gittes's earlier expression: "That's Chinatown!"

As soon as he hangs up on Walsh, Jake is greeted by Escobar and Loach. "Looks like she flew the coop," he tells Escobar, never bothering to reveal that he sent Evelyn on her way with instructions. The wily Jake tells Escobar that Evelyn has retreated to her maid's house. "I think she knows something's up," he plays innocent.

CURLY'S RETURN

When Gittes informs Escobar that Evelyn's maid lives in San Pedro, alert viewers are tipped off to his emerging strategy. The Towne ploy is for a character from the film's initial scene to return. Curly was crestfallen to discover the incriminating photographs documenting his wife's indiscretions as well as embarrassed that he was unable to pay Gittes, who assured him he was not after his last dollar. Now Curly is in a position to assist the detective in a moment of need.

Jake plays an excellent poker hand with Escobar. To avoid arousing his suspicion, he tells Escobar that he will write down the San Pedro address of the fictitious maid. Towne has supplied another example of Raymond Chandler's Philip Marlowe at his wiliest. In that Gittes is a former policeman himself who has worked with Luis Escobar and knows his methods well, he seeks to present a feigned picture of his own motivations to influence an erroneous response from the lieutenant. Believing that Gittes is eager to dodge him, Escobar replies, "No, Gittes, you'll show me." The following exchange reveals the determination of Escobar contrasted with the cagey deceit of a private detective of equivalent motivation:

ESCOBAR: If she's not there, you're going downtown, and you're gonna stay there til she shows up.

GITTES (deliberately petulant): Gee, Lou, I'm doing the best I can.

Jake knows that his resourcefulness must continue if he is to pull off his ploy and make contact with the San Pedro fisherman rather than be escorted downtown by Escobar and Loach. When the unmarked police vehicle pulls to a stop in front of Curly's home, Gittes asks what he hopes will be interpreted as one final favor. Insisting that Evelyn Mulwray is not armed, he beseeches Escobar to allow him one minute alone with her. "You never learn, do you, Gittes?" Escobar disgustedly replies. Jake wonders if his response means he will refuse his request. Escobar ultimately grants him three minutes and no more.

The first thing the detective does is to talk his way nonchalantly inside Curly's house when his wife answers the door. The black eye she wears is an obvious aftermath of Curly's reaction after viewing the photographs in Gittes's office. Curly and his children are at the kitchen table in the middle of dinner when Gittes arrives. Curly is honored by Jake's presence. When he introduces him to his wife, her cool reaction indicates what she thinks of his detective work, which resulted in the discovery of her infidelity and a resulting black eye.

Gittes speedily maneuvers Curly into another room, explaining that he needs the fisherman to drive him somewhere fast and that it cannot wait until dinner is finished. Curly maneuvers his car out of an alley and Gittes ducks down in the front seat next to him, avoiding the sight of Escobar and Loach.

Curly has a boat and Gittes has a use for it. Negotiations quickly conclude between the men as Gittes agrees to pay Curly $100 along with canceling his debt to the detective if he will transport two passengers to Ensenada, Mexico, that night.

Curly has his game plan in place, being told where to pick up Evelyn and Katherine. The fisherman picks up the maid at the Mulwray house. Gittes stands by the pond, waiting for his climactic meeting with Noah Cross in the approaching dusk.

When Cross arrives, he remains consistent with his image. A clever script ploy is to have Cross consistently mispronounce the detective's name during the entire film. In their earlier meeting, he made an attempt to set the power-hungry mogul straight, but he persists in referring to Jake as "Mr. Gitts" rather than Gittes. The obvious inference is that not only does Cross have a great deal on his mind; from a psychological standpoint, the salient conclusion is that names mean as little as the people behind them. Here is a master manipulator who spends what he deems is a necessary portion of his vast wealth buying people off for his own purposes. Noah Cross would agree with the worldview of the equally corrupt Harry Lime of *The Third Man*: The people observable far below Vienna's Great Wheel constituted no more than "dots" to be manipulated or dispensed with, depending on the occasion and purpose. Cross, who wants his daughter-granddaughter back, immediately asks Gittes about her. He tells her she is with her mother, then moves on to the central

John Huston, left, portrays a mogul who believes anybody can be bought for the right price in *Chinatown*, an explosive noir drama set in Los Angeles in 1937. The nose patch worn by Jack Nicholson was a souvenir provided by the film's director, Roman Polanski, who appears in one scene playing one of Huston's henchmen, who cuts a slice from Nicholson's nose. Huston as Noah Cross seeks unsuccessfully to buy off Detective Jake Gittes, played by Nicholson, who falls in love with Cross's daughter, played by Faye Dunaway.

point of the glasses he found in the pond. While Hollis Mulwray did not wear bifocals, Noah Cross does. Jake also tells Cross that the victim had salt water in his lungs, and that the mogul killed him.

The treacherous multimillionaire then delivers what sounds like an impromptu eulogy for Hollis Mulwray, explaining his fascination with tide pools, marshes and sloughs, and about how "he made this city." Cross points with pride to his continuation of Mulwray's grand vision, not bothering to point out that he killed him over the fundamental issue of whether the citizenry or a private monopoly, namely himself, should control the city's water supply. When Gittes asks how Cross plans to achieve his master stroke, aware that the San Fernando Valley is not a part of the city and that citizens will be paying for water they are not obtaining, the amoral master planner coolly responds, "That's all taken care of. You see, Mr. Gittes. Either you bring the water to L.A.—or you bring L.A. to the water." When Jake asks how this will be accomplished, Cross explains that the valley will be incorporated into the city, so the water will go to Los Angeles after all. "It's very simple," he concludes.

As Towne explained, while Jake Gittes considered himself world wise and believed himself too experienced to be shocked by outrageous behavior, the cool and blatant amorality on a grand human and economic scale practiced by Noah Cross leaves him aghast. While he had previously dealt with numerous criminal types, his experience had never alerted him to the existence of anyone like Noah Cross. When Jake asks, "How much are you worth?" he is greeted with the response, "I have no idea. How much do you want?" Once more the Cross consciousness of buying people off is manifested through a misunderstanding with Gittes, who is genuinely concerned about what motivates a man like the wealthy mogul. Cross concedes he is worth over $10 million. Gittes follows up, displaying his exasperation: "Then why are you doing it? How much better can you eat? What can you buy that you can't already afford?" Once more Noah Cross has a swift response: "The future, Mr. Gittes—the future."

Cross then demands to see Katherine, explaining that she is the only daughter he has left since "Evelyn was lost to me a long time ago." Gittes replies with sarcasm, "Who do you blame for that? Her?"

Noah Cross once more displays himself as a man who has an instant answer for anything. He also makes it abundantly clear that nothing will thwart him from achieving his objective of controlling all people and situations he deems vital to his interests. Cross makes no pretense of being even remotely influenced by conscience. "I don't blame myself," he promptly replies. "You see, Mr. Gittes, most people never have to face the fact that at the right time and right place, they're capable of anything." One could envision a defiantly grinning Orson Welles as Harry Lime delivering those identical words.

Tired of conversation and eager for action, Cross calls out to an old nemesis of Gittes's to take the potentially incriminating bifocals from the detective. Claude Mulvihill moves into view. Jake demonstrates initial reluctance, but it is swiftly overcome when Mulvihill points a gun at the detective's head. The inclusion of Mulvihill into the mix of characters is instructive. Gittes revealed earlier that Mulvihill is a former sheriff of Ventura County, L.A. County's neighbor to the north. He reveals himself to be under the control of Cross, a bought-off former policeman. Mulvihill is a sharp contrast to Gittes, a man who furiously tells Escobar that extortion is where he "draws the line" and comes close to a fistfight with the mortgage banker in the barber shop who questions how he makes his living.

An Ending Replete with Symbols

One of the fascinating aspects of *Chinatown* is the intricacy of the script, beginning with Towne's clever use of the word that embodies the title as a symbol for the best of intentions being thwarted and the corruptibility of the system through domination at the top by financial might being unscrupulously applied.

The story utilizes so many symbols, beginning with its title, that extra care needed to be applied to the story's conclusion. With a sophisticated two-tiered story built around Gittes's investigation of a control grab by Cross of the city's water rights and an obscene $30 million San Fernando Valley land windfall profit on the one hand and the unraveling account of Evelyn Mulwray marked by the detective falling in love with her and seeking to help her out of her tragic dilemma with her father on the other hand, without meticulous care being applied at the film's close, it could fall into the unfortunate category of so many promising suspense films whose effectiveness are blunted at the end by a screenwriter being too clever by a half, creating fascinating plot twists, then not being able to satisfactorily resolve them.

As so frequently occurs, there was much discussion between director Polanski and scenarist Towne. One major conflict occurred over the writer's proposed ending in the original draft to have Evelyn go to jail after killing her father with her daughter escaping to Mexico. Towne revealed that a major disagreement between himself and Polanski was over the director's preference for having Evelyn Mulwray die at the end of the film. "You're kidding," Towne replied when Polanski revealed his idea. "Well, think of something else," Polanski replied. Towne supplied an alternative ending "about four or five days before shooting." He took his altered script to Polanski, who replied, "Well, it's too late. We're going to shoot in a week and I can't change anything. I just can't do it." That was the last time that Towne and Polanski spoke prior to filming.

"It was very quiet, subdued, although we'd had several fights in which I'd blown up and yelled at him, and he at me," Towne recollected. "But I must also say that except for Arthur (Penn), Roman taught me more about screenwriting than anybody I've ever worked with, both in spite of and because of our conflicts. Roman is great at elucidation of the narrative—to go from point A to B to C. In that sense, he is excellent."

As earlier revealed, Towne heard a police officer describe the hands-off strategy of the Los Angeles Police in Chinatown. He decided to use the term as a code name for a system that does not work amid corruption at the top, a controlling influence personified by Noah Cross. A debate raged over justification for the film's proposed title when the action occurred outside of Chinatown. The problem was resolved by setting the film's final scene in Chinatown. Towne remembered one particularly heated discussion:

"These guys sat around like Harry Cohn saying, 'How can you call a movie *Chinatown* when there's no Chinatown in it?' Roman led the way. One highly sensitive man whom I *love* went so far in this discussion—and things had gotten so out of hand—that he actually said, 'Well, maybe if Gittes liked Chinese food.' At which point I blew up. It was one of those story conferences with the best of men, I'm afraid, saying these crazy things."

Many things are often said, often with intense anger under great pressure, before a final shooting script is delivered and filming begins. When Robert Towne comments on Polanski's astuteness in moving a story from point A to point B to point

C, he focuses on why screenwriting instructors such as Syd Field have selected the *Chinatown* script as a model along with why Towne secured an Academy Award. It is a work of symmetrical beauty, richly symbolic, and, while Towne believed that the film's ending was "harsh," it was masterful in the manner in which characters and symbols were effectively unified in an inventive and highly plausible manner. The two-tiered story involving the corruption and control of Cross on one side and Jake Gittes's romantic feelings toward Evelyn Mulwray on the other reaches a dramatic merger.

Here are some of the elements at work in the film's evocative final scene:

1) A showdown in the very section of the city where control is said to be virtually nonexistent and in which Gittes's law enforcement career came to a screeching halt amid tragedy.

2) A dramatic confrontation involving Cross and his daughter over control of the child they created, who sits by helplessly, saying nothing.

3) A return by Gittes to his old terrain, an area replete with meaning and steeped in tragedy.

4) A meeting of three levels of law enforcement, each heavily cloaked in symbolism—Escobar, the successful policeman Gittes conceived of becoming, someone who has just made lieutenant, and with whom the private detective worked; the symbol of Gittes himself, a former officer who, despite his status as a private detective specializing in peeping on cheating spouses, bristles at any hint of corruption on his part or suggestion that he is in a tawdry profession; and Claude Mulvihill, a former Ventura County sheriff who represents a body for hire, casting his lot with Noah Cross, someone capable of outbidding rivals for his services.

5) As exemplified in Towne's basic theme, in Chinatown, control is ultimately exerted not by the police but by Cross. When Gittes emphatically explains to Escobar his correct conclusions about Cross being a ruthless killer who will do anything to solidify his power base, including killing his own son-in-law, the city's water chief, he is ignored. This is the only segment of the film in which Gittes is blatantly a desperate man. Even when his life was in danger, he retained a measure of control. Now that he has all the answers concerning Cross's nefarious dealings, he is powerless to do anything, a spurned man.

6) Gittes's total helplessness as an individual doomed to see tragedy repeated in the same section of town, and in the same manner, losing a woman he profoundly loved.

7) The symbolic meaning of Evelyn Mulwray's death. With all of the major characters and significantly featured characters, such as Claude Mulvihill, Gittes's partners Walsh and Duffy, Evelyn's Chinese butler, her daughter Katherine, and Escobar's Gittes-hating assistant, Loach, all assembled together, combined with the heavy use of symbols, the concluding scene of *Chinatown* is representative of the resolution of a Greek tragedy. An important symbol is the manner in which Evelyn is killed by police gunfire as she seeks to escape with Katherine. She is shot in the eye, an important concluding symbol. It is important, particularly within Chi-

natown, not to see too much. A person can lose one's life by observing and knowing certain information.

It is also a bitter pill for Gittes that the officer firing the fatal shots is Loach,
his archenemy.

8) A final concluding symbol, delivered in an almost whispered tone by Gittes,
a sparkling touch by the brilliantly instinctive Nicholson, which gives the statement
more power than if it were stated loudly or even at moderate volume. As delivered
by Jack Nicholson, the all-important phrase "as little as possible" carries the tragic
ring of fate asserting itself as well as an unanswered prayer. How Gittes would have
preferred Escobar to pounce on his fresh information about Noah Cross, which he
barely lived to reveal. Instead he is ignored, investing a seemingly simple-sounding
phrase with profound meaning.

The film's final scene moves so quickly that it is necessary to stand back and
reconstruct events as well as principals to discern the brilliant poetry and meaning
of its composition. Gittes, escorted to Chinatown by nemesis Cross and enforcer
Mulvihill, is immediately placed under arrest by his former co-worker Escobar, the
man who wears the lieutenant's badge he had once hoped to gain. This happens in
the very section of town he and Escobar had worked together, and which he would
love to forget, but never can. The private detective has come to realize through bitter experience how difficult it is to tackle the might of a millionaire power broker
like Noah Cross, knowledge that is reinforced when his accurate observations
obtained at continuing risk of death are ignored by Escobar. When Evelyn, in a final
brief meeting with her father, refuses to give up Katherine, shooting him in the arm
and driving off rapidly as Escobar shouts "Halt!", the handcuffed Gittes's helplessness extends to peak level as he watches Loach, the officer he loathes, fire the fatal
shots at Evelyn Mulwray while an overcome Katherine sobs uncontrollably and a
crestfallen Cross plaintively wails, "Lord, oh Lord!"

A totally distraught and helpless Gittes mumbles the fateful words in the
manner of a character in a Greek tragedy or a French drama by Sartre or Camus:
"as little as possible." Equally significant is the swift and angry response of Perry
Lopez as Lieutenant Luis Escobar. The bristling reaction demonstrates that Escobar is as familiar with the expression as Gittes and knows its heavily laced, dou-
ble-barreled meaning of leaving well enough alone not only regarding Chinatown
but with highly influential, albeit ruthless, persons of influence such as the megalomaniac Noah Cross. Escobar initially reacts in disbelief over what Gittes has
said:

ESCOBAR: What's that? What's that? You want to do your partner a big favor, you
take him home. Take him home! Just get him the hell out of here. Go home, Jake. (Lowers
voice.) I'm doing you a favor.

It remains for Gittes's faithful associate Walsh, played by Joe Mantell, to deliver
a final parting message of wisdom: "Forget it, Jake. It's Chinatown!" Walsh seeks

to get Jake in touch with where he is, the territory where policemen and private investigators like himself might patrol, but will never control.

Irony is piled atop irony up to the closing comment, that of a policeman shouting with imperious authority as sirens sound and local Chinese curiously gather: "All right. Come on, clear the area. On the sidewalk. On the sidewalk, get off the street." By then it is plainly obvious that the bluster is no more than feigned control. The officers might have the authority to clear the streets, but when it comes to Noah Cross, he is able to walk away with the object he sought, Katherine, and will later gain $30 million through his nefarious dealings, resulting in three murders, at least one of which he committed personally, that of Hollis Mulwray. The absence of control by the police is so pervasive that Gittes, who is prepared to offer proof of Cross's murder of Mulwray and assorted lucrative corruption, is told by Lieutenant Escobar that he is doing him a big favor by releasing his handcuffs and allowing him to go home without arresting him!

SOME FUTURE OSCARS?

Chinatown received an astounding total of 12 Oscar nominations, winning but one, that of Best Original Screenplay with Towne the recipient. It lost out in the Best Picture category to Francis Ford Coppola's *The Godfather, Part II*. Polanski lost out to Coppola in the Best Director category. Keeping things very successfully in the family, the director's father, Carmine Coppola, triumphed in the Best Musical Score category, in which Jerry Goldsmith had been nominated for his movingly moody, trumpet-oriented *Chinatown* effort.

While the film's leads, Nicholson and Dunaway, did not secure Oscars, an argument could be made that their compelling performances in *Chinatown* had carryover impact, as they both won statuettes shortly thereafter. While Nicholson did not secure an Oscar for *Chinatown*, his performance won Best Actor laurels from the New York Film Critics Circle in tandem with his role in *The Last Detail*. The following year, Nicholson garnered his first Academy Award, winning in the Best Actor category for *One Flew Over the Cuckoo's Nest*. He more recently won an Oscar in the Best Actor class for the 1997 comedy hit, *As Good As It Gets*, while his co-star Helen Hunt was honored as Best Actress. He won a New York Film Critics Circle Award for Best Actor in 1985 for *Prizzi's Honor*. One of his finest overall efforts came in a supporting role opposite Tom Cruise and Demi Moore in the 1992 release, *A Few Good Men*, for which he received an Oscar nomination. More recently he received a Best Actor nomination for *About Schmidt* (2002).

Nicholson's staying power stems from his ability to adjust. Starting as a disillusioned youth in the sixties, his brilliant flexibility has enabled him to develop into a wise cynic, a more mature type of rebel, or an interesting oddball. Nicholson has endured by nurturing a great natural talent, adapting it to the times and circumstances.

Dunaway, with her elegant look and the high cheekbones of a fashion model, was perfectly cast as Evelyn Mulwray, the woman Jake Gittes, the private detective from the other side of the tracks, lusts for, yet finds intimidating. The Florida native, daughter of an Army officer, discovered her talent early. By 1962, the year she became eligible to vote, she joined the Lincoln Repertory Company under the direction of Elia Kazan and Robert Whitehead. Her major film break came opposite Warren Beatty in Arthur Penn's 1967 jackpot success, *Bonnie and Clyde*, a production with which Robert Towne became associated as script doctor. The next year, she received plaudits for *The Thomas Crown Affair* opposite Steve McQueen. While Nicholson won an Oscar one year after his performance in *Chinatown*, Dunaway took but two years to garner a statuette in Sidney Lumet's scorching social commentary drama, *Network*, in 1976. The great performances of Dunaway and Nicholson could not help but leave favorable impressions that conceivably had a bearing on their Oscar triumphs not long thereafter.

A major reason for *Chinatown's* success was the authentic thirties' Los Angeles feel. The cinematography of John A. Alonzo, a fellow Roger Corman alumnus along with Nicholson and Towne, contributed mightily to conveying a thirties' impression, as his deeply shaded blendings of yellows and browns conveyed an essence of time and place.

Director Polanski also left a rich imprint on the film. The eerie edge of tragedy that permeated the film, accented by Jake Gittes slowly but surely moving closer to a repeat disaster involving a woman he loved in the area of the city he can barely even think about, much less discuss, is comparable in many facets to Polanski's life.

Polanski was born on August 18, 1933, in Paris, the son of a Polish Jew and Russian immigrant. When he was three, his family moved to the Polish town of Krakow, which the Germans invaded in 1940. After the Nazis established the Krakow ghetto, Polanski's parents were taken away and placed in a concentration camp. His mother would ultimately die at Auschwitz. Before his father was seized, he helped his young son escape, where he managed to survive through a combination of help from kindly Catholic families and his own ingenuity. At that point, he became an ardent cinephile, seeking to shut out the dark world outside. At one point, the Germans used Polanski for idle target practice.

His father survived the war and remarried. The adolescent left home at that point and became a bigger cinema devotee than ever. Two movies that greatly influenced him at the time were Carol Reed's *Odd Man Out* (1947) and Laurence Olivier's *Hamlet* (1948).

Another of Polanski's close brushes with death occurred when he barely escaped being a victim of a man who had just killed three people. His father enrolled him in a technical school at that point, but he left in 1950 to attend film school, concurrently becoming an actor with the Krakow theater. He made his screen acting debut in Andrezj Wajda's 1954 release, *A Generation*. That same year he became but one of six applicants accepted at Lodz's prestigious State Film School. *Two Men and a Wardrobe*, a student film, won the young director five international awards. In

1962 he made his feature film debut with the one and only movie the director would make in his native Poland, *Knife in the Water*, on which he collaborated in the screenplay with Jerzy Skolimowski and Jakub Goldberg. Considered the first Polish postwar film not to deal with the conflict, the story, set on a sailboat, involves a husband's attempts to impress his wife and his potential rival, a young hitchhiker he brings aboard on a whim.

Polanski moved to England to make two films, one of which was the 1965 psychological thriller, *Repulsion*, his declared personal favorite. He then journeyed to America and directed the 1968 horror classic, *Rosemary's Baby*, starring Mia Farrow and John Cassavettes. After that, he tried his hand at adapting Shakespeare to the screen in 1971 with *Macbeth*.

In 1969 Polanski encountered another close brush with death. He happened to be away on business that tragic night when the diseased, robotic followers of Charles Manson descended on the residence he was renting. They were looking for the previous occupant of the home, Terry Melcher, son of actress Doris Day, angered over not receiving a rock and roll recording contract from the record producer. Instead they brutally slashed to death Polanski's beautiful young blonde wife, Sharon Tate, along with other assembled guests.

Polanski's next American effort following a sex comedy he made in Italy was *Chinatown*. With an Oscar nomination in tow and acclaim for not only his association with a truly great film but also helping to bring back the then-dormant film noir movement, his future in American filmmaking appeared bright. At that point, a severe roadblock appeared with his conviction of statutory rape regarding sex with a 13-year-old girl. The director forfeited bail and fled the country rather than face the prospect of a jail term. Polanski fled to France, became a French citizen, and did not make another film until the highly acclaimed 1979 release, *Tess*, starring 17-year-old Natassja Kinski, with whom he was romantically involved. His output level having dropped off, Polanski's 1986 release, *Pirates*, was a spoof while the erotic thriller *Bitter Moon* (1992) received notice as a showcase for a then-unknown Hugh Grant.

Polanski received an Oscar in absentia with his superb direction of *The Pianist* (2002), a biographical film of a great Warsaw artist who, through assistance from an active Polish underground and his own courage and resourcefulness, avoids death in the Nazi Holocaust, the fate which was grimly visited on other members of his family. Given his own background and his mother's death at Auschwitz, this was a project which was understandably near and dear to the director's heart. Adrien Brody also secured an Oscar in the Best Actor category while Ronald Harwood received Best Screenplay honors for his adaptation of the powerful autobiography by Polish concert pianist Wladyslaw Szpilman.

Robert Towne's successful career generated considerable momentum after his Oscar effort with *Chinatown*. He received an Oscar nomination for Best Original Screenplay the following year with *Shampoo*, directed by Hal Ashby, which he co-penned with the film's male lead, Towne's close friend Warren Beatty. In 1982 Towne made the jump to directing. He also handled the writing chores for *Personal Best*, an intimate look into the world of female track athletes starring Mariel Hemingway. He would later write and direct the 1988 Robert Redford starrer, *Tequila Sunrise*, and the 1998 release, *Without Limits*. A Towne script that received high praise was the 1984 release, *Greystoke: The Legend of Tarzan, Lord of the Apes*.

Towne once more joined forces with former roommate Nicholson, as the actor starred again as Jake Gittes as well as directing the 1990 *Chinatown* sequel, *The Two Jakes*. The film encompassed Gittes's Los Angeles career a decade after *Chinatown* in 1947 when, as a result of post-war prosperity and continuing migration to the city, the divorce rate increased, and with it, the detective's business.

NINE

In Search of Rollo Tomasi

Merry Christmas to you, Officer.

L.A. Confidential (1997)

It was like a scene from a movie. A 10-year-old boy, after spending a weekend with his father, returns home on a Sunday afternoon to be reunited with his mother in the suburban community of El Monte, just east of Los Angeles. The youngster's parents were divorced, and this was a routine followed regularly, living with his mother during the week and seeing his father on weekends; but this time, something was different, radically out of the ordinary.

On this occasion, when young James Ellroy returned home, there were police cars on the premises. The grim message he received was short and to the point—Ellroy's attractive, 40-year-old mother had been strangled to death, her body discovered on a road beside a playing field at Arroyo High School. Some alert Babe Ruth League baseball players working out observed a shape in the ivy strip just off the curb. Their coaches, walking behind the young baseballers, observed loose pearls on the pavement, then the lifeless form of Jean Ellroy.

The youngster's tragedy would, as in the case of so many writers, result in efforts to achieve a form of peace and understanding through applying pen to paper. Even within the sometimes-familiar vicarious pursuit of writing, however, the story of James Ellroy stands as a unique and fascinating chapter in the world of letters in the latter part of the twentieth century. A key element in understanding the path that Ellroy treaded on the journey to becoming an internationally acclaimed chronicler of the Los Angeles netherworld of night and mystery in a fashion similar to the great master, Raymond Chandler, lies in comprehending his initial response to his mother's death. Ellroy, whose author's journey through some of Los Angeles's most darkened haunts would result in the novel from which the 1997 noir classic, *L.A. Confidential,* would be adapted, harbored an initial resentment toward his mother and was initially delighted that he would, as a result of Jean's tragic death, be able to live with his father. As the years passed and he reached maturity, over-

209

coming a tragic youth amid problems with the law, Ellroy achieved success as a mystery writer of unique style and substance. The longer he lived, the greater the mystery became concerning his mother, her death, and his search to understanding her as well as his relationship with her. The result was a memoir as distinctive in its own way as his fictional writings. The cover bore a picture of his mother taken not long before her tragic death. It was called *My Dark Places*, a journey into James Ellroy's troubled past, extending beyond his successful career as a crime novelist highlighted by a fascinating search with a crack former homicide detective of the Los Angeles County Sheriff's Department. Despite the fact that the combined efforts of Ellroy and the man who would become his best friend, Bill Stoner, failed to solve an almost four-decade-old unsolved homicide, the effort enormously benefited Ellroy in other ways. He came to understand his mother as never before and became able to reconcile his former feelings for her and understand her in a manner he never could when she was alive.

That quest for understanding the brutal murder of his mother and its impact on him, culminating with the publication of *My Dark Places*, took Ellroy through his own personal hell, in the course of which he turned to writing as a means of expression. By the time he found a natural penchant for storytelling with a strong mystery flavor, he had already developed an expert's grasp from his encyclopedic reading into the Los Angeles crime scene.

When young James went to live full time with his father, he encountered a man on a tragically downhill spiral that would never be reversed prior to death. Once an impressive man described by his son as "drop dead handsome," Ellroy's father at one point became successful enough to serve as Rita Hayworth's business manager. According to Ellroy, he put together arrangements for the red-haired actress' wedding to Prince Ally Kahn. In that his mother was also a redhead, Ellroy observed that his father's life revolved around them. Eventually Hayworth fired Ellroy as her business manager. His world began toppling cataclysmically not long thereafter, motivated in large measure by alcoholism.

A turning point in the life of a youngster struggling for his own identity occurred less than a year after his mother's murder. On his eleventh birthday in 1959, his father gifted him with a book written by Los Angeles legend Jack Webb entitled, appropriately, *The Badge*. As mentioned earlier, Webb's enormous success with his popular *Dragnet* series, in which he played hard-working and righteous Detective Joe Friday, arguably had an influence on Stanley Kubrick in *The Killing* with its documentary narrative approach. Mark Hellinger, as noted, was an influence on Webb. *The Badge* provided Webb's take on some of the more famous criminals and crimes committed in Los Angeles. Ellroy developed an immediate fascination for "The Black Dahlia" case and the murder of young Elizabeth Short from Massachusetts, who was part of the long parade of young women who flocked to Hollywood in search of stardom, only to fall on hard times and become ultimately a murder victim.

The determined pursuit of Ellroy as a Los Angeles crime case aficionado served a dual purpose for a young man caught in the underbelly of the city and in a sad domestic situation with an equally troubled father. Crime case pursuit was a form of therapy and an attempt at understanding the tragic plight which befell his mother late one El Monte night on the one hand and a convenient escape route from a world he did not comprehend on the other.

In the manner of a tortured youngster, Ellroy responded by seeking attention in the most outrageous manner, the sole objective being noticed. He resided in the Fairfax area, one of the most heavily Jewish-populated sections of Los Angeles. Ellroy, whose own father was anti-Semitic, picked up the cue and pursued a hostile, uncompromising right-wing line with a strongly negative bias toward Jewish people. He rode his bike into Hollywood and purchased the latest extreme right-wing anti-Semitic hate tracts from a local bookstore specializing in such reading material and sought to wave them at his predominantly Jewish classmates. Ellroy might have been a source of negative attention, but it was notice he craved above anything else, and his outlandish behavior accomplished that goal.

Criminal activity entered the picture for Ellroy beyond his vicarious appreciation for the subject in book and magazine form. He began shoplifting as well as casing houses at night when their occupants were gone. An attempt to straighten him out by Ellroy becoming a Marine met with disaster.

Ellroy obtained a job caddying at Hillcrest Country Club in West Los Angeles. He was fired after an altercation with the son of a member, after which he got a job at nearby Bel-Air Country Club. He began hitting the marijuana and alcohol hard. On the surface, James Ellroy appeared to be on the road to disintegration with prison or death looming on the near horizon.

Before such a prediction could be realized, things began changing for Ellroy. Armed with a huge repository of information clicking within his brain, reflective of the Los Angeles Police Department's computer bank, this walking encyclopedia of L.A. criminal activity began tapping his vast informational repository. Eventually this would prove to be much more than helpful therapy. Ellroy's natural propensity for crime research happened to be integrated with a talent apparatus enhanced by a highly distinctive style. Ellroy's sentences were short and contained the kick of a mule. His chapters as well as his characters had a snippet pungency that carried the reader from chapter to chapter in the hungry quest of exploring in greater depth. He understood the direct, forceful language of policemen and criminals, a testament to his own background as well as his voracious reading.

When Ellroy's distinctive crime novels began selling, it was only a question of time before he would tackle the trauma pertaining to his mother's death in a graphic way. This happened when he wrote the runaway bestseller, *The Black Dahlia*. A lovely young brunette who came west to sample the palm trees and neon glitter of Hollywood, Elizabeth Short ultimately experienced instead the dingy darkness of bars and pickups with numerous men, no doubt hoping that a relationship would somehow emerge that would put her on the right track. If not stardom, perhaps a relationship of promise would emerge. Instead she ended up a highly publicized murder statistic, a young woman whose nude body was abandoned on a vacant lot several miles west of the Los Angeles Coliseum and the University of Southern California campus.

Many homicides were being committed in a city as large with a culture as diffuse as the Los Angeles of January 1947, but seasoned crime journalists can smell a good story, and the Beth Short murder had the ingredients to sell newspapers. Her mysterious aloofness on the one hand coupled with her prowling the darkened reaches of the city by night was one fascinating angle. Enhancing the picture further was that Elizabeth Short was an attractive young brunette and an aspiring actress. The Paramount drama starring Alan Ladd and Veronica Lake, *The Blue Dahlia*, had debuted in 1946 and become a success. Raymond Chandler wrote the screenplay. An alert local reporter played off the neon-catching title of the movie, and before long, Elizabeth Short was a name that faded into the past. From that time forward, she would be known as "The Black Dahlia." The name became so imprinted in the public mind that only the more alert readers would even know who Elizabeth Short was. After all, this was the territory of the movie capital, the great widescreen dream factory, and the obvious ingredients for generating interest in an always drama-hungry local populace were 1) a beautiful and mysterious young woman, 2) an exotic name, and 3) the elements of a brutal unsolved murder.

In *My Dark Places*, Ellroy concedes that writing about Elizabeth Short was a natural step in his progression of leaving the past behind by confronting its elements through his prolific writing facility. There were similarities between the young woman from Massachusetts and Ellroy's mother Jean. Each had striking beauty that had been recognized, leading them to believe that perhaps Hollywood's studios would welcome them into the fold and stardom could ultimately be theirs.

Jean Ellroy was a Wisconsin farm girl. Her good looks acknowledged in her own small community, her picture was sent to a newspaper, and she won first prize in a photo beauty contest. The first prize was a trip to Hollywood and a screen test. After traveling to the movie capital, Jean Ellroy discovered she was not so fond of the business that she would make the sacrifices and endure the hard work required in the competitive film world. The movie people were not those with whom she wished to mingle, and eventually, she married and had a son instead. Elizabeth Short came from Massachusetts in pursuit of stardom and ended up a creature of a sordid world of evening, flashing neon lights and darkened bars with an overhanging ozone of smoke.

The successful crime novelist and former prowler with a penchant for breaking and entering homes certainly needed to come to grips with the haunting city he prowled by night. Ellroy's psyche would rest only after tackling that project in the same forthright manner that he had his mother in *The Black Dahlia*. The name he chose for his sweeping, Chandleresque tome about the city where he grew up was an adroit merging of the city's name interlinked with its insatiable curiosity for gossip, one that has been long extended to the national citizenry through the efforts of Hollywood columnists Louella Parsons and Hedda Hopper continuing to the current diet of tabloid magazines and television journalism. One of the main characters of the book and the film from which it was adapted, played brilliantly by Danny De Vito, is an oracle who shamelessly dishes out dirt to a hungrily devouring public. The name *L.A. Confidential* conjures up an image of public curiosity for the low-down on the famous of Tinsel Town as it was provided within the fifties period in which the book and film are set by *Confidential Magazine*. De Vito's unforgettable Sid Hudgens reigns as conductor virtuoso, seeking to satisfy the insatiable urges for informational dirt on the famous.

Ellroy's tales of the dark side of humankind contain a complex series of characters. Director Curtis Hanson, in his collaborative scripting effort with Brian Helgeland, mastered the challenge of winnowing down the labyrinth of characters and plot situations from the Ellroy bestseller, winning a Best Adapted Screenplay Oscar in the process. Ellroy's writing is profoundly visual. The challenge for Hanson and Helgeland resided in simplifying the story to conform with the film's ultimate 137-minute time frame. A major concern of the adaptive process was not losing the rich essence of a story focusing on the nihilistic side of a rapidly burgeoning Los Angeles in the early fifties. One large hurdle successfully surmounted by the Hanson-Helgeland tandem was reducing the enemy list of the novel to one major figure representing the essence of evil, the avaricious Lieutenant Dudley Smith of the Los Angeles Police Department, played with a cool, polished mercilessness by James Cromwell, whose father John was the director of *A Tale of Two Cities* (1935), Bogart suspensor *Dead Reckoning* (1947), and many other films.

The first paragraph of *L.A. Confidential*, consisting of one sentence, shows Ellroy in pulse-pounding form. He provides the story thread around which both the novel and the movie will revolve, the death of a former policeman gone bad:

"An abandoned auto court in the San Berdoo foothills; Buzz Meeks checked in with ninety-four thousand dollars, eighteen pounds of high-grade heroin, a 10-gauge pump, a .38 special, a .45 automatic and a switchblade he'd bought off a pachuco at the border—right before he spotted the car parked across the line: Mickey Cohen goons in an LAPD unmarked, Tijuana cops standing by to bootjack a piece of his goodies, dump his body in the San Ysidro River."

Meeks, a former policeman and later hired muscle, had stolen 18 pounds of heroin from Mickey Cohen's operatives during the anarchistic period following the L.A. crime boss' legal derailment and ticket to McNeil Island Federal Penitentiary. Meeks is ultimately killed for the heroin by another former policeman, who in turn suffers an identical fate. The deaths trigger a spate of killings and cover-ups in a tangled web of corruption and violence in which the sworn presumed upholders of the law, the badge wearers, frequently outdo the hardened criminals in corrupt and violent activity.

ELLROY CONNECTIONS

Ellroy's fascinating background is revealed in the characters and situations emerging both in his book and the faithful adaptation to the screen by Hanson and Helgeland. The film begins with a narrative containing the same type of clever cynicism of *The Third Man*. In the 1949 British film, director Reed is the narrator. The narrator, as *New York Times* film reviewer Bosley Crowther said, comes across like a crafty and not altogether honest tour guide. There is the suggestion that he looks anything but unfavorably toward Vienna's thriving black market and is linked himself. *L.A. Confidential* begins with a breezy narrative from Danny DeVito, who plays a profound role in the film. DeVito is Sid Hudgens, editor and publisher of *Hush-Hush* magazine, which bears a striking resemblance to *Confidential*, the fifties' tabloid publication with a penchant for delivering the lowdown on the higher-ups.

Mickey Cohen is introduced into the picture with DeVito's narrative, in which he focuses on the tremendous migration to Los Angeles, which burgeons with population increase, freeway development to meet expanding needs, and the presence of the film industry. While the narrative is reminiscent of Carol Reed setting the stage for post-war Vienna in *The Third Man*, Los Angeles is depicted with supreme cynicism by a sleazy journalist intent on dispensing dirt about the famous, the near-famous, and others interesting enough to arouse curiosity. The cynicism is also reminiscent of Jack Nicholson as Jake Gittes in *Chinatown*, which focused on a Los Angeles in transition a little better than a decade earlier than the Christmas Eve of 1950 when *L.A. Confidential* begins.

In addition to showcasing Cohen, an L.A. legend Ellroy read about in his youth, another figure from a 1958 tragedy appears as a character in the film. Johnny Stompanato was Mickey Cohen's bodyguard. The handsome Italian developed a major reputation with the ladies and successfully pursued blonde screen bombshell Lana Turner. His temper was mercurial, and during one rage, when he was allegedly pummeling Turner and threatening her life, her teenage daughter, Cheryl Crane, came to her rescue with a knife. In the ensuing fracas, Stompanato was stabbed in the stomach and died. This was one of the cases that Ellroy studied with interest.

Sergeant Jack Vincennes, portrayed with the proper measure of coolly detached cynicism by Kevin Spacey, is a hip officer who gravitates between narcotics and vice. His activities arouse keen interest from dirt collector pseudo-journalist DeVito, who pays Spacey for leads while he in turn tips off the officer to facilitate first-class collars. Vincennes is billed as the officer who arrested Robert Mitchum on his 1948 marijuana charge. Smooth operator Jack Vincennes supplements his police income and dabbles in show business by serving as technical adviser for a popular television program called *Badge of Honor*. Once more Ellroy is tapping that repository of learning initiated during his troubled boyhood. *Badge of Honor* is evocative of Jack Webb's popular *Dragnet* series covering the exploits of the Los Angeles Police Department. The oft-repeated line on *Badge of Honor*, which Sid Hudgens mouths, is "Just the facts." This was the operative phrase of Jack Webb as Sergeant Joe Friday, a line that was satirically repeated by television comedians of the fifties.

The Ellroy tortured youthful psyche is thematically depicted in two-fisted police detective Wendell "Bud" White. After the film's opening narrative concludes and viewers are given a brief summary of some of the city's current happenings at the close of 1950, the scene shifts to a concerned White observing a battery in progress, a man who has just been released from San Quentin beating up his wife. White watches the developing action from the unmarked vehicle he shares with partner Dick Stensland, played by Graham Beckel, a veteran officer whose blase attitude is evidenced by the manner in which he sips from a bottle of

Danny De Vito prepares another searing article exposing famous figures of early fifties Los Angeles in *L.A. Confidential.* De Vito plays the editor and publisher of a tabloid reminiscent of *Confidential,* which achieved notoriety in the fifties with its exposes of celebrities. De Vito uses tips from well-placed LAPD Detective Kevin Spacey as the bases for articles exposing some of the city's biggest names. De Vito and Spacey are ultimately eliminated by corrupt Police Captain James Cromwell after proving too adept in their underground investigations.

whiskey. Stensland suggests that the concerned White call in the battery and let the uniformed officers confront the problem, adding that they need to pick up the liquor for the Christmas Eve party at the station. His tone suggests, however, his realization that White will not do this.

White, played by Russell Crowe, immediately gets the enraged husband's attention by pulling down a Santa Claus with reindeer display from the roof. When it falls with a crashing thud on the lawn, the man storms outside to confront White, who suggests that he fight with a man for a change. A brief confrontation ensues as White knocks the man down, handcuffs him, and leaves him for the uniformed patrol.

White has achieved a well-deserved reputation within departmental circles for his muscle and willingness to put it to work. His short fuse is perceptibly aroused by abusers of women, as graphically delineated in the film's first scene. While partner Stensland is bored and anxious to get to the alcoholic merriment of the Christmas Eve office party, White is transfixed on meting out swift punishment to a wife beater. White, it is later explained, underwent a tragedy in his youth that prompts him to see red whenever a woman is abused. His father chained him to a sink and beat his mother to death in front of White's eyes. The Bud White character closely resembles the young James Ellroy, who arrived home on a Sunday afternoon following a weekend with his father, learning that his mother had been murdered. In *My Dark Places*, Ellroy traces the story of an emotionally scarred youngster and the long, tough road he faced before ultimate recovery. White endures the pain of losing a mother in his youth, and in this instance, was a spectator to the gruesome slaying. He takes out his angry frustration on the malefactors of society he encounters in his police work, with special emphasis on woman beaters.

AN ODD COUPLE PAIRING

A clever dramatic ploy is the invocation of an odd couple pairing, creating a natural conflict of opposites merging and working together, albeit difficultly, to obtain a common objective. Two promising young actors who appeared convincing as Los Angelenos while products of Australian films interacted to achieve a dynamic result. Bud White was played by Russell Crowe, who was born in Auckland, New Zealand, and raised in Australia from the age of four. His parents catered movie shoots. When young Russell accompanied them to work, he developed an interest in movies, obtaining his first role in *Spyforce*, an Australian television series, when he was six. By age 18, he pursued acting earnestly and won Australian Film Institute awards for *Proof* in 1991 and *Romper Stomper* a year later. Sharon Stone helped bring Crowe to Hollywood to play a gunfighter-turned-preacher opposite her in *The Quick and the Dead* (1995). Stone, much renowned for her screen sensuality, called Crowe "the sexiest guy working in movies today."

The film provided Crowe with a ticket to the Hollywood fast lane, on which he capitalized with relish. By 1999 he received a Best Actor Academy nomination for his portrayal of whistle-blowing scientist Jeffrey Wigand opposite Al Pacino in *The Insider*. One year later, he copped the Best Actor statuette for *The Gladiator*. The New Zealander's breakthrough role in *L.A. Confidential* enabled him to showcase a rugged physicality which he reprised in subsequent roles combined with an inner sensitivity revealed in his relationship with Kim Basinger. The physical side of his role is reminiscent of Ralph Meeker as Mike Hammer in *Kiss Me Deadly*.

Crowe's nemesis through most of the film, who becomes his eventual ally, is Guy Pearce. Born in Cambridgeshire, England, Pearce's life took a tragic turn when he was eight and his father died in a plane crash. The Pearces moved to Australia when Guy was three, and his mother decided to keep the family there. As with Crowe, Pearce launched his acting career early, landing at age 19 a regular role on the popular Australian soap opera *Neighbours*, in which he appeared from 1986 to 1990. His breakthrough film opportunity came in a role far removed from that of Police Lieutenant Edmund Exley in *L.A. Confidential* when he portrayed flamboyant drag queen Adam/Felicia in the 1994 sleeper hit, *The Adventures of Priscilla, Queen of the Desert*. After his triumph in *L.A. Confidential*, Pearce captivated audiences with his sensitive portrayal of a man who has lost his short-term memory and seeks to resolve the mystery of his wife's murder and the beating which put him in his dilemma in Christopher Nolan's *Memento* (2000), an unconventionally fascinating noir venture in which he appeared opposite Canadian actress Carrie-Anne Moss.

The seething mutual antagonism between Pearce as Exley and Crowe as White had its genesis on the Christmas Eve of 1950 when the film opens. Exley is a departmental whiz kid who made lieutenant at 30, three years before his illustrious father, a legend killed in the line of duty. He is invested with watch commander duty that evening due to the fact that the older married officers were given the opportunity to spend Christmas Eve with their families. When a group of Mexicans are brought into the station, Dick Stensland, White's veteran partner, spreads word, contrary to other evidence, that they had badly beaten some officers. Stensland, already under the influence of alcohol, suggests that the police dispense their own kind of "justice" and leads an assault against the Mexicans with encouragement from fellow officers, who throw Exley into a room and lock the door when he seeks to halt the misadventure. Eventually partner White, at first seeking to restrain Stensland, becomes angry when one of the Mexicans curses him out, joining the fray.

The police chief, livid over the conduct of the officers and the field day the local newspapers enjoy, replete with glaring headlines, decides that "heads must fall." Exley, considering both Stensland and White to be nothing more than street thugs on the police payroll, offers to testify against each man. White, on the other hand, refuses to cooperate in any way, detesting what he considers "snitching" on fellow officers.

Not wishing to go to the grand jury with young officer Exley as the department's only material witness, Sergeant Jack Vincennes becomes the wild card in the equation. Initially balking at the prospect of testifying against colleagues, when the chief mentions severing him from his technical adviser's status on *Badge of Honor*, the astutely pragmatic officer has second thoughts. Always thinking, Vincennes covers his flank by giving evidence against some veteran officers who "will be fishing in Oregon next week." Exley, on the other hand, incurs great wrath by testifying against White's partner Stensland, who was a year and a half removed from his pension. Exley's plans to deliver White to the grand jury as well are thwarted when the powerful Captain Dudley Smith uses his influence to prevail on the chief to send his message that brutality and hooliganism will not be tolerated within police ranks by delivering Stensland as a symbol. Smith regards White as his kind of officer and wants him to remain on the force.

As it appears that Stensland is about to fade out of the story, he becomes an integral part of a complex mystery. On his final day, Stensland truculently trudges out of the station, showing his animosity toward Exley by knocking a box containing paperwork out of the young lieutenant's hands. White runs after his former partner, catching up with him in the parking lot, asking him if he would like to have a few beers after he finishes his shift. The older officer declines with a grin, explaining that this particular evening he has a hot date. This response will later serve as a clue to White when he seeks to unravel a perplexing mystery.

BRUTAL KILLINGS AND THE
APPEARANCE OF ROBBERY

Later the same evening that Stensland has left the police station for the last time, a call comes in about a brutal execution-style mass murder of presumed robbers at a seedy all-night Hollywood restaurant, the Nite Owl Cafe. Exley is the first ranking detective on the scene and protests when Captain Smith arrives and announces he is taking over the case. The reason for Smith's anxiety to elbow his way into command through using his rank will be revealed only when the mystery is unraveled. Department concern intensifies when Stensland is identified as one of the victims.

Another of the deceased is a young red-haired woman bearing such a close resemblance to actress Rita Hayworth that operatives in the coroner's office initially believe the star to be the homicide victim. The young woman, Susan Lefferts, can only be identified by her mother through a birthmark on her leg. She is recognized by White, who is there to obtain information about the death of his former partner.

The site of Lefferts immediately jogs White's memory. At the film's outset, following the altercation with the wife beater, White made a stop at a Westwood liquor store to pick up the liquor for the station Christmas Eve party. White's memories are made increasingly vivid by the dazzling blonde also waiting for an order. Breathlessly, White intones to Kim Basinger, "Merry Christmas." The blonde perceptively responds, "Merry Christmas to you, Officer." Her recognition of his officer's status only increases his fascination toward her. As events reveal, ultimately it will become a painful obsession.

Outside the liquor store, White's suspicion is aroused by the sight of a woman in the backseat of a parked car. The bandage on her face arouses concern with the acutely sensitive White that a beating has been administered. The young woman assures White that she is all right. Basinger has returned from the liquor store and personally vouches as well that the redhead, later discovered to be Susan Lefferts, is not in danger. This happens after White has disarmed the group's hired muscle, who is Buzz Meeks, subject of the first paragraph of Ellroy's novel. There is a distinguished, dark-haired man wearing a mustache in the backseat with Lefferts, Pierce Patchett, who will play a major role in the drama. When he returns to his car, Stensland informs his partner that Meeks used to be a policeman.

As Bud White begins to explore the mystery, the general department attitude that he is all muscle with nothing above his neck begins to dissolve. He starts to display the kind of analytical prowess associated with an intelligent homicide detective. Returning to the liquor store, he obtains the address where the blonde has the bills sent. White visits the exclusive Los Feliz area address of Pierce Patchett, a high roller involved in freeway development, played by David Strathairn. He concedes "off the record" to White that he also runs a high-class prostitution business called *Fleur-de-Lis*, the motto of which is "Whatever you desire." The women receive reconstructive surgery operations paid for by Patchett so they resemble famous film stars. When White spotted Susan Lefferts wearing a bandage, it was shortly after she had undergone surgery to become a Rita Hayworth look-alike. *Fleur-de-Lis* was another example of Ellroy, the Los Angeles historian, at work in that a similar business was run by a local woman in the thirties in which the high-priced call girls were selected by resemblance to major stars of the period, such as Jean Harlow.

After making contact with Patchett, White's life takes a major detour when he visits Lynn Bracken, a pillar of Patchett's operation and the woman who placed him on a cloud upon meeting her at the liquor store, and whose intuitive intelligence impressed him when she recognized the plainclothes officer's policeman's identity. When Bracken expresses surprise that White did not, like most other men, immediately tell her how closely she resembled Veronica Lake, he responds emphatically, "You look better than Veronica Lake." The chemistry is perfect, and the two begin a torrid affair, the high-priced call girl and the tough cop.

THE SETUP

Clever mystery dramas turn on pivotal plot twists that promote surprise, turning the story around and carrying it in another direction, enhancing suspense. A pivotal moment is reached in *L.A. Confidential* after, following police leads, three African American young men are gunned down. Exley, who gunned down one of the suspects by shooting him in the back as he sought to escape the apartment shootout where the men were cornered, became a decorated hero, winning the department's highest honor, its Medal of Valor, for presumably leading the raid on the brutal perpetrators of the Nite Owl Cafe massacre. At the time the thugs were apprehended, they were holding a young Hispanic woman they had kidnapped and were raping repeatedly. Exley, who is already entertaining misgivings about whether the African Americans were the perpetrators of the Nite Owl Cafe massacre, asks the young woman when she is released from the hospital whether any of the deceased mentioned the Hollywood slayings. The rape and kidnapping victim concedes that she falsely claimed they had discussed the Nite Owl Cafe killings, explaining that this was the only way that any attention would be paid to such mistreatment of a young Mexican woman.

A SETUP GONE AWRY

Jack Vincennes has established a cozy relationship with Sid Hudgens, editor and publisher of *Hush-Hush*. While both are attending a campaign benefit kickoff for the reelection of L.A. County District Attorney Ellis Lowe, the impish Hudgens approaches the super-cool Vincennes, informing him that he intends to set up none other than the officeholder himself, using a young actor named Matt Reynolds as bait for gay sex. Reynolds had previously been arrested for marijuana possession by Vincennes. He has just been released from jail and is seeking a way to get back into acting. The cunning Hudgens offers to help him, slipping him some money to entice D.A. Lowe into motel sex later that night. Hudgens introduces Reynolds briefly to Vincennes on the pretext that the officer can help the struggling actor obtain a role on *Badge of Honor.*

As soon as Reynolds is out of earshot, Hudgens ridicules his offer of help, telling Vincennes that by the time the actor has been busted on a morals charge, his career will be over. Hudgens supplies Vincennes with the name of the motel and the room number where the anticipated assignation will occur later that night.

When Spacey arrives at the appointed hour at the designated motel room, he finds Matt Reynolds lying dead on the floor, his throat slit. Even the incredibly cool Vincennes feels emotion when he finds the vulnerable young actor dead, having met such a barbaric end. He is determined to solve the case, convinced that Reynolds's murder will uncover a much broader chain of activity.

DeVito as Hudgens and Spacey as Vincennes provide fascinating screen chemistry in their unethical relationship. The contrast is fascinating. Both men are professionally linked to the seamy side of Hollywood life, but one profound difference emerges. DeVito conveys every impression of what he is, an overbearing double-dealer profiting from Hollywood corruption. Spacey, on the other hand, is cool with a detached air of elegance, well dressed and supremely calm. He appears totally baffled by an emotional man of violence such as Crowe. Spacey can scarcely conceive of breaking a sweat, much less getting caught up in a torrent of violence.

Kevin Spacey represents for the late nineties and perhaps a significant part of the new millennium the kind of role model in mystery films that Robert Mitchum typified from the late forties to the sixties and Jack Nicholson embodied from the Vietnam- and Watergate-conscious sixties through the seventies. The Mitchum from *Out of the Past*, appearing at the outset of the film noir movement, was a survivor determined to "die last." He was a man who could be driven to outrage if he believed he was being crossed. While Mitchum's persona was developed in the early stages of the Cold War, Nicholson, who typified a cooler type than Mitchum, had emerged from a world in which Vietnam battlefield bloodshed became prime-time news footage and Watergate revealed the level of government and corporate corruption. Nicholson's persona was accordingly more accustomed to wrongdoings and tragedies of every type as opposed to Mitchum. By the time Spacey emerged, society had reached a point where Internet websites extolled mass murderers and terrorists destroyed airplanes and large buildings alike. Spacey's "Cool Jack" portrayal in *L.A. Confidential* embodies a man who has adapted to the corruption around him, wearing a "no big deal" expression wherever he goes. He has seen it all and realizes that the only way to survive in a considerably imperfect world is by adapting.

Spacey is the unruffled product of an advanced technological age. Even when he portrayed a serial killer in *Seven* (1995), being slain by policeman Brad Pitt after Spacey had killed Pitt's wife, his method relied on a cool and resourceful intelligence with anger and emotion never entering the picture. Having performed on Broadway in David Rabe's *Hurlyburly*, in the film version, Spacey was the coolly ruthless opposite to Hollywood Hills roommate Sean Penn, who was given to waves of emotion.

Spacey won an Oscar for Best Supporting Actor by portraying a cool, unruffled con artist in *The Usual Suspects* (1995) who ends up outsmarting everyone, including the police, with his well-conceived gambits. He impressed as a foul-talking real estate con man selling worthless Florida land in David Mamet's *Glengarry Glenn Ross* (1992). In addition to starring in *Midnight in the Garden of Good and Evil* (1997), Spacey took London and New York by storm in Eugene O'Neill's *The Iceman Cometh*.

The talented Spacey, a New Jersey native who migrated to the San Fernando Valley with his parents, getting his first touch of grease paint in Chatsworth High School productions, garnered a Best Actor Oscar with his impressive portrayal of a dysfunctional man seemingly doomed to encounter tragedy in the highly acclaimed 1999 release, *American Beauty*. The film's British director, Sam Mendes, making his film debut, also received an Oscar, as did Alan Ball for Best Original Screenplay and Conrad Hall for Best Cinematography.

Despite Vincennes's disinclination to work with Exley, they form an odd couple, a mutually beneficial relationship akin to the one the young officer who plays by the rules will later form with his hated nemesis Bud White. It is not so much that Vincennes hates Exley, as White searingly loathes him. The eternally cool pragmatist would consider such emotional expenditure foolishly wasteful. What bothers Vincennes is that the snitch stigma attached to the ambitious young lieutenant will injure him.

The more Exley looks into the Nite Owl Cafe killings, the greater his skepticism becomes that something is tragically wrong. The police were led to the suspects by a call informing them that African Americans were shooting guns in Griffith Park, and that the same Mercury that was seen transporting them in and out of the park was parked in front of the Nite Owl. When the leads dry up and nothing can be corroborated, Exley connects the Nite Owl Cafe mystery to the death of his father, who was allegedly killed by a purse-snatcher he was seeking to apprehend. No evidence of such a person could ever be found, motivating Exley to join the force to solve the crime. He even provided a name to the phantom mystery man of "Rollo Tomasi." This story element can be related to author Ellroy's real-life pursuit of his mother's killer.

Recognizing Vincennes's investigative savvy along with his knowledge of the subterranean city scene, Exley shrewdly concludes that the sergeant can help him solve the Nite Owl case, which his gut instinct tells him is connected to Rollo Tomasi. He persuades a reluctant Vincennes to join forces with him and spy on Bud White, correctly concluding that White is on to something, in exchange for helping the sergeant with the case that perplexes him, the throat-slitting of young actor Matt Reynolds.

When Vincennes begins pursuing White, he learns about his relationship with Lynn Bracken and discovers the *Fleur-de-Lis* operation. In the meantime, White has pieced together a good deal of information on his own. A visit to Mrs. Lefferts enables him to learn that her daughter Susan had an older boyfriend of whom she disapproved. When White shows her a picture of his former partner Stensland, she identifies him as the boyfriend. She mentions a loud argument with another man. White's instincts tell him to look beneath the house, at which point he finds a rotting corpse that turns out to be Buzz Meeks.

When Exley learns that White visited Mrs. Lefferts, he retraces his steps. He learns from Vincennes about the *Fleur-de-Lis* connection and visits Pierce Patchett. An aware Patchett telephones Sid Hudgens before Exley visits Lynn Bracken. A grinning Hudgens stands outside and takes pictures of the officer succumbing to the abundant charms of the blonde call girl.

A CRUCIAL CHARACTER TWIST

A problem that occurs in many poorly done films is when a character undergoes an implausible change. In the case of Bud White, he actually does not change; other dimensions, of which his colleagues were unaware, are brought out. Not wanting to be considered a brainless behemoth, White is determined to demonstrate that he has sound detective instincts. His confidence is enhanced by Bracken, who tells him that he was bright enough to find Patchett and herself, and that he should also be able to resolve the murder of his partner Stensland, which White believes is linked to the mystery of the Nite Owl Cafe slayings.

Another characteristic of White brought to the fore by his relationship with Bracken is the boyish tenderness that resides beneath his broad-shouldered police toughness. He becomes so enamored toward the sexy call girl that he sits in his patrol car in the rain, tears streaming down his cheeks as he watches male clients enter and exit her house.

His relationship with Bracken and the concurrent opportunity to demonstrate tenderness occurs at a time when White is reeling with distaste from the special assignment provided by the sagacious Captain Smith. Under the guise of keeping Los Angeles free of mob influence, Smith practices police vigilantism. He sets up a room at the Victory Motel and takes incoming mobsters there, those who arrive in the city from places like New Jersey and Cleveland, hoping to fill the vacuum created by the imprisonment of local crime boss Mickey Cohen. White is trotted out as Smith's enforcer, working over the mobsters. Ultimately they are convinced to return to their respective homes. White becomes increasingly resentful of being no more than an enforcer. He longs for legitimate police work.

THE ROLLO TOMASI LINK

If there is one important requisite that Cool Jack possesses, it is the ability to think, and in the most dispassionate manner. Once he is turned loose by Exley, he develops a link between Stensland and Meeks extending years back into L.A.P.D. annals. He deems it perfectly logical, therefore, to present his evidence to Dudley Smith, arriving late at his home to discuss the subject. Smith begins by joking that it is a good thing that his family is vacationing in Santa Barbara, meaning that otherwise Vincennes would be in trouble for calling so late.

A shrewd Machiavellian, his unruffled manner and analytical skills make Captain Dudley Smith an older Jack Vincennes, with one exception; Smith, despite his deceptive carefree Irish brogue, has a dark side and a penchant for control extending well beyond the modest designs of the resourceful sergeant. When Vincennes explains his theory linking Stensland and Meeks to the Nite Owl Massacre with the concurrent implication that much more lies beyond, Smith concludes that decisive action is needed. Vincennes is much too shrewd to be taken lightly. While Vincennes sits comfortably at the kitchen table, Smith gets the drop on him and shoots him fatally. Just as Vincennes draws his last breath, he gasps, "Rollo Tomasi."

The next day, Smith supervises the cover-up of Vincennes's murder, stressing that a thorough investigation will be launched to find his killer or killers. He makes what proves to be a fatal miscalculation when he curiously asks Ed Exley if he has ever heard the name Rollo Tomasi. As the camera closes in on Exley, the young officer, despite an inevitable volcanic inner reaction, reveals a clever poker face. He tells Smith that the name means nothing to him, realizing that Vincennes, with whom he shared his secret about the reason he joined the force, to solve the mystery of his father's murder, had uttered the name before dying. Smith, seeking to cover all bases, curiously wonders about the significance of the name.

Now Exley will ultimately make a pact with his severest enemy in the department, Bud White; but before that, the resourceful Machiavellian Smith launches a clever ploy to drive an even wider wedge between the two enemies. He hopes that the wedge will drive White's mercurial temper to the point where he kills Exley.

AN EXPLODING TRIANGLE

Romantic triangles are often used in dramas for the simple reason that they are emotion generating. A veteran officer such as Dudley Smith recognizes this and uses his Machiavellian instincts to "divide and conquer," reasoning that if he can destroy the opposition, he will be free to operate unimpededly. Knowing that White passionately hates Exley for testifying against his former partner Stensland, resulting in his dismissal from the force, he knows that by making his Victory Motel enforcer aware of the tryst between the young lieutenant and the woman he passionately loves, Lynn Bracken, he might be pushed to homicidal rage. Should he actually kill Exley, White would be imprisoned or perhaps executed, putting him out of harm's way.

Inveterate sleaze merchant Sid Hudgens is used to bait Exley into a rageful trap. On the pretext of serving in his normal enforcer's role at Room 6 of the Victory Motel, Hudgens discloses, through apparent physical duress, that he has taken some pictures of Lynn Bracken that are in the trunk of his car. White is unstoppable, running into the rain, prying open Hudgens's trunk. He finds the infuriating photographs of his sexy blonde girlfriend making passionate love to Lieutenant Exley.

As Smith watches White drove off in a rage, he smilingly gloats, "I wouldn't trade places with Edmund Exley right now for all the whiskey in Ireland."

White's first stop is not the police station, but Bracken's Westwood home. He tearfully shows her the photographs, then beats her up. His expression displays a man whose entire world has been crushed. The reason for White's devastation was a bedrock belief in Lynn Bracken and their relationship. Clever Machiavellian Smith knew precisely how to trigger the full ferocity of White's legendary temper. As for Hudgens, who believed that by cooperating with Smith he would be spared trouble by the police, the conniving police captain has a surprise in store for the sleazy journalist. Believing him to be a major liability, Smith has Hudgens beaten to death shortly after White leaves in a rage, intent on seeking vengeance upon Lynn and Exley.

The role of Lynn Bracken, the independent-minded and resourceful call girl, provided an opportunity for Kim Basinger to move out of the realm of a beautiful and alluringly sexy woman into a meaty role of dramatic substance. The result produced a well-deserved Academy Award for Best Supporting Actress. The Georgia native's radiant blonde hair, creamy complexion, beautiful features and eye-popping figure, helped her win the Georgia Junior Miss title and enabled her to move into the high ranks of modeling early as she became a television fixture on Breck home permanent ads.

Basinger became one of *Playboy* magazine's all-time favorite centerfolds. Her starring debut was, appropriately, in the 1978 television film, *Katie: Portrait of a Centerfold*. One year later, she moved away from her typecast starring debut into a role in some ways similar to that of Lynn in *L.A. Confidential*, as she played the sensitive prostitute Lorene Rogers, who romances a troubled soldier with adjustment difficulties in the television miniseries *From Here to Eternity*. She received major attention in a role that showed her off revealingly in a formfitting bikini with Sean Connery in the 1983 James Bond film, *Never Say Never Again*.

Basinger's *L.A. Confidential* role fell into a something old, something new vein. While her role as popular favorite among the glamorous call girls in the posh pulchritude stable of Pierce Patchett was typical of roles accenting Basinger's physical attributes, this part represented a partial change of pace. Lynn Bracken is a shrewd and resourceful woman with a strong degree of independence, someone who operates professionally on her terms. A native of Bisbee, Arizona, Bracken's game plan is to return to the small town after making enough money to buy a dress shop. Her prideful independence is showcased when she tells Bud White that, unlike the other Patchett call girls who have been surgically cut to resemble famous movie stars, her Veronica Lake "look" was natural. All she had done was to dye her hair blonde. Basinger's relationship with Russell Crowe is one of the most dramatically evocative of the film as she brings out the tough policeman's natural sensitivity. She also supplies him with the confidence to rise out of the stereotypical tough cop image that Dudley Smith attempted to exploit and perpetuate for his own purposes, and he begins to behave in the manner of a thinking detective, detesting the enforcer role he performs for the corrupt captain at the Victory Motel.

THE ODD COUPLE TRIUMPHS

The worst fears of Dudley Smith are ultimately realized. He seeks to avoid a formidable team of the fearsome muscle of White merging with the canny resourcefulness of Exley. After White works over Lynn, he rushes to the police station and physically attacks Exley. At one point, Exley momentarily stops the rageful White by pulling a weapon, but the bullish officer wrests it away from him and renews his attack. Exley ultimately convinces him to stop his angry assault after the young lieutenant, aware of Smith's ploy, relates enough details to White to make him see that he is being used to further the captain's personal aims.

When the former enemies join forces, they learn how quickly Smith is liquidating anyone standing in his path to total power. Exley and White find Pierce Patchett dead in his living room, slumped over next to a phony suicide note expressing his guilt and dismay over his involvement in prostitution. Exley calls the sheriff's office and has Lynn placed in immediate protective custody.

Exley and White, hell-bent on getting answers, barge into the office of District Attorney Ellis Lowe, played with an appropriate insouciant arrogance by Ron Rifkin. When Lowe initially laughs off the inquiries of the officers, Exley watches while White performs one more strong-arm duty. White grabs the uncooperative Lowe and, after shoving his head into a toilet bowl, holds him out the window by his trouser leg, which begins to gradually tear, leaving him increasingly exposed to a precipitous fall many floors below. Finally a terrified Lowe provides information, resolving the mystery that Jack Vincennes was seeking to solve before being gunned down by Smith. It was Smith who was responsible for killing Matt Reynolds, using the damaging information to blackmail Lowe, who was helpless to move against a power-lusting officer determined to take over the local drug and prostitution empire of Mickey Cohen.

The moment of ultimate truth occurs, appropriately enough, at the Victory Motel. Exley and White are given identical messages to meet there, prompting each to conclude that the other person delivered the message. They grab weapons and take their positions in the infamous Room 6, where White served Smith's efforts to discourage interloping crime figures from other states, never knowing that it was a self-serving effort on the captain's part to destroy competition.

The two officers are able to stave off the mighty efforts of rogue officers under Smith's control who are determined to kill them. Eventually Smith himself surprises them by making a stealthy entrance from a rear door, getting the drop on them. White saves Exley's life by pushing him out of the line of fire. He takes bullets from Smith in the process. White saves the life of his former enemy for the second time in rapid succession when he is able, even in his weakened state, to reach up and grab Smith's leg, giving Exley the chance to gain the upper hand.

Once Exley holds the gun on Smith, the endlessly crafty opportunist seeks to convince him that they can become partners. Exley is told that Smith can make him chief of detectives. As the sound of approaching police sirens are heard, Smith walks outside and holds his badge above his head in the traditional manner following a shootout, preparing to weave yet another spell with his captivating blarney. Exley faces a decision. It was none other than Captain Dudley Smith who had repeatedly told Exley that he should confine his detective career to cerebral crime solving, stating that he did not have the stomach for procedural aberrations such as shooting an obviously guilty criminal in the back or planting evidence. Smith believed that the mercurial, highly physical White was a better candidate for field action, solving crimes on L.A.'s mean streets. Not wanting to give Smith the chance to weave his spell once more, Exley instead shoots him in the back, bringing his Machiavellian plans to an instant halt.

If White had revealed a surprising side as his sensitivity blossomed under the tender loving care of Lynn, so did Exley, who adopts some of the tough pragmatic thinking of Captain Smith. Exley silenced Smith permanently by shooting him in the back, a tactic he found previously abhorrent. Recognizing the continuing stigma of disclosures concerning Smith's extensive activities, Exley recommends and the department concurs that the easiest way of handling events is to give Dudley Smith a hero's sendoff as a dedicated officer killed in the line of duty.

Exley and Smith are given Medals of Valor by the department. Exley receives his in a ceremony while White, recovering from the gunshot wounds inflicted by Smith, waits in a car nearby. It belongs to Lynn, who will take them both to Bisbee. Exley walks over to the car with her, saying his final goodbye to White. Badly injured from the Victory Motel shootout and unable to speak, White says his farewell symbolically, pressing his hand against the backseat window of the automobile while Exley does the same from outside the car.

The longing expression Exley displays as he looks at Lynn demonstrates that he would like to be the man traveling to Bisbee with her. She seeks to soften the blow by telling Exley, "Some men get the world. Others get ex-hookers and a trip to Arizona."

L.A. Confidential provided a journey back to the fascinating realm of film noir for audiences hungering for more of the same kind of adventure provided in the past by so many talented creative artists who made the evening darkness come alive with

Guy Pearce is shown in a scene from the climactic gun battle which resolves the issue of control of the Los Angeles Police Department. Pearce is pitted opposite corrupt cop James Cromwell in the 1997 screen adaptation of James Ellroy's best-selling novel, *L.A. Confidential*, directed by Curtis Hanson, who won an Oscar with collaborator Brian Helgeland for Best Adapted Screenplay. Kim Basinger also secured a statuette for Best Supporting Actress. The muted color hues of cinematographer Dante Spinotti evoked the Los Angeles of the early fifties in the same manner that John A. Alonzo's cinematography displayed the city in the late thirties in *Chinatown*.

suspenseful anticipation. Like other great noir masterpieces, it blended those salient elements of a story that keep audiences absorbed and guessing: fascinating characters, crisp dialogue, dramatic performances and shocking conclusions that leave patrons emotionally spent when "The End" flashes on the screen.

The road traveled in *L.A. Confidential* has been recently revisited by former Los Angeles Police Department homicide detective Steve Hodel in his book, *Black Dahlia Avenger*. Unearthing fresh evidence, Hodel has linked the killing of Elizabeth Short, known as "The Black Dahlia," to his father, Dr. George Hodel, revealing that the family home on Franklin Avenue in Hollywood had been bugged and that his father, possessor of an Einstein-level genius IQ, was about to be arrested, but was allowed to escape from Los Angeles and America. The reason for the great reluctance of the police to move in on the wealthy Hollywood doctor was the hazardous trail of corruption and neglect attributed to the LAPD during a time of great corruption amid anarchy. This fascinating, well-researched volume adds further credence to the position taken by James Ellroy in his gripping novel *L.A. Confidential* and carried forward to the screen by scenarists Hanson and Helgeland concerning the myriad problems of the Los Angeles Police Department at mid-century. Steve Hodel displays a photograph of Fred Sexton, an accomplice of his father's whom he suspects might have been involved with the elder Hodel in the brutal slaying of Elizabeth Short. The photo of Sexton is displayed alongside a Los Angeles Sheriff's Department composite sketch of the suspected killer and presumably last person to see James Ellroy's mother Jean alive. The sketch closely resembles the photo, indicating the possibility that, when Ellroy was disposed toward writing a novel about the murder of the Black Dahlia, he was proceeding even eerily closer to home than he realized.

   L.A. Confidential embodies the best of chilling noir with the additional flavor of Los Angeles history at mid-century. The characters represent a flavor of a fascinating city immersed in corruption and conflict, a perfect mix for successful film noir.

Synopsis of the Films

The Big Sleep (1946) is one of the most influential detective and noir movies ever made, but even director Howard Hawks found the script confusing. What Hawks knew, however, was that the cast of characters adapted from the novel, which was Raymond Chandler's first, were so colorful that they would insure cinema success. Hawks began by re-teaming his blockbuster combination from his screen adaptation of the Ernest Hemingway novel *To Have and Have Not*, Humphrey Bogart and Lauren Bacall. They once more produced intense on screen dynamite. Bogart, playing Chandler's legendary detective Philip Marlowe, attempts to track down ruthless gambling house proprietor Eddie Mars, played by John Ridgely. In addition to the superb starring duo, *The Big Sleep*, like *The Maltese Falcon*, which also starred Bogart as a detective, owes much to its colorful ensemble of character actors, beginning with noir favorite, Elisha Cook Jr., along with Dorothy Malone, Martha Vickers, Bob Steele and Regis Toomey.

Criss Cross (1948) was highlighted by the appearance of steam team lovers Burt Lancaster and Yvonne De Carlo. Lancaster, once a law-abiding armored truck driver, offers to cooperate in a holdup with the gang of Dan Duryea, a hoodlum he despises, to help ex-wife De Carlo. She has subsequently married Duryea after her brief marriage to Lancaster resulted in divorce. Lancaster cannot get her out of his system, and his effort to help De Carlo is actually part of a criss cross engineered by Duryea to enlist his assistance in the armored truck theft, which is believed to be impossible without inside assistance.

D.O.A. (1950) was one of the greatest low-budget sleepers in film history. It is a unique story of an accountant from the Southern California desert community of Banning who, on a visit to San Francisco, learns that he has been fatally poisoned. Edmond O'Brien has but one day to solve his own murder and makes the most of the opportunity, tracking down and killing his own killer, William Ching, just before facing his own end. To succeed O'Brien must run the gauntlet by eluding the efforts of Luther Adler and his gang, who realize that if the accountant unravels the case

229

the mob boss faces a stretch in prison. O'Brien is able to turn the tables on psychopathic Neville Brand, Luther's designated executioner, who delights in inflicting pain, to provide O'Brien with one final chance to square matters with Ching. Pamela Britton is properly empathetic as O'Brien's secretary and lover. Their last meeting is the romantic high point of the film.

In a Lonely Place (1950) stars familiar noir leading man Humphrey Bogart, who plays a brilliant but unpredictable screenwriter with a short fuse and corresponding penchant for violence. When a young woman who was last seen in his Beverly Hills apartment is found strangled, he becomes a suspect in her death. Investigating the case for the Beverly Hills Police Department is Frank Lovejoy, whose commanding officer in World War II was Bogart. Coming to Bogart's assistance is Gloria Grahame, a neighbor of Bogart's, who tells the police that she saw the woman leave the actor's apartment alone. Her assistance leads them to get better acquainted, and love ultimately blossoms between Grahame, a down-on-her-luck actress, and the screenwriter. The more that Grahame sees of Bogart's less sensitive, often brutal side, however, the more ambivalent she becomes in the face of his marriage proposal.

The Blue Gardenia (1953) features a terrified young woman, played by Anne Baxter, who is wanted for the murder of playboy artist Raymond Burr. All she can remember after going to his apartment in an intoxicated state is fighting him off, then passing out and, upon awakening, seeing his lifeless body on the floor. Richard Conte plays an ambitious headline hunting columnist who achieves fame exploiting the wanted woman he calls "The Blue Gardenia," coined from the name of the Hollywood Polynesian nightclub where playboy Burr had taken Baxter for dinner and potent drinks, which he hoped would render her vulnerable. Eventually Baxter turns herself in to Conte, but before he can take any action, she is arrested by police captain George Reeves. Conte then sets out to prove Baxter's innocence.

Kiss Me Deadly (1955) was, like *D.O.A.*, a low-budget sleeper that ultimately scaled the ranks of enduring classic. Ralph Meeker stars as tough-guy detective, Mike Hammer, in an adaptation of a novel by Mickey Spillane. Director Robert Aldrich takes advantage of dark hallways and cavernous streets in the Bunker Hill section above downtown Los Angeles to achieve brilliant noir black and white effects. Meeker picks up a hitchhiker (played by Cloris Leachman in her film debut) who has escaped from a mental institution; then he finds that she is wanted by a ruthless gang. She is killed and he barely survives. Determined to gain revenge and find the individual responsible for what happened, Meeker soon learns that he is confronting a mad scientist, played by Albert Dekker, who is determined to possess a bomb capable of unleashing great destruction. The well-crafted script by A.I. Bezzerides plays on Cold War fears of nuclear catastrophe.

The Killing (1956) was a low-budget sleeper that pushed previously unknown Stanley Kubrick into filmdom's leading ranks. Sterling Hayden stars as an ex-con determined to obtain the good life by holding up a racetrack on the day of its biggest race. He enlists the help of offbeat types outside the realm of regular criminal enterprise. One member of the group, played by Elisha Cook Jr., gets Hayden's gang into serious trouble when he confides too much to his nosy and disloyal wife, Marie Windsor. Femme fatale Windsor drags enough out of Cook to whet the appetite of boyfriend Vince Edwards, who plots a double cross with criminal accomplices to turn the results of the holdup in his direction.

Chinatown (1974) is based on actual Los Angeles history, with John Huston playing the role of an unprincipled financial magnate who cannot make enough money or secure enough power to satisfy himself. Huston's character is based in part on Los Angeles pioneer William Mulholland. Screenwriter Robert Towne, who won an Oscar for Best Original Screenplay, crafted a story set in 1937 Los Angeles about Huston's effort to control the city's water supply and make a fortune from a corresponding property swindle. Determined to succeed at all costs, Huston seeks to have detective Jack Nicholson killed after his bloodhound scent smells corruption. In a manifestation of symbolically graphic film noir, Nicholson, in one of the film's most memorable scenes, has a piece of his nose sliced off, a reminder of the cost of nosiness, by the film's director, Roman Polanski, in his only speaking scene in the film. Nicholson's progress in the case notably increases after his involvement with Huston's daughter, Faye Dunaway, with whom he falls in love, learning in the process the dark and deadly secret she conceals regarding her relationship with her father.

L.A. Confidential (1997) depicts Los Angeles in 1950 in a graphic manner comparable to the depiction in *Chinatown* of the city thirteen years earlier. Like the earlier film, the story is based on certain historical circumstances. Director Curtis Hanson and Brian Helgeland won a Best Adapted Screenplay Oscar in crafting a script from the best selling novel of James Ellroy, who focused his story on the turbulent early fifties, when the Los Angeles Police Department faced a corruption scandal. The story involves a clash for power, which ultimately results in former enemies Guy Pearce and Russell Crowe joining forces to bring down megalomaniacal police captain James Cromwell, whose goal is total control of the Los Angeles vice scene. Pearce and Crowe form their alliance with great difficulty, thanks to their disparate views of police investigation along with a common love interest in a high-priced prostitute, played by Kim Basinger (who won an Oscar for Best Supporting Actress). The film includes characters drawn from L.A. fifties history such as mobsters Mickey Cohen and Johnny Stompanato. Stompanato's then girlfriend, superstar Lana Turner, is also depicted in one hilarious scene in which she throws a drink in Guy Pearce's face after he mistakenly believes her to be a prostitute in a famous stable then in operation, which features movie star lookalikes (Basinger's character resembles Veronica Lake).

Bibliography

All-Movie Guide. Internet Film Site and Database, allmovie.com.

Annakin, Ken. *So You Wanna Be a Director?* Sheffield, England: Tomahawk, 2001.

Arts and Entertainment Network. "Murder He Wrote," Biography of Raymond Chandler, 1997.

Bacall, Lauren. *By Myself*. New York: Knopf, 1979.

Behlmer, Rudy, editor. *Memo from Darryl F. Zanuck*. New York: Grove Press, 1993.

Bogdanovich, Peter. "What They Say about Stanley Kubrick." *New York Times Magazine*, July 4, 1999.

Bosworth, Patricia. *Anything Your Little Heart Desires: An American Family Story*. New York: Simon and Schuster, 1997.

Brady, John. *The Craft of the Screenwriter*. New York: Simon and Schuster, 1981.

Brooks, Richard. *The Brick Foxhole*. Garden City, New York: The Sun Dial Press, 1946.

Brown, Peter Harry, and Broeske, Pat H. *Howard Hughes: The Untold Story*. New York: Dutton, 1996.

Buford, Kate. *Burt Lancaster: An American Life*. New York: Knopf, 2001.

Cain, James M. *Cain x3: The Postman Always Rings Twice, Mildred Pierce, Double Indemnity* New York: Knopf, 1969.

Caute, David. *Joseph Losey: A Revenge on Life*. London: Faber and Faber, 1994.

Cement, Michel, with Adair, Gilbert and Bonnono, Robert, translators. *Kubrick*. London: Faber and Faber, 2001.

Chandler, Raymond. *Four Complete Philip Marlowe Novels: The Big Sleep, Farewell, My Lovely, The High Window, The Lady in the Lake*. New York: Crown, 1986.

_____. *The Little Sister*. Boston: Houghton Mifflin, 1949.

Cotten, Joseph. *Vanity Will Get You Somewhere*. San Francisco: Mercury House, 1987.

Crockett, Art, editor. *Celebrity Murders*. New York: Pinnacle, 1990.

De Carlo, Yvonne, with Warren, Doug. *Yvonne: An Autobiography*. New York: St. Martin's, 1987.

DiOrio, Al. *Barbara Stanwyck: A Biography*. New York: Coward-McCann, 1983.

Dirks, Tim. *The Greatest Films*. Internet Film Site and Database, filmsite.org.

Drazin, Charles. *In Search of the Third Man*. London: Methuen, 1999.

Ellroy, James. *L.A. Confidential*. New York: Warner, 1990.

_____. *My Dark Places*. New York: Knopf, 1996.

Feeley, Gregory. "The Masterpiece a Master Couldn't Get Right." *New York Times*, July 18, 1999.

Field, Syd. *Screenplay: The Foundations of Screenwriting*. New York: MJF, 1994.

Friedrich, Otto. *City of Nets*. New York: Harper and Row, 1986.

Goodman, Dean. "Cathy O'Donnell." *Films of the Golden Age*, Fall 1996.

Hanna, Thomas. *The Thought and Art of Albert Camus*. Chicago: Regnery, 1958.

Hare, William. "Mervyn LeRoy: 'You Shoot the Picture, not the Money.'" *Films of the Golden Age*, Spring 1998.

_____. "The Ken Annakin Story." *Films of the Golden Age*, Fall 1998.

_____. "Rouben Mamoulian: Impeccable Style." *Films of the Golden Age*, Spring 1999.

Higham, Charles, and Greenberg, Joel. *The Celluloid Muse: Hollywood Directors Speak*. Chicago: Regnery, 1969.

Hiney, Tom. *Raymond Chandler: A Biography*. New York: Atlantic Monthly Press, 1997.

Hirschhorn, Clive. *The Warner Bros. Story*. New York: Crown, 1979.

Hodel, Steve. *Black Dahlia Avenger*. New York: Arcade, 2003.
Holden, Stephen. "Stanley Kubrick, Film Director with a Bleak Vision, Dies at 70." *New York Times*, March 8, 1999.
Hoopes, Roy. *Cain: The Biography of James M. Cain*. New York: Holt, Rinehart and Winston, 1982.
The Internet Movie Database. Internet Film Site and Database. us.imbd.com.
Larkin, Rochelle. *Hail Columbia*. New Rochelle, New York: Arlington House, 1975.
LeRoy, Mervyn, as told to Kleiner, Dick. *Mervyn LeRoy: Take One*. New York: Hawthorn, 1974.
MacFarlane, Brian. *An Autobiography of British Cinema*. London: Methuen, 1997.
MacShane, Frank. *The Life of Raymond Chandler*. New York: Dutton, 1976.
Maltin, Leonard, editor. *TV Movies and Video Guide*. New York: Signet, 1990.
McGilligan, Patrick. *Fritz Lang: The Nature of the Beast*. New York: Griffin, 1998.
Meyer, Jim. "Marie Windsor: A Shining Light." *Classic Images*, November 1999.
Milne, Tom. *Mamoulian*. Bloomington: Indiana University Press, 1969.
Morella, Joe, and Epstein, Edward Z. *Lana: The Public and Private Lives of Miss Turner*. New York: Citadel Press, 1971.
_____. *Rita: The Life of Rita Hayworth*. New York: Delacorte Press, 1983.
Nolan, William F. *Hammett: A Life at the Edge*. New York: Congdon and Weed, 1983.
Oliver, Myrna. "Hollywood Blacklist's Abraham Polonsky Dies." *Los Angeles Times*, October 28, 1999.
Perry, George. *The Great British Picture Show*. Boston: Little Brown, 1985.
Rabe, David. "Admiring the Unpredictable Mr. Kubrick." *New York Times*, June 21, 1987.
Raphael, Frederic. *Eyes Wide Open: A Memoir of Stanley Kubrick*. New York: Ballantine, 1999.
Reisner, Marc. *Cadillac Desert*. New York: Penguin, 1993.
Schlessler, Ken. *Ken Schlessler's This is Hollywood: An Unusual Guide*. Redlands, California: Ken Schlessler, 1993.
Sennett, Ted. *Warner Bros. Presents: The Most Exciting Years—from The Jazz Singer to White Heat*. New Rochelle, New York: Castle Books, 1971.
Server, Lee. *Screenwriter: Words Become Pictures*. Pittstown, New Jersey: Main Street Press, 1987.
Sperber, A.M. and Lax, Eric. *Bogart*. New York: Morrow, 1997.
Spoto, Donald. *The Dark Side of Genius: The Life of Alfred Hitchcock*. Boston: Little, Brown, 1983.
Taylor, John Russell. Introduction. *Masterworks of the British Cinema*. New York: Harper and Row, 1974.
Thomson, David. *A Biographical Dictionary of Film*. New York: Morrow, 1976.
_____. *Showman: The Life of David O. Selznick*. New York: Knopf, 1992.
Tierney, Gene, with Herskowitz, Mickey. *Self-Portrait*. New York: Wyden, 1979.
TV Guide, Motion Picture Database. Internet Film Site and Database, tvguide.com.
Vaughn, Robert. *Only Victims*. New York: Limelight Editions, 1996.
Wakeman, John, editor. *World Film Directors: Volume One, 1890–1945*. New York: H.W. Wilson, 1987.
Wapshott, Nicholas. *The Man Between: A Biography of Carol Reed*. London: Chatto and Windus, 1990.
Weiler, A.H. "'The Killing': Film at the Mayfair Concerns a Robbery." *New York Times*, May 21, 1955.

Personal Interviews

Ken Annakin
Beverly Garland
Jane Greer
Robert Kendall

Index

235